The ANCIENT
MAGICK
of TREES

ABOUT THE AUTHOR

Gregory Michael Brewer (Bloomington, IL) has practiced Wicca/Paganism for more than twenty-five years and has served as a board member of the Pagan Pride Project Worldwide for seven years. He has taught workshops and facilitated rituals at Pagan Spirit Gathering, Chicago Pagan Pride Day, and Central Illinois Pagan Pride Day. Additionally, he has given lectures about Paganism at Heartland Community College and Illinois State University.

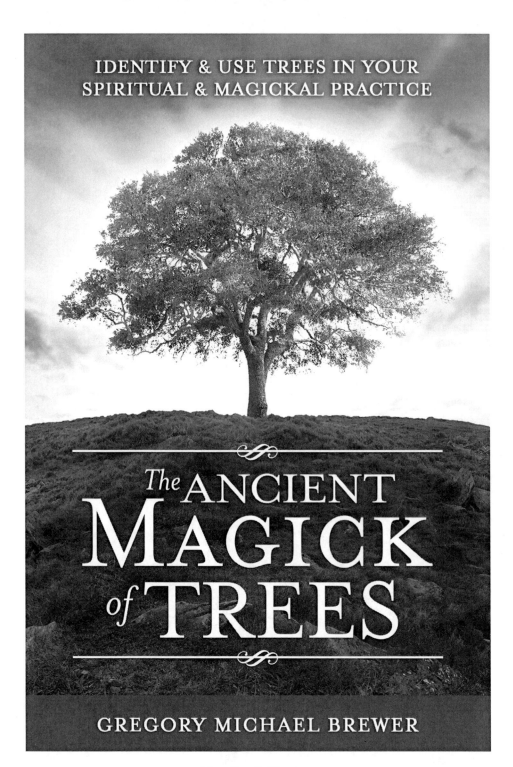

IDENTIFY & USE TREES IN YOUR
SPIRITUAL & MAGICKAL PRACTICE

The ANCIENT MAGICK of TREES

GREGORY MICHAEL BREWER

Llewellyn Publications
Woodbury, Minnesota

FIRST EDITION
First Printing, 2019

Cover design by Shannon McKuhen
Editing by Brian R. Erdrich
Interio rtree illustrations by Mary Ann Zapalac; other art by Llewellyn Art Department.

Llewellyn Publications is a registered trademark of Llewellyn Worldwide Ltd.

Library of Congress Cataloging-in-Publication Data (Pending)
ISBN: 978-0-7387-6162-6

Llewellyn Publications
A Division of Llewellyn Worldwide Ltd.
2143 Wooddale Drive
Woodbury, MN 55125-2989
www.llewellyn.com

Printed in the United States of America

DEDICATION

To come.

TREES

I think that I shall never see
A poem lovely as a tree
A tree whose hungry mouth is prest
Against the earth's sweet flowing breast;
A tree that looks at God all day,
And lifts her leafy arms to pray;
A tree that may in Summer wear
A nest of robins in her hair;
Upon whose bosom snow has lain;
Who intimately lives with rain.
Poems are made by fools like me,
But only God can make a tree.

—Joyce Kilmer

CONTENTS

TREES

EXERCISES

INTRODUCTION

Relax. Take a deep breath. Now let's go on an adventure!

See yourself walking in a forest or woodland. You feel the vibrant energy of nature surrounding you. It's a summer evening and the sun is beginning to dip below the horizon. The day has been hot and humid, but a steady breeze is now cooling the landscape. The sky is transforming into a mystical blue. It is the time of evening twilight.

Nearby stands a tall mighty tree. Its creaking branches make it seem as though the tree is watching *you*. Fireflies are flashing, crickets are piping, but you take no notice of them. The terrifying oak has won your attention.

October arrives and the air is cooler. The scenery shifts to shades of red, orange, and yellow. Halloween is nigh, and we give thanks for the harvest. Images of haystacks, scarecrows, and pumpkins abound. Ghosts and skeletons lurk around. But the true joy is the scent of the fallen leaves that crunch and crackle beneath our feet.

Winter approaches. A brilliant cascade of blanketing snow covers the ground and bough of every tree. It is the time of the spruce, fir, holly, and pine. The scents of the evergreens bring merriment and we see life enduring through the darkest times.

Spring brings renewal and greenery fair. Daylight increases, and the perfume of nature fills the air. It is the work of regeneration and the divine hand of expression manifesting across the land. The aromas, the natural therapy of budding and flowering trees, proclaim life in bloom once more and whisper the mysterious joy of renewal.

Suddenly, a loud car rushes by with the stench of exhaust and fumes. Your mind becomes filled with images not so wonderful—pollution, exploitation, and contemporary neighborhoods where each house looks like the other and is built from the same cookie-cutter blueprint. How much better would that house look—that one over there—with a birch, maple, spruce, or lilac in the yard?

Take a deep breath and master your focus. While there is a comforting mystery to be discovered amid the trees, their magick reaches far beyond comfort and imagination. Planting trees in a yard, in a park, or near a place of business can increase the value of the property and provide aesthetic pleasure and shade, but trees are much more valuable than this. Life on our planet cannot exist without them!

Trees supply oxygen, moderate temperature, cleanse the air by removing carbon dioxide (helping to combat the greenhouse effect), purify our waters, decrease soil erosion, minimize dust, absorb noise, conserve energy, furnish birds, humans, and various forms of life with food and shelter, and provide us with lumber, paper, medicine, and much more. Of all the plants on earth, trees have been the most victorious, enduring for over 370 million years, and there are more than eighty thousand known species. In our modern day fast-paced world of science and technology, our diminishing trees are incredibly valuable, and sadly, many see dollar signs in them rather than their sacredness and magick.

Since the dawn of humanity, in all cultures and religions across the globe, trees have been revered not only as a life-sustaining source of food and medicine but also as a place where spirits dwelt, awaiting to reveal great mysteries to those who sought their wisdom, knowledge, and magick. From the ancient Celts, Israelites, Egyptians, Greeks, and Norse to the Native Americans, including the Aztec and Maya, all across the world there have been both written and oratory accounts of numerous myths and legends of great spiritual symbolism to be discerned amongst every type of tree.

If you are like me, there have most likely been times when you gazed upon a tree and wondered what it was. Or perhaps you wanted to find just the right type of wood for making a wand or staff to utilize in a magickal working or ritual. As a lover of nature and practitioner of Pagan spirituality for over twenty-five years, the day came when I decided to set out to learn the names of the trees and how to identify each based on their unique individual properties. Although I have a BA in Spanish and am currently working on my MA in Spanish literature and culture, my passion for trees is so great that it led me to study tree identification and taxonomy during my undergraduate studies simply to quench my thirst for knowledge. I have taught a Pagan study group in my home on a weekly basis for the past fifteen years and often take students out on a nature walk and teach them how to identify the local trees. I compiled this book about trees so that you too may not only learn to identify them, but also how to experience their magick.

The Ancient Magick of Trees is split into four main sections: mythology and legend, field guide to the trees (including the medicinal and magickal properties), tree correspondences within various spiritual systems, and magick, activities, and craft. The ultimate goal of this work is to help you learn to identify the trees and how to incorporate them into your spiritual practices; however, taking a brief examination of the sacredness of trees through the eyes of many ancient cultures of the world will enrich your study and make your experience much more meaningful. Together we will explore myths, legends, and symbolism of trees from the past to present, as well as practical, magickal, and divine correspondences, astrological symbolism, magickal activities, meditations, and how to make a personal connection with the trees and even to communicate with them. Let's experience the magick together!

WARNING—Before moving forward, it is of great importance to understand that there exist in nature a great deal of poisonous look-alike trees and plants. Don't eat or employ the medicinal properties of any type of fruit, berry, wood, flower, root, bark, or leaf without consulting a doctor first. Some plants, as harmless as they may appear, can cause nausea, vomiting, problematic and uncomfortable skin conditions, dementia, paralysis, and even death!

Section One

TREE MYTHOLOGY
AND LEGEND

Hidden below two crossing boughs
Shadows fell before the eve
Pointing where shamans stood in rows
Tales now buried beneath a tree

Chapter I

SACRED SYMBOLISM
OF TREES IN THE BIBLE

The study of trees is relevant and worthwhile for all people around the world regardless of one's spiritual path and cultural upbringing. The sacred magick of trees has been shared throughout every culture and religion since the beginning of recorded history and is not limited to one faith or belief system. Let us put aside any differences to hear not only what the trees have to say but also what the teachers and wise ones from various religions and cultures of the past have willingly shared with the world and its future generations.

TREES AND THE BIBLE

Many Pagans, based on my own observations, sometimes choose to avoid the magick, wisdom, and tales of profound mystery that reside in the pages of the Bible. There are also those who sometimes take the Bible a bit too literally and miss the point or the message and are not willing to realize that some of the narratives in the Bible are tales, a good number of which are a retelling of different takes on earlier Pagan myths. These are myths and tales that were written to explain human existence from a spiritual perspective and a way to answer questions such as: who are we, where did we come from, why are we here, and what happens after death? While many of these tales contain wisdom and mysteries that need to be understood as metaphors residing within the collective unconscious and/or the individual subconscious, many others had some basis of truth regarding historic events of the past, and most of these teachings were originally passed down in an oratory manner long before being written and altered from storyteller to storyteller. Regardless of whether or not one views the Bible as a divinely inspired sacred text, as mythology it has much to reveal regarding how peoples of the ancient world interacted with the spiritual nature of trees.

Other sacred texts throughout history were possibly as divinely inspired as the Bible and all are extremely ambiguous. To gain a greater understanding, it is important to keep in mind that the writers of the Bible were exactly that—writers.

The Christian theologian and prominent author Northrop Frye in his book called *The Great Code* states; "The emphasis on narrative, and the fact that the entire Bible is enclosed in a narrative framework, distinguishes the Bible from a good many other sacred books." This statement was intended to give praise to the Bible, and clearly it does, but why don't we take a closer look?

Frye states that the Bible was written in a narrative structure. What is narrative? It is the art of telling a story or describing events, either fictional or nonfictional, by employing literary techniques; in other words, a telling, or retelling of stories based on events that may or may not have occurred. Frye also declares that the Bible is set apart from other sacred texts. What does this imply? There exist other sacred texts apart from the Bible.

Regarding the sacredness of trees found in the Bible, there are more than 525 accounts, representing a total of 22 different trees, and as previously stated, each passage is quite ambiguous. Below are a few selected verses I have chosen to write about because I feel they best present a possible lost and forgotten symbolic meaning of the tree as a reflection of our connection to the divine.

Many are aware of the story of the Garden of Eden and the tree of the knowledge of good and evil, but a proper examination of this tale would require perhaps an entire book in and of itself, or at least an extended essay involving the study of history, archetypes, mythology, and the literature of the Bible from an academic and historical perspective. Although important to keep in mind and I encourage you to explore the topic further, this would stray from the point.

We will later be taking a brief look at the Qabalistic Tree of Life. But this may not be quite the same as the Tree of Life found in the pages of the

Bible, though I am deeply suspicious. The following verses have been taken from *The New Student Bible: New International Version* and followed by my own personal brief commentary.

Genesis 2:9—"And the Lord God made all kinds of trees grow out of the ground—trees that were pleasing to the eye and good for food. In the middle of the garden were the tree of life and the tree of the knowledge of good and evil."

This verse suggests trees were divinely created as a source of beauty and food and whispers a hint of symbolic esoteric knowledge. It is important to note that the Tree of Life grew in the middle or center of the garden.

Leviticus 27:30—"A tithe of everything from the land, whether grain from the soil or fruit from the trees, belongs to the Lord; it is holy to the Lord."

This speaks of the divine sacredness of trees, and if you think about it, mirrors the libation of the simple feast in some Pagan rituals that is when the first cake or piece of bread and measure of ale or juice are given as an offering to the Goddess and the God. A tithe means ten percent. The obvious found in this verse is the statement that fruit from trees are holy and sacred.

Deuteronomy 20:19—"When you lay siege to a city for a long time, fighting against it to capture it, do not destroy its trees by putting an axe to them, because you can eat their fruit. Do not cut them down. Are the trees of the field people, that you should besiege them?"

This speaks of the nourishing value of trees, but also more. At first glance, this verse clearly states that trees are not people, but another verse found in the Bible, Isaiah 55:12 states: "You will go out in joy and be led forth in peace … and all the trees of the field will clap their hands." Even more interesting is Ezekiel 31:8–9, which mentions a tree that grows in the Garden of God that is so beautiful that all the other trees are envious of it. How fascinating! I also want to point out, on a side note, that many Native American myths describe trees as "tree people." This is not meant to be taken literally of course, trees are not people, but it could imply that they have a spirit or awareness of sorts. Why does the creator, as found in the former verses, not mind so much that people are slaughtered in times of war, but forbids the destruction of trees while also personifying them? Obviously, the answer is because life as we know it cannot exist without trees and it implies that trees are sacred and may possibly have a spirit of their own. I cannot help but notice the coincidence—or synchronicity—that this happens to be verse 12. Just keep it in mind and take it with a grain of salt and at the same time consider the fact that numbers are significant in the Bible, so much that there is an entire book called "Numbers." As you read further, you will begin to understand why I have mentioned this.

Job 12:7, 8—"But ask the animals, and they will teach you, or the birds of the air, and they will tell you; or speak to the earth, and it will teach you, or let the fish of the sea inform you."

Although this verse, my favorite, does not mention trees, it does share the Pagan/magickal/occult concept of animism and spirit revealed through nature, as above so below, or that which is without is within, and that which is within is without. It is the microcosm in the macrocosm and vice versa. Animism is the belief that everything has a spark of life and spirit, such as crystals, wood, dirt, etc. All things are animated with life or energy from the great source. Another way to look at it is that what can be seen in nature is representative of that which is in the spirit. It also implies that great mysteries and knowledge are hidden in nature and can be discovered if only we seek them. Read the verse again if needed.

Isaiah 6:13—"And though a tenth remains in the land, it will again be laid waste. But as the terebinth and oak leave stumps when they are cut down, so the holy seed will be the stump in the land."

To begin, this verse reveals the sacredness of the oak and the terebinth tree. Ancient Hebrews considered the oak tree as holy. In this verse is a hint of the continuation of life after death, or possibly reincarnation or recreation if you think about it, for if the stump of the tree remains it will grow again. The stump is used as an analogy of the holy seed mentioned. So, what is a holy seed? A seed provides a means of new life or birth. Holy implies divinity, purity, innocence, and spirit, hence the divine rebirth of the soul; and within the seed can be found DNA, the unique blueprint of life. However, a seed alone cannot produce life. Fertilization of the egg is required. This symbolism is the true meaning of coloring eggs for Easter celebrations in the springtime as it reflects fertility / reproduction of the physical body and the continuation of life and the eternal soul. The stump can be seen as phallic and the earth as a womb, and we should ponder here on the duality of the divine as having both masculine and feminine aspects. Of course, this could also imply that at some point in human evolution, we shall once again return to our connection with nature and the divine. This verse may also be a prophetic foretelling of the coming end of an age. Whatever was intended in the analogy presented by the writer we may never know, but most great myths and legends contain symbolism that can be reinterpreted again and again each time they are read while unveiling a different meaning each time. If you are curious, the terebinth tree is that which produces the pistachio nut.

Ezekiel 47:12—"Fruit trees of all kinds will grow on both banks of the river. Their leaves will not wither, nor will their fruit fail. Every month they will bear, because the water from the sanctuary flows to them. Their fruit will serve for food and their leaves for healing."

This verse indicates a divine revelation of the healing and medicinal properties of trees. It also states that these trees will bear fruit each month. There are twelve months in our common year, twelve traditional signs of the zodiac, and coincidentally this is the twelfth verse of the chapter.

Most trees do not literally bear fruit all year round, so this verse may be suggesting something more, something deeper. This verse also states that trees will grow on both banks of the river. Let's take a look.

In various ancient cultures, rivers have sometimes been used as a metaphor for a journey, and many times that journey was the passage from life to death and into the afterlife, such as the River Styx of Greek mythology. The Egyptians viewed the Nile in a similar manner. Ancient Egyptians buried their dead on the west side of the Nile, and daily life commenced on the east. It may be important to consider the statement that trees of all kinds grow on both sides of the river. Again, we can see the duality of male and female because in some cultures left is considered feminine and right is considered masculine, much like the two halves of the human brain. Is this a reflection of a divine masculine and feminine?

Many ancient cultures of the Middle East and Europe viewed the west as the land of the dead because the western world, or the Americas, had not yet been "discovered" and many thought the world was flat; therefore, the Atlantic Ocean to the west was where the world ended and where the spirits of the dead crossed over. The west is also the direction where the sun and moon set. This verse may hint of an ancient hidden knowledge of other cultures, peoples, and civilizations. Could this verse additionally imply the equality of all peoples of all cultures, religions, color, language, gender, class, and sexual orientations?

Of course, this is quite ambiguous, and the context of all passages should be considered, but it is possible to view the portion of the above verse, which states the leaves will never wither as a metaphor for eternal life. But that's not all.

The verse declares that these trees never die, nor do the leaves wither because the water from the sanctuary flows to them. This is the water of the spirit, of the divine. Water has often been considered a symbol or metaphor for life, love, intuition, emotion, eternity, mystery, and the astral plane. Just think about it while moving onto the next verse taken from the last chapter of the Bible.

Revelation 22:2—"… on each side of the river stood the tree of life, bearing twelve crops of fruit, yielding its fruit every month. And the leaves of the tree are for healing of the nations."

There is so much going on in this verse and it is incredibly similar to the verse in Ezekiel while also reminding us of the story in Genesis.

Understand that the above verses of the Bible are parts of a larger story being told. Here I am only pointing out the symbolic use of the tree within the texts. First, this verse mentions the Tree of Life, which we will eventually examine. Also, this suggests there may be a tree to represent each month of the year, as well as the twelve signs of the zodiac and the roughly 2,000-year cycle of the ages.

It has been suggested that there may be a forgotten or lost sign of the zodiac that ancients of various cultures were supposedly aware of called

Ophiuchus (O-fee-cuss), the serpent. There is much debate about this possible thirteenth sign, and I only mention it because I feel it is unfair to ignore the possibility.

There does exist what is called the great year, or Platonic year, when our sun and planet pass through each sign of the zodiac. To complete one cycle of the great year takes about 26,000 years, give or take a few. Some say that the passing from one sign to the next takes 2,167 years, placing the Age of Pisces from about 155 BCE to 2012 CE when the new age of Aquarius is thought to have begun. However, like I said, there is debate. Some say that each age takes 2,000 years to complete. If there are only twelve signs of the zodiac, or twelve ages enduring roughly 2,000 years each, the cycle of the Great Year would take 24,000 years to complete, but it takes approximately 26,000 years which could possibly imply a thirteenth sign of the zodiac.

Shortly before the birth of Jesus and up to the turn of the twenty-first century, we have experienced the Age of Pisces, the two fish, and the fish happens to be a common Christian symbol. Jesus was a "fisher of men." But now we have shifted, or are shifting, into the "new" or next age of Aquarius, and yes, the shifts move backward through the signs if you are curious. As previously mentioned, there is great debate regarding the exact time and arrival of the Age of Aquarius, but in my opinion, we are certainly close. It is also no coincidence that Jesus had twelve disciples, and when you add Jesus, we have thirteen. There were twelve tribes of Judah, but there were also the "lost" tribes—another story—and there are thirteen full moons in each twelve-month cycle. It is also interesting to note that the Jewish high priest, before entering the sacred temple called the Holy of Holies, wore a breastplate made of twelve sacred stones but also carried two other stones: Urim and Thummim.

In Hindu religion, there are twelve gods associated with the sun, each representing a different month, and perhaps the ages and the great solar year. The Greek pantheon as well includes twelve Olympian gods, though sometimes there is fourteen.

I do not claim to be an expert on this topic, and this book is not intended to explore prophecy, astrology, or theories that we will not truly be able to understand until the time comes and we look back, but this book is about the sacred symbolism of trees throughout the ages and how the tree is and has been a symbol of our connection to the universe and the divine.

There are some modern Neopagans, in the name of ancient Celtic/Druidic lore, that have assigned a tree to each month of the year, and this is often based on the works Robert Graves who possibly invented this system.

Robert Graves, already a successful author at the time, published his well-known book *The White Goddess* in 1948. While this tree calendar has been labeled as an ancient Druidic system of time and correspondences, it may or may not have been used by the Druids, but that doesn't mean it's not valid today as a new system. In addition to much Celtic legend, lore, and mythology, Graves also drew upon biblical texts. My guess is that he found a way to link biblical scriptures with Pagan lore, and his version of the tree calendar includes thirteen not twelve. This tree calendar may or may not be an ancient Druidic system, but I think he was certainly onto something.

I also want to say that knowledge does not need to be of ancient origin to be valid. Many Pagans fantasize about the recreation of ancient spirituality, or the old ways, and indeed the ancients knew a few things that we have likely lost or forgotten, but they were not ancient in their day. We, here and now, will one day be the ancients of another time and age. Truly, if knowledge is divinely inspired or channeled, it matters not if it is ancient or contemporary. Everything has a beginning and today is nothing more than tomorrow's history.

I would also like to mention that in the Bible many passages refer to the sacredness of the willow, though some versions have replaced the willow with the poplar tree. Palm trees were also considered holy and the cedar tree is mentioned often.

There are many other scriptures in the Bible referring to the trees. If you feel the need, please do additional research. Knowledge is power, or should I say liberation?

There is, however, a bit more to think about before moving on. I knew you would be excited! As seen in the verses above, in the beginning of the Bible is mentioned the sacred and divine creation of the trees; they are mentioned throughout the Bible and again mentioned at the end.

A tree has roots reaching deep into the soil, a trunk covered with bark, and branches stretched up toward the sun: the beginning, the middle, and the end.

In contemporary Pagan theology, as well as ancient, the tree employed as a symbol of the three basic realms of existence: the lower or underworld, the physical realm, and the higher or divine realm. These can also be viewed as our subconscious, normal/daily conscious, and superconscious. In many cultures around the world, this collective universal model is referred to as the "World Tree," the "Sacred Tree," or the "axis mundi" and is sometimes depicted as a ladder or tower.

The other idea to chew over, one which I mentioned briefly, is that the divine feminine aspect of the universe, generally referred to as the Goddess, is sometimes called Mother Earth, while the God, the divine masculine aspect of the universe has been called the lord of the hunt, the god of the forest, the Green Man, Jack in the Green, and countless other names. A tree—tall, long, and hard—penetrates the soil. A tree can be viewed as phallic and governed by the God, while the earth is receptive and represents the womb. Together, a tree planted deep in the soil gives birth to all life and reveals to us the mystery of the united force of the divine masculine and feminine.

Let us now move on to myths, legends, sacred writings, and wisdom of other ancient cultures regarding the symbolism, mysteries, and the magick of trees. As you read on, you may begin to see a link between the myths and legends presented to formulate a bigger picture.

Chapter 2

SACRED SYMBOLISM OF
TREES ACROSS CULTURES

TREES AND THE NATIVE AMERICANS

In Native American mythology and legend, just as in the Bible and myths of countless other cultures, there are numerous tales regarding the magick and sacredness of trees. Here are two I feel are most beneficial to examine in the endeavor of formulating a larger picture. Before moving forward, please keep in mind that if I were to gaze upon a tree while sitting down beneath it and looking up, I could say this perspective is how a tree looks. If you are standing on top of a building and looking down upon the same tree, it will appear differently, and you could say this is how a tree looks. Both are correct, both are true, and there are also other viewpoints, but one cannot say his or her viewpoint is the only truth because that is not true.

Legend of the Sacred Tree

In the book *The Sacred Tree: Reflections on Native American Spirituality*, authored by Judie Bopp, Michael Bopp, Lee Brown, and Phil Lane Jr., one can find the story of the Sacred Tree. This tale states that the Creator has given to the peoples of the earth a sacred tree under which all can gather, and under this tree can be found healing, wisdom, and refuge. This tree has roots reaching deep into Mother Earth and tall branches climbing up toward Father Sky like hands in a gesture of prayer. The fruits of the Sacred Tree are love, compassion, generosity, patience, wisdom, justice, courage, respect, and humility. The story goes on to share a great prophecy as taught by the ancients of North America. The prophetic portion of this tale suggests that if humans stray too far from the tree and forget to eat of its fruit, or should they turn against this tree and attempt to cause it harm, great troubles would fall upon humanity. People will become sick in the heart, body, and spirit and lose the ability to receive visions and dreams. They will begin to quarrel and war with each other and become unable to tell the truth or function as honest beings. Lives will become filled with anger, sadness, and depression. The prophecy states that this will come to pass, but that the Sacred Tree will never truly die, and if the Tree lives, so shall humankind. The prophecy concludes with the foretelling of a time when all people shall awaken from a long deep sleep during a time of great need, and many will fearfully search for the tree once more. This tree will be found in the hearts of the honest and wise.

What an amazing tale! Generally, when the heart is referred to in spiritual or mystical writing, it is not in reference to the literal, physical heart but is symbolic of our emotional self or perhaps the heart chakra, which is a bridge between our lower and higher selves. The heart chakra is located just above the center of our bodies, the solar plexus chakra. Could this tree, found in our hearts, be a mirror image of the Tree of Life found in the center of the Garden of Eden?

I cannot help but see a parallel between this prophecy, those of the Bible, and so many others. To me, it certainly seems as though we are living in the times of this prophecy. Let us open our hearts to the Sacred Tree and to each other once more.

The Sacred Cottonwood

I found the following story in a book called *Myths of the Sacred Tree* by Moyra Caldecott. It is a Sioux story of the cottonwood tree. This is indeed a sacred tale. A wise and knowledgeable shaman was granted a vision in a time when the people had been drifting away from their roots and sacred rites. The vision was a ritual to be performed, one that would bring the people back to the sacredness of nature and the divine. It was a ritual to be called the Sun Dance.

The shaman, or spiritual leader of the people, announced that in the ritual they were to perform, a "standing person" would be chosen to occupy the center of the ritual circle. This "standing person" was the cottonwood tree and was chosen because the tree represents the way of the people because it appears to reach from earth to heaven.

Again, the tree is located at the center of a sacred space and we see the need to reconnect with the Sacred Tree, the World Tree, or our higher self in order to realize what we have forgotten: we are all connected to each other, to the earth, and to the divine. God, Goddess, the Great Spirit, the Creator, our heavenly father and mother, or whatever you prefer to call the higher power, is truly neither up nor down, but is all around and within. We are part of the divine and the divine is part of us. All you must do is contemplate upon the mystery of a tree.

NIGERIAN MYSTERY OF THE TWELVE TREES

I also found this tale in the book by Caldecott and it was so fascinating that I had to share it. It is brief but enriched with much symbolism and meaning. In this tale, a hunter ventured into the woods to gather food, and the spirit of the forest revealed to him a potent formula to render oneself invisible. He was to take the bark of twelve particular trees (the tale does not specify which trees) and grind the bark into a powder to be mixed with water. This paste, when applied over the body, would render him invisible to the animals of the forest.

Clearly, the formula mentioned will not literally turn anyone invisible, therefore it is not of great importance to know which trees were to be used. What matters is the symbolism. Once more we encounter the number twelve, here being the combination and unity of different types. This could be referring to the zodiac and the ages, but it more than likely refers to the unity of all peoples and our connection with nature and the divine. I feel that the invisibility spoken about here may better be phrased as a blending in of sorts. If someone blends in with the background or the environment, they may move about unnoticed. Additionally, to "blend in" can mean to be a part of the environment, to be one with nature. Another possibility is that by blending in, we lose our pride and ego, shed our differences, and we lose the evil of discrimination and judgment. By blending in with the environment, we see each other as equals. The tale also states that one will be rendered invisible to the animals, and I suspect that this could imply placing emphasis on our higher selves and the divine in a way that our earthly/mundane concerns, or our animal selves, become less important and disappear into the background, hence the beginning of spiritual enlightenment.

I believe this tale is suggesting the power and importance of rediscovering our connection to nature, to each other, to spirit, and reminds us that we are a part of nature not above it. Just give it a thought and see what it means to you.

SACRED TREES OF THE EGYPTIANS

Trees held a very special place in Egyptian mythology, religion, and art, and many if not all trees were considered sacred. Let's begin with the sycamore tree.

Although a variety of trees have been found in ancient Egyptian art and mythology, the hieroglyph indicating a tree seems to be a sycamore and is called *nehet*. Found in the Egyptian Book of the Dead, two identical sycamore trees stand at the eastern gates of heaven. Between these two trees is where the sun god Ra, or Re, rises each morning. The sycamore tree, according to Egyptian mythology, was also viewed as an earthly manifestation of the goddesses Isis, Hathor, and Nut. It is interesting to note that the sun god rises between the trees of the goddesses. Again, we see the equality and union of the feminine and masculine aspects of the divine. I also find it quite interesting, though nothing to do with trees, that one of the Egyptian names of the sun god is Ra, or Re, while the god of the underworld or darkness is called Set (who may, although debatable, possibly have later become known as Satan). Today we have sunrays in the day and as night approaches we call it sunset.

The willow tree, Tcheret, was considered sacred to the god Osiris, and the willow was thought to contain the body of Osiris after he was slain and later resurrected. An interesting similarity with the Bible is that Jesus was buried in a tomb and three days later rose from the dead after descending into hell to conquer eternal death. Osiris was also buried in a tomb, actually a few tombs since myth has it that his body was dismembered, and rose from the dead after descending to the underworld. It is said that the tombs of Osiris were located near groves of willow trees.

Other trees considered sacred to the ancient Egyptians were the myrrh, pomegranate, and palm. Palm was sacred to the Egyptian god Heh. The palm was also a holy tree of the Bible and deeply connected with Jesus, as was myrrh. Palm branches were thrown at Jesus in a reverent manner shortly before the crucifixion and symbolized his triumph over death, and myrrh was one of the gifts presented to Jesus by the three wise men, the magicians or wizards, from the east.

In the Old Testament, originally written in Hebrew (and it is important to keep in mind that the ancient written Hebraic language contained no vowels), the sacred name of God, the tetragrammaton, is simplified as YHWH, from which we get the names Yahweh and Jehovah. YHWH stands for *Yod Heh Vau* (or *Vav*) *Heh*. *Yod* represents the divine masculine aspect of the spirit; *Heh* represents the divine feminine; *Vau* represents their union; and the final *Heh* represents the physical universe and creation as a product of that union which is you and I, the earth, and all creation. It has also been said that YHWH contains an aspect or representation of earth, air, fire, and water.

Remember as previously stated, the palm tree was sacred to the Egyptian god Heh. Just think about it. The Israelites were at one point in linear history slaves and subjugates to the Egyptian and Babylonian empires. Is it possible that the mythology and sacred teachings of the Egyptians and Babylonians influenced the later writers of the Bible? The possibility cannot be ignored.

Additionally, the Hebrew letter *Y*, standing for *Yod*, (pronounced "Yode" like "mode"), is generally thought to mean the fingers or hand of God, perhaps symbolic of hands pointing up in prayer just like a tree. This comes into greater importance when we look at the Qabalistic Tree of Life. It is quite possible that a tree is symbolic of the hand of a god and our connection with the divine and our divine selves. The *W* of YHWH is pronounced "Vav" or "Vau" and represents the joining of earth and heaven and makes a connection between the matters of spirit and the physical realm. If you put it all together, the tree may be a seen as a symbol of our earthly connection to the divine.

BUDDHA AND THE BODHI TREE

The story of the Buddha is not only interesting but also relevant to the study of the sacredness of trees. It is important to note that there are many accounts and variations of this story, but it is said that sometime between 563 and 623 BC, Siddhartha Gautama (who later became known as the Buddha), was born in Nepal. One version of this legend, in brief, recounts that his mother dreamt she was soon to give birth to a holy man, a great spiritual leader. Shortly after being born, Siddhartha is said to have taken seven steps in each of the four directions; east, south, west, and north (although which direction he started from is not clear) and then pointed one hand up to the sky and the other down to the earth below while simultaneously declaring that he had come to relinquish suffering. His mother died seven days after giving birth. He was then raised by his aunt and rich, powerful father who intended him to have all the luxuries of the world and to shelter him from grief, pain, and religion.

Siddhartha became married at the age of sixteen and all was well until he reached the age of twenty-nine when he had four disturbing real-life encounters that opened his eyes to the suffering of the world. The first encounter was with an elderly man who was broken-down, slobbering, and near death. The second was with a young man who was perishing from an unknown disease. The third encounter was with a decaying corpse, and the fourth was with a monk practicing a life of scrutiny. Due to these experiences, Siddhartha became disinterested in luxury and wealth in fear that he too would suffer from age, disease, and death; therefore, he decided to pursue a life of spiritual contemplation much like the monk. He sought out other teachers as well, but they were unable to satisfy his thirst for understanding and knowledge. He then chose to live a life of very extreme asceticism. He denied every carnal pleasure including food and grew so weak that he himself grew close to death. Eventually, Siddhartha realized that the path of asceticism was also not providing him with the answers he sought. But soon, all he was seeking to understand was about to be made known.

Siddhartha came upon a large bodhi tree and sat beneath it for forty-nine days. During that time, he became one with the tree and was sustained by the nutrients of the soil below and the energy of the sun above. He was the tree, and the tree was he. He realized that all are one, all are connected, all are equal, and we are all a part of the divine. Once we realize this, there truly is no suffering. Thus, he became the Buddha.

This is an incredible legend and I cannot help but notice the coincidence between the four directions that the newborn Siddhartha took, seven times each, and the four encounters that changed his perspective. But wait, there is a bit more.

Another version states that many local prophets predicted the arrival of the Buddha twelve years prior to his birth. These prophecies, along with the dream that his mother experienced before passing, were the reasons why his father sheltered him from the outside world. Interestingly enough, this sheltering is what led to the young Siddhartha's exploration of the world and to the discovery of the tree where he found peace. For the record, there is some debate regarding what tree Buddha rested under. Some accounts claim that it was a fig tree, others a banyan, but it is most commonly referred to as the bodhi.

Another interesting parallel is that while Buddha received enlightenment while sitting under a tree, Isaac Newton was also sitting under a tree when enlightened with the theory of gravity. What is the theory of gravity? What goes up must come down—up and down, much like a tree. We can see the macrocosm in the microcosm via the symbolic image of the tree. As above, so below.

A JAPANESE FOLKTALE OF THE SACRED WILLOW

The following Japanese folktale expresses the sacredness of the willow tree. This tale has been taken from the book *Ancient Tales and Folklore of Japan* written by Richard Gordon Smith and published in 1918. The tale itself is likely to have originated in or near the year of 1132 AD There are many versions of the story and these are sometimes called "The Willow Wife" or "The Spirit of the Willow Tree." Below is a summary.

Heitaro, a very poor man, had nothing but a willow tree growing near his home. He thought himself wealthy for having such a fine tree and often listened to the sound of the blowing wind through its leaves and branches. This willow kept him company year after year, and he loved it greatly. He felt a deep devotion to this tree and thought of it as his sacred temple.

Eventually the day came when others of the village sought to cut down the tree because they needed the wood to build a bridge. Heitaro pleaded with the people and offered to gather the necessary wood from the nearby forest for the creation of this bridge on the condition that his willow was left unharmed. It was agreed.

Later that evening while the moon was shining, Heitaro stood under the willow and gave thanks for the tree being unharmed when suddenly something moved nearby! He looked around and saw a beautiful woman. He believed she was waiting to meet her lover and apologized for intruding. She watched him as he departed.

The following evening, he saw her again, and the next as well. In time, he realized it was he that she had been anticipating. Indeed, she had been waiting to meet her lover. Soon they married and had a child.

Then one day the emperor decreed that a temple to the goddess Kwannon be built in the area, and for this the villagers demanded the wood from the willow. Heitaro was saddened, but his grief was lessened because he now had a wife and a daughter. As the tree was being cut, chopped, and axed, his wife began to cry that the world was growing dark. As she fell, she twisted her arms and covered her face, attempting to shield the cuts and blows. Heitaro could do nothing as he watched his wife die. Upon the final blow to the tree, he stood alone with his daughter.

The first time I read this story I was deeply moved. The irony and lesson found in this story is that Heitaro considered the willow as his temple, but eventually the tree was cut down to build, you guessed it, a temple. Do we really need to destroy nature to have a place of worship? Piety is found in the heart not in a building, and nature is the true temple. We can worship anywhere. Let faith be in our hearts and let us learn to see the divine and the sacredness within and all around us.

YGGDRASIL—THE NORSE WORLD TREE

The following summarized tale is a Norse story of creation. The Norse were a Germanic people that inhabited a region in Northern Europe known as Scandinavia.

In the beginning was the emptiness of chaos, and before anything existed there was only cold and heat. Eventually cold and heat collided and creation began to manifest. First was Ymir and then came Bor; the father of the god Odin. In time, Ymir was destroyed and transformed into the earth, sky, and sea by his progeny. This realm, halfway between the heat and the cold, was called Midgard. The realm where Odin and the twelve aesirs (one of two groups of gods in the Norse pantheon) dwelt was called Asgard.

Growing at the center of all realms, from the lowest to the highest, was the great ash tree called Yggdrasil (eeg-dra-sil), and each day the gods met beneath its branches. This tree would have perished if it had not been watered daily from the well of life. This great tree had nine branches that represented the nine worlds. Living amongst the leaves was Mimir, the god of knowledge, wisdom, and memory. An interesting note is that at one time, Odin, the father god, hung upon the tree for nine days and nights while his side was pierced and bleeding. From this sacrifice, he gained knowledge and power over all things.

In time, according to the legend, at the end of the first age, a battle was fought between good and evil and the tree shook. Eventually the tree was destroyed by fire, but from the ashes grew a man and a woman.

The above tale was a brief version, but again we see numbers in play. The number twelve seems to be dominant in many sacred myths concerning trees and the divine, and once more we find a tree representing the lower, middle, and upper worlds. This symbol reappears over and over throughout history and is not limited to any culture or civilization. I find it fascinating to yet again discover parallels with this story and the Bible. Jesus, while hanging on the cross, was pierced in the side and three days later rose from the dead and victorious over death. Odin hung on the tree for nine days and nights with his side pierced as well. Both in this tale and the verses in the Bible, the Sacred Tree was watered from a river or well of life. The tale also mentions the end of an age with a tree at the center, and in the tree, there can be found knowledge and wisdom. There are many other similarities with this tale and the stories of Genesis such as the creation, a battle between good and evil, the recreation of the earth, and the first man and woman.

THE MAYAN WORLD TREE

Numerous depictions of a great Sacred Tree, or World Tree, representing the union of the lower, middle, and higher realms have been discovered in the art and surviving texts of the ancient Maya and their predecessors.

One such piece, a stone carving found in the ancient Mesoamerican site of Izapa (stela 5) located in southern Mexico close to the modern border of Guatemala, predating the Maya, depicts a great tree of creation and has been dated a century or two prior to the birth of Christ. It is possible that this visual depiction, as well as many others found throughout Mesoamerica, is the same tree written about in one of the very few surviving books of the Maya called the Popol Vuh. Interestingly, upon a very close examination, one can see twelve human or intelligent beings and possibly twelve animals and birds as well. This stone carving has been called the Tree of Life Stone.

In the Popol Vuh is found the tale of a life-giving tree. It is the story of a champion hero named One Hunahpu.

One Hunahpu spent much time with his brother playing an ancient ball game, but eventually the game became so loud that it upset the lords of the underworld. Two of the chief lords, lord of death one and lord of death seven, were so disturbed by the ruckus that they became determined to destroy the two brothers and so consequently sent them to the underworld where they would endure many trials. One Hunahpu was then beheaded and his white skull was placed upon the branches of a dead tree. Instantaneously the tree was regenerated with life and the tree sprouted white flowers resembling his skull.

The renewed life of the tree so threatened the lords of the underworld that all were forbidden to approach it. But the story spread throughout the lands below and above, and in time a young woman, a daughter of the lords of death, learned of the tree and made a journey to obtain a fruit from the tree. After a great search, she found the tree, and while reaching up to pick the fruit, the skull of One Hunahpu warned her against doing so unless she was sure of her desire and intention. She convinced One Hunahpu that she was indeed certain, but as she reached to take the fruit, One Hunahpu spat into her hand and she became pregnant. Because of this immaculate conception, life would be restored and never to be lost again. She climbed the tree up to the world of the living and gave birth to two sons who in time defeated the lords of death and resurrected the bones of their father One Hunahpu.

Again, we encounter an ancient myth of a tree representing the unification of the upper, middle, and lower realms, as well as a tree that gives life. Much like the stories in the Bible, it is a woman who picks the fruit from a forbidden tree and a man who hangs upon the tree as a sacrifice granting victory over death and is later resurrected. It is interesting to note that Adam and Eve also gave birth to two sons.

Additionally, this tale may suggest the unity of all peoples—that is: under the skin, everyone's bones are white and all of us will share the same fate. In literature and sacred texts throughout the ages, the color white, which is a combination of all colors (just shine a white light through a prism) has been used as a symbolic representation of the divine, purity, hope, life, and innocence. We all have red blood, we all shall die, and underneath our layers of human flesh, pride, and ego, our bones and blood are the same colors. We are all equal!

What is going on here? Why do we keep finding the same tales and stories being retold again and again throughout various ancient cultures, religions, and sacred texts across the world and throughout history? Before these questions can be answered, and I'm not sure they can, we must yet examine a few more. I will say that the symbolic meanings of the tree can be found not only in nature, not only in mythology, not only in all cultures and times, but can be found within our own heart and spirit.

As previously stated, and before we draw a conclusion (one that is ultimately left for you to ponder), there are other accounts of the Sacred Tree to be examined.

THE SACRED TREE OF THE BOOK OF MORMON

The reason for jumping ahead through history to examine the use of the tree as sacred in the Book of Mormon is directly due to the associations of the Mormon faith with those of the Mayan World Tree. This is about to get interesting.

The Mormon faith is a branch of Christianity that not only reveres the Bible but also an additional book of scriptures called the Book of Mormon.

This book is based on the golden tablets supposedly discovered in the Americas and is an account of the teachings of Jesus after his death and resurrection to the native peoples of ancient America.

According to Mormon doctrine, Jesus came to the Americas and not only revealed his status as the messiah, but also taught the people about the history of the Jews, such as the stories of creation and the Tower of Babel. These "latter-day" teachings of Jesus are said to have been inscribed upon golden tablets and hidden or buried upon a hill. In time, a glorified resurrected being, often referred to as an angel, appeared to a man named Joseph Smith and revealed to him the location of the golden tablets on the fall equinox of 1823. The equinox happens to be the balance of light and dark.

Many Mormons are fascinated by the art and widespread stories of the Mayan World Tree. Remember, the surviving accounts of this tale revealed the death and resurrection of a man upon a tree, a tree that bore white flowers. In the Book of Mormon can be found the following scriptures:

1 Nephi 8:10–13—"And it came to pass that I beheld a tree, whose fruit was desirable to make one happy. And it came to pass that I did go forth and partake of the fruit thereof; and I beheld that it was most sweet, above all that I ever before tasted. Yea, and I beheld that the fruit thereof was white, to exceed all the whiteness that I had ever seen. And as I partook of the fruit thereof it filled my soul with exceedingly great joy; wherefore, I began to be desirous that my family should partake of it also; for I knew that it was desirable above all other fruit. And as I cast my eyes round about, that perhaps I might discover my family also, I beheld a river of water; and it ran along, and it was near the tree of which I was partaking the fruit."

1 Nephi 15:21–22—"And it came to pass that they did speak unto me again, saying: What meaneth this thing which our father saw in a dream? What meaneth the tree which he saw? And I said unto them: It was a representation of the tree of life."

The similarities between the above verses in the Book of Mormon and the story of the sacred tree found in the Popol Vuh are obvious, but I doubt these are one and the same. If Jesus visited the Americas, the tablets found at Izapa predate the birth of Jesus, which would make it impossible. There are also many similarities between the verses in the Book of Mormon and those found in the creation story of the Bible as well as those of other ancient cultures. Yet again we encounter a tree representing life, death, and rebirth, a tree that stands as the axis of all worlds, and a tree of knowledge that is watered by a sacred river of life. Let us now move on, or perhaps I should say move back, to another Mayan myth.

MAYAN FOLKTALE OF THE CACAO TREE

This is a brief summary of the Mayan tale of the sacred chocolate tree, the cacao. It is where we get the name cocoa. Kukulkán was a highly venerated god of the Mayan people and was also worshipped by the Aztecs and their predecessors known as the Toltecs, however the Aztecs and the Toltecs knew him by the name of Quetzalcoatl. Kukulkán was not only a god but is also believed to have ruled as a king in physical form and was depicted as being dressed in snake skins and bright colorful feathers like the tropical bird known as the quetzal. The Mayan people worshipped this god/king and in the ancient city of Chichén Itzá, they built a temple in his honor. This temple was a pyramid with many steep steps that rose to the sky like a ladder and it faced the morning star. It is said to have been the dwelling place of Kukulkán on earth. For the record, the morning star was a reference to the planet Venus.

Each morning, Kukulkán would descend from the realm of the gods to guide and watch over his people. Many mornings he was greeted with numerous offerings such as fruits, vegetables, and crafts. He thought that the Mayan people should in turn be given a very special gift. He decided to ascend back to the realm of gods where they enjoyed a very special drink called chocolatl (hot chocolate). The gods sweetened the beverage with honey and added chili powder to make it taste just right. This drink was made from the seeds of the cacao tree, but the tree did not grow on the earth, so Kukulkán decided to steal a small cacao tree from paradise and bring it to the Mayan people. According to the legend, many of the gods were very angered by this and so they banished him from paradise forever. Today the cacao tree is considered very sacred to the Mayans and the world now enjoys the gift of chocolate.

How fascinating! Once again, we see a tree as not only sacred but also as a bridge between the worlds. It is also interesting to note that both Jesus and Satan of the Bible have been called the bright morning star. It is now time to examine the sacred and divine correspondences of trees in other cultures.

SACRED TREES OF THE ANCIENT GREEKS

Concerning Greek mythology regarding the sacredness of trees, there are far too many tales to present here, so rather than giving accounts of each, below are some correspondences, divine associations, and sacred trees related to the Greek pantheon:

- Adonis—laurel, vine
- Aphrodite—myrtle, apple, birch, apricot, cherry, elder, linden, pine, cypress, hazel, myrrh, pomegranate
- Apollo—ash, laurel, plane tree (sycamore), cedar, olive, date palm, cypress, vine
- Ares—oak, cherry
- Artemis—cypress, cedar, palm, hazel, willow, laurel, fir, walnut, oak, myrtle, chestnut, cherry, yew
- Astarte—pine, alder, cypress, juniper, cinnamon
- Athena—cedar, cypress, oak, olive, and possibly mulberry
- Cronus/Kronos—yew, beech, cypress
- Daphne—laurel
- Demeter—fig, oak, elm, pear, apple, alder, cottonwood, and pomegranate
- Dionysus—vine, fig, pomegranate, apple, pine
- Gaia—all trees and especially fruit trees
- Ganymede—olive, coconut
- Hades—oak, yew
- Hecate—yew, willow, cypress, myrrh, alder
- Helios—laurel
- Hephaestus—laurel

- Hera—apple, pear, hawthorn, willow
- Hercules—Cypress (as a symbol of rebirth), aspen, oak
- Hermes—palm, aspen, willow, hazel
- Leuce (Poseidon's daughter) after death became the poplar tree
- Nymphs—poplar, pine, and all trees
- Orpheus—elm, willow
- Pan—oak, pine, lilac, and many others
- Persephone—pomegranate, willow, alder, cedar
- Poseidon—ash, olive, pine, cedar
- Rhea—oak, myrrh
- Zeus—oak, plane tree (and sycamore), cedar, juniper, chestnut, olive, apple, black walnut, linden, aspen, poplar, fig

In Greek mythology, it is interesting to note that there are twelve Olympian gods, though the lineup changes from time to time and a total of fourteen are presented in all, ten of whom are consistent. Once more the number twelve enters the picture, and each god and goddess has one or more trees associated with them.

It is also important to mention that in several Greek myths, as well as those of various other cultures, men and women have been transformed into trees, such as the transformation of Atys to pine, Smilax to yew, Dryope to lotus, and Daphne to the laurel tree. Much like in the Bible and tales of Native Americans, we once again encounter tales of the personification of trees.

THE SACRED HAWTHORN OF BRITISH LEGEND

This is the summary of a tale of the infamous mythological figure known as Merlin, or Myrddin. It is not known for certain whether Merlin was an actual person or mythical figure only.

When Merlin was well-aged (no one knew exactly how old he became), a young, desirable woman came to visit the court of King Arthur. This woman was said to be a maiden of the Goddess who had emerged from the lake to give Arthur the infamous sword known as Excalibur. Though she was beautiful beyond words, none could discern the nature of her heart and true intentions. Her name was Vivien and she watched the court of the king piously. In time, she grew jealous of Merlin's wisdom and power and set out to learn as much as she could from him by charming him with flattery and sex appeal. She was so beautiful that, in time, Merlin succumbed to her and revealed many secrets, some that he should not have. For Vivien, however, this was not enough. She desired more.

Knowing that some mysteries are too powerful to be revealed, Merlin fled across the sea and into a sacred forest, fearing that he would not be able to resist her charm any longer. But Vivian followed. She cried and pleaded that her heart was broken because he had not trusted her. Once again Merlin yielded and revealed a most precious secret; how to transform and imprison a man within a tree. Immediately after learning this sacred knowledge, she turned against him and the great wise magician became imprisoned forevermore as the hawthorn tree.

Again, we encounter a tale of the personification of the tree. In this myth, it is possible to once more view the tree as a symbolic vessel of hidden / concealed wisdom. It is no coincidence that the hawthorn, per Druidic tree lore, is a symbol of hardship and times of trial much like the Tower and Death cards of the tarot. Following a hardship or trial, one that will not last long, the hawthorn tree represents a new beginning or awakening.

CONTEMPORARY AMERICAN TALE OF THE GIVING TREE

In 1964 the well-known American writer and author of many children's books, Shel Silverstein, wrote a story called *The Giving Tree*. This story is a tale of the life-long relationship between a boy and a tree.

While very young, the boy forges a bond with an apple tree and they love each other greatly. The tree gives the boy everything that he needs and wants such as fruit to eat, shade from the hot summer sun, branches to climb and swing on, and companionship, and they played many games together. The tree loved him very much.

As the boy grew into a young adult, he visited the tree less and less until years had passed. This greatly saddened the tree.

In time, the young man came back to visit. The tree invited him to climb and swing again from its branches like he did as a child, but the young man said he was too big for that now. He told the tree that what he needed now was money, and so the tree offered its apples so that he could take them to the market to sell. They agreed, and the tree was happy again.

Many additional years passed until once again the boy, now a grown man, came to visit his tree friend. This made the tree very happy. He told the tree that now he needed a house, and the tree told him it could not give him a house because its house was in nature but offered its branches so that he could build one. He accepted, and both were happy.

After much more time, he came back again to visit his old friend and he told the tree that what he wanted now was a boat to sail away from all the stresses of society. The tree in turn offered its trunk to make a boat and so he cut it down. Both were happy.

Eventually, as a very old man, he returned one last time to his childhood tree companion, now nothing but a stump. The tree told him that it could not offer anything else, but all he wanted now was a place to rest and so the tree invited him to sit down on its stump and relax. He did, and both were happy.

What a wonderful tale! This story is both sad and comforting. It describes the most vital give-and-take relationship humans have with trees and all of nature. Can we live without them? We use trees for nourishment, wood, shade, oxygen, paper, to build bridges, houses, and boats that cross water—yet another symbol of our journey into the next life and our yearning to rejoin spirit. This anecdote raises many questions. Do we take too much from nature or does nature gladly provide us our greedy needs selflessly? Must we cut down trees to build temples or is nature our temple? Is the tree passively or actively giving? Can mankind learn to find a balance and love for our environment? Is the true temple within our hearts? What questions does this story inspire for you?

OTHER IMPORTANT MENTIONS AND ASSOCIATIONS

It is worthwhile to point out other representations of the sacred symbolism and lore of trees throughout history.

- The Chinese Tree of Life is called *Kien-Luen*, the Moslem Lote tree, and stands as a boundary between humanity and the divine.

- The Japanese sakaki tree represents the central axis of the universe, or the pillar between all worlds.
- The Japanese deity Uku-No-Chi is said to live in the trunks of trees, and the tree god Hamori protects the leaves.
- Ancient Pagan Germanic tribes once created pillars resembling tree trunks, and these are thought to represent the "Tree of the Universe" but the true purpose of these pillars has been debated by scholars for centuries. These were called the *Irminsul*, or "giant columns." Many of these were destroyed in the conversion of Paganism to Christianity beginning in the year 772 under Charlemagne.
- Many Greek and Roman columns, well known today in the field of architecture, were also based on the model of a tree trunk.
- The Tibetan tree Tarayana grows near the side of a great river and divides the worlds.
- Sacred to the Hawaiian goddess Pele is the Ohia Lehua tree. Ohia was a handsome warrior and Pele desired to marry him. However, Ohia had already promised himself in marriage to his lover Lehua. Pele became so furious and jealous that she turned him into a tree. Lehua was deeply heartbroken by this and legend says that the gods took pity on her and turned her into the flowers that grow upon the tree so that the two lovers could always be together. It is an evergreen tree in the myrtle family.
- The bodhi tree is also sacred to Vishnu in Hindu.
- The Scandinavian "elder mothers" are tree spirits believed to reside within the elder tree and possess very powerful magick. These tree spirits, however, were thought to be malicious. I suspect that the myth arose from the fact that the elder tree is toxic and can cause sickness when burned or if the berries are consumed when unripe.
- The Scottish myth of the tree spirit Ghillie Dhu, sometimes called GilleDubh, is thought to be a guardian spirit of trees and takes residence in the birch tree. He loves children (innocence and imagination) and is likely a twist upon the Green Man.
- The Hindu god Soma is both a god and a plant and is a bridge between heaven and earth.

• Yaxche is the name of the Mayan Tree of Life and was believed to hold
up the heavens on its branches while penetrating the underworld (or
the subconscious) by its roots and balancing all the realms from our
physical perspective in the trunk. In other words, the Mayan Tree of
Life was seen a bridge and a connection to the divine.

Before drawing a conclusion, in chapter 5 we will be looking at other
divine tree associations throughout history, the Druidic tree ogham and calendar, and the Qabalistic Tree of Life. Until then, let us take a moment to
examine the sacredness of the tree as can be found in contemporary society.

Chapter 3

THE SACRED TREE TODAY

Although the majority of contemporary society may have seemingly forgotten the meaning and sacredness of the tree, the magick of the tree continues to thrive and influence us today. Here are a few modern examples to ponder:

The Yule Log: Yule is a Pagan holiday of pre-Christian origin in celebration of the winter solstice and the return of the sun. Since the winter solstice is the longest night of the year, it marks the time when the light of the sun will begin to last a bit longer each day until the summer solstice. In earlier times, before we had indoor plumbing, heat, electricity, cars, supermarkets etc., the common folk relied on farming and hunting for survival. For many, depending on where one lived, winter was a time of dread, and only those who gathered and stored enough food and firewood to endure the long, hard, and brutally cold winter months survived. The return of sunlight meant the promise of warmth, light, and easier access to food. It only stands to reason that the return of the sunlight and warmth was certainly something to celebrate and to be thankful for. For many Pagans, the sun was a symbol or representation of the masculine form or aspect of deity, and therefore Yule also served the purpose of celebrating the birth of the sun god. It is easy to see why the later Christians adopted the holiday to celebrate the very same thing, only in this case the birth of the son rather than the sun. One ancient Pagan tradition that is still practiced today is that of the Yule log.

The Yule log is a surviving custom of pre-Christian Celtic traditions and is a fun and wonderful way to celebrate the return of the sun and the hope of eternal life. It is generally thought that the log was made from oak and gathered earlier in the year. There are many traditions and ways of creating/utilizing a Yule log, and so here I will only share two.

On the night of winter solstice, the log is burned in the hearth (fireplace), but a small portion of the log is saved and kept to rekindle the fire for the next winter solstice and the new Yule log. This is a symbolic gesture of the continuation of life and/or the cycle of life, death, and rebirth. It is also thought to have brought protection to the home. The ashes of the log can be saved and used for protection or other magickal workings.

Another way to incorporate a Yule log into solstice celebrations is to gather a log, one that has good balance and that does not tend to roll over, then carve or drill one, two, or three holes in the log just big enough to hold taper candles. A log with one lit candle can represent the return of the sun or any other symbolic meaning, such as the Great Spirit. Two candles can represent the masculine and feminine aspects of the divine, the darkness and the light, or life and death. Three candles can represent life, death, and rebirth or the Goddess, the God, and their union. There are many possibilities and even more when it comes to choosing the colors of the candles and what those colors may mean to you. It is reasonable to have one green candle to represent Mother Earth, one red (or orange or yellow) candle to represent the light of the sun, and a white candle in the middle to represent the Great Spirit. I prefer this second method because this way the same log can be used again and again and therefore represents longevity and eternal life. While it may be traditional to use oak wood for the Yule log, and that certainly is a great choice, there is no reason to limit it to oak alone. Pine, fir, or spruce can be used to represent protection and eternal life, or birch can be used to represent new beginnings. Apple wood can be used to represent love and abundance, willow for ease of suffering and magick, and there are many other options and possibilities as well. Please refer to section 2 or chapter 12 for more information regarding the magickal and mythical correspondences of trees.

The Christmas/Yule Tree: A representation of eternal life and rebirth. It is almost always an evergreen tree that is used to festively decorate the home, whether it be real or artificial. The evergreen tree represents endurance through hardships and the promise to survive the cold months of winter. Due to the fact that an evergreen tree maintains green leaves (typically needles) all year round, these trees have historically represented eternal life and longevity. Ancient Pagan Rome used evergreen trees during the feast of Saturnalia to symbolically celebrate and welcome the birth of a new year.

Many years back, a friend I met on Facebook, Ian, once shared with me his take on pine trees by saying they reminded him of rocket ships pointing toward heaven. He mentioned that perhaps when people or animals are buried near a pine tree, the tree acts as a facilitator to send the soul out into heaven. I cannot help but think his analogy could possibly be similar to the concept the ancient Egyptians had in mind while constructing the pyramids. Not only that, but an evergreen tree such as spruce, pine, or fir makes me think about Christian lore, which has it that Jesus was crucified on a wooden cross, a tree, and his sacrifice represents eternal life. I think that this may possibly be one reason why the Christian faith incorporated ancient Pagan Yule traditions of an evergreen tree into contemporary practice. In fact, I decided to do some research on the possible types of wood that could have been used by the Romans for crucifixion. While it is not known for certain which trees they used, it is largely agreed that the crosses were likely constructed from a few types of wood that were locally available. The consensus includes cedar, cypress, palm, olive, pine, and box. However, according to Dr. Alexander Roman in his article "Feast of the Exaltation of the Cross," the longest going legends support the notion that Jesus was crucified on either cedar, pine, or cypress. All three of these are evergreen trees, except for the bald cypress, and therefore again we see the evergreen as representing eternal life or life after death.

The Christmas/Yule Wreath: Think about the meaning of a circle. There is no beginning and no end, only a continuation. The wreath represents eternal life and a way to view time apart from a linear viewpoint as well as a symbol of hope and protection. The wreath can also represent the wheel of the year and the natural cycle of life, death, and rebirth. These holiday wreaths are almost always made from either real evergreen trees or artificial representations of them.

The Maypole: A celebratory symbolic representation of the balance of male/female and of reproduction. Maypoles can be made from many types of wood.

The Family Tree: A family tree is a record of the continuation of life after death or the passing of blood from generation to generation. The family tree not only reveals the most recent members of a family, but also the family's roots. Again, this represents the continuation of life after death.

Walking Stick/Magickal Staff: A symbol of wisdom, age, and a bridge symbolically connecting the past, present, and future. A walking stick also symbolizes a journey. I have included more information about this in chapter 11.

Flagpoles: These lift our pride from below and into the air above for all to see. While most modern flagpoles are made usually made from steel or aluminum, they were originally made from various types of wood and the practice of constructing flagpoles dates to at least two thousand years ago. Although not related, whenever I see a flag pole I automatically think about the Native American practice of creating totem poles.

The Cross: This symbol commonly represents the death and rebirth of Jesus, but it also represents the four directions, the four elements, and the procession of the sun. This symbol predates Christianity.

The Ladder of Transmigration: The Ladder of Transmigration is a pictorial symbol from medieval Christianity and looks much like a pine tree. It is a representation of the transmigration of the soul from its earthly form and into heaven or paradise. I suspect that the staff of the Pope, called the papal staff, is based on this very image.

The Tree House: As a child, or even as an adult, did you ever play in a tree house or dreamed of having one? Did you ever stop to think about it? Probably not, because that would defeat the purpose to begin with. A tree house can represent not only innocence and escape from the stresses of responsibility but can also represent our lost heritage—a time when we once lived in harmony with our environment. The tree house represents a childhood fantasy but also is a symbol of our journey from childhood to adulthood, and then into the ever after.

General Sherman: General Sherman is the largest living tree on earth and is located in the Sequoia National Park of California. Over a million people visit the park each year to see not only General Sherman but the many government-protected giant sequoia trees. Many people still find beauty and awe in our trees.

Tying Ribbons around Trees: I am not sure when this tradition started, but perhaps in the 1970s the popular song "Tie a Yellow Ribbon Round the Ole Oak Tree" by Tony Orlando and Dawn inspired the custom. The song told a tale of a man who served time as a prisoner of war and wanted his girlfriend to give him a sign that he was still wanted when he came home. If he saw a yellow ribbon tied to the oak tree, it meant that she was still faithful to him, but if it was not there, he would simply go on with his life and try to forget her. The song was likely inspired by a nineteenth-century practice of women tying yellow ribbons in their hair to make a public statement proclaiming that she was still loyal and devoted to her husband or lover who went away to war. Nowadays, there are many customs of tying ribbons around trees. I have seen pink ribbons tied around trees to symbolically stand against breast cancer, red ribbons for AIDS, blue ribbons for freedom, and even ribbons tied on trees to celebrate Earth Day. Could these practices be a modern form of folk magick?

Carving Love Affirmations on Tree Trunks: We have seen it in movies and in real life. You know what I'm talking about; a heart-shaped image carved into a tree trunk that often includes initials proclaiming one's love for another such as "P &J forever." On the campus where I earned my BA and where I am currently working on my MA is the Fell Arboretum, which was founded in 1867 and granted status in 1995 into the International Society of Arboriculture. It contains thousands of trees on a 490-acre site and represents over 154 species. When I first began studying the trees that thrive there, I noticed that on the bark and trunks of a large beech tree, there were years and years of carved images, mostly love affirmations, that students had engraved. At first, I was rather appalled by the blatant desecration of the tree, but at second glance it seemed as though the tree was still quite healthy and had suffered little as a consequence.

A few years later, I learned about an old folk tale suggesting that carving into the bark of a beech tree makes honest requests or dreams come true. After thinking about this for a while, I am inclined to believe that the practice could be applied to most types of trees, however, the trunk and bark of older beech trees is very smooth and makes carving a very easy process.

On that note, I simply must share a brief and true story. It must have been well over ten years ago when a great friend of mine, former member of our group, and fellow lover of trees shared with me that she had met a boy on campus that she instantly took an interest in. The feeling seemed mutual. Every day they began to meet each other before and after class beneath the large weeping beech tree on campus (a weeping variety has branches and leaves that reach down to the ground rather that up into the air) where they would talk, read to each other, and make out. Today they are happily married and recently gave birth to their first child. As I was writing this little section, I contacted her to ask if they had ever carved upon the tree, and while the answer was no, she reported to me that the tree seemed to have a very unique character and vibe to the point that the tree seemed to have chosen them and that only those the tree permitted were given access to enter its sacred space.

I challenge you to find more examples of the sacredness of the tree that can be found today, for there are many others. Dare yourself to imagine.

SUMMARY

From the beginning of recorded history, both ancient and contemporary cultures across the world have viewed trees as a means of nourishment, healing, magick, and balance and as a symbol of our connection to the divine as well as the divine's connection to us.

In numerous myths and tales concerned with the sacredness of trees, we have encountered the number twelve repeatedly and this can be a representation of the heavens above, the world below, and the ages of time. From the heavens to the earth, the tree stands in the center as a symbol of the Goddess and the God both within us and without, representing not the beginning of time nor the end, but eternity and our place within it. The tree is a symbol of life, death, and the promise of rebirth.

Regarding the number twelve, I leave you with a few things to ponder. The number twelve may symbolize the cosmic order, at least from our planet Earth, and twelve is a sequence of the numbers one and two. If you point one finger up, it looks like a phallic shape, and if you point two fingers like the peace sign, it resembles the form of the female counterpart. The number twelve thus can represent a balance of male and female and it is the same with a tree. The number twelve represents the zodiac and the twelve constellations. There were twelve tribes of Judah/Israel, twelve sons of Jacob (the same Jacob who ascended the ladder to heaven), twelve disciples of Christ, twelve stones on the breastplate of the Jewish High Priest, twelve knights of the round table, twelve tasks of Hercules, twelve Olympian gods, and in the American court system a jury consists of twelve members. There were also twelve staffs to represent each tribe of Judah/Israel. The New International Version of the Bible has the following verse: "So Moses spoke to the Israelites, and their leaders gave him twelve staffs, one for the leader of each of their ancestral tribes, and Aaron's staff was among them" (Numbers 17:6). It is said that the staff of Aaron was made from the almond tree, and possibly that of Moses as well, but I suspect that these twelve staffs were made of twelve different types of wood and that these trees correspond to each sign of the zodiac, which would therefore help support Robert Grave's claim that there was in ancient times a tree associated with each month.

As found in the *Three Books of Occult Philosophy* by Henry Cornelius Agrippa, originally written over five hundred years ago, Agrippa shared the following concerning the number twelve:

- There are twelve orders of blessed spirits as well as twelve degrees of devils
- Twelve angels that rule over the signs
- Twelve tribes
- Twelve prophets
- Twelve apostles

- Twelve signs of the zodiac
- Twelve months
- Twelve principal members of the body
- Twelve deities
- Twelve consecrated birds
- Twelve consecrated animals
- Twelve holy stones
- Twelve plants
- Twelve sacred trees
- Twelve members of man distributed to the signs

Speaking of Agrippa, I couldn't help but share this quote from the aforementioned book, "It is thought that natural magic is nothing else but the highest power of natural sciences..."

Each of us are a leaf on the great World Tree and it is high time that we once again connect to the trees and rediscover the sacred magick of the divine within our hearts.

Section Two
FIELD GUIDE TO TREES

I am the tree
I have witnessed the ages
I have witnessed the gods
I have witnessed creation
I invite you to learn my secrets
I am the tree

Chapter Four
GUIDE

This chapter is a field guide to help properly identify many of the common trees that can be found in North America and Europe as well as to provide the medicinal and magickal properties of each. Unfortunately, it is just not possible to represent every tree in the world, and so therefore I have chosen to represent one hundred. However, I have also included many additional trees as important mentions at the end of chapter 12. If there is a tree near you that is not found in this book, please do some research to learn about the tree because all of trees are sacred. Regarding tree lingo and terminology, refer to the appendix at the end of the book, and by all means, enjoy your studies and get out there and experience the magick the and wonder of the trees.

— ALDER, BLACK —

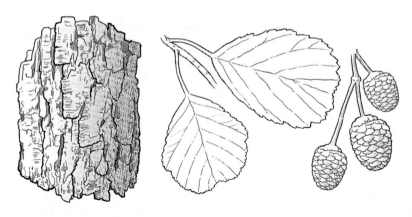

Other Names: Black alder, European alder, hazel alder, tag alder, and *fearn* (Celtic)

Number of Species: About 35 species of Alnus

Family: Betulaceae

Genus/Species: *Alnus glutinosa*

Leaf: Simple alternate, deciduous, 6–8 pairs of veins, oval to circular-shaped, sharp teeth. The leaves stay green long into the fall.

Bark: Smooth greenish-brown on young trees; brown or gray and deeply fissured and rough on older trees

Fruit: Small, woody, egg-shaped cone that resembles a pinecone

Magickal Properties and Lore: Shielding, protection, defense against psychic/magickal attack whether intended or not, confidence, courage, and strength to face hardships. Place flowers, leaves, or twigs in your pillow or near your bed to stimulate prophetic dreams and keep you safe. The message of the alder is to pay attention to the things that may be hidden around you. Alder wood makes an excellent wand.

Practical Uses: Wood is durable under water and many foundations for bridges have been made from alder.

Medicinal Properties: Leaves can be used to reduce swelling and as a natural insect repellant, especially against fleas. The bark can be used to treat inflammations, rheumatism, and diarrhea. The leaves and bark can be used as a mouthwash for treating the gums, throat, and dental problems. The essence of alder helps to calm the nerves and reduce anxiety.

— APPLE —

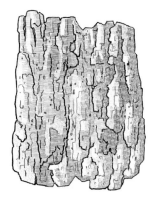 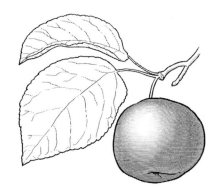

Other Names: Fruit of the gods, silver bough, tree of love, and *queirt* (Celtic)

Number of Species: Over 35 species and 7,500 varieties. All apple trees owe their existence to the crabapple.

Family: Rosaceae

Genus: *Malus*

Leaf: Simple, alternate, deciduous, oval-shaped, usually between 2 and 4 inches long with fine-toothed margins

Bark: Brown or gray and scaly

Fruit: Edible (other than the seeds), delicious, very healthy, 2 inches or more in diameter

Magickal Properties and Lore: Health, healing, fertility, love, youth, sex, immortality, food for honoring the dead, magickal and otherworld journeys, used for protection on the astral plane such as in dreams. Use the wood to make a great wand. Blossoms can be added to love sachets or used in a ritual bath for purification. Cut an apple in half and share with a loved one. If cut in half horizontally at the middle, you will discover a five-pointed star. Plant an apple tree to honor the Goddess and nature spirits. Apple trees are known to be quite friendly, and apples were thought to be the fruit of Avalon—granting people with magickal abilities.

Practical Uses: Use apple trees to adorn the yard, for they provide beautiful flowers in the spring. Grow apple trees simply for the enjoyment of their edible fruits.

Medicinal Properties: Apples are a good source of nourishment providing antioxidants, vitamins E, A, C, B-6, niacin, potassium, and iron. Apple is beneficial to the bowels, liver, and the brain. Eating an apple can relieve a headache, help with blood pressure and heart problems, and ward off fever. An apple helps clean the teeth and gums and will kill bacteria in the mouth. The boiled fruit can be applied to the skin to help remove burn marks.

— ARBORVITAE, AMERICAN —

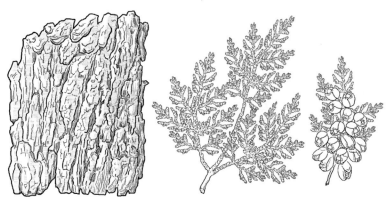

Other Names: Eastern arborvitae and often called white cedar, though not a true cedar

Number of Species: 5

Family: Cupressaceae

Genus/Species: *Thuja occidentalis*

Leaf: Evergreen, simple opposite in 4 rows, short-pointed and scale-like

Bark: Dark reddish-brown, finely fissured, and scaly

Fruit: Small egg-shaped cones, oval and round, color depends on the season

Magickal Properties and Lore: Protection, banishing, exorcisms, releasing the unwanted, confidence, divination, curse-breaking, strength, scent can ward off grief and sadness, a symbol of immortality, and used in funerals. Dried leaves can be burned along with sage to clear an area of unwanted energies.

Practical Uses: Used as an ornamental tree or hedge to adorn a yard or landscape and planted to serve as a natural fence. Wood is soft but resists decay, repels moths, and is used to make fence poles and chests.

Medicinal Properties: Needles have been used to make a tea that contains 50 mg of vitamin C per 100 g and can used to treat scurvy—a disease formed as a result of vitamin C deficiency. It can be used to treat many kinds of warts and ringworm.

— ASH, GREEN —

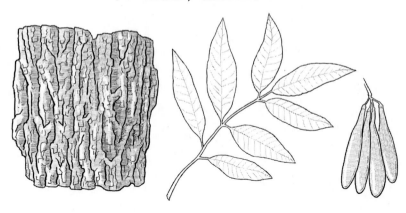

Other Names: *Nion* (Celtic), red ash

Number of Species: About 70 species of ash, although many have been lost due to the emerald ash borer

Family: Oleaceae

Genus/Species: *Fraxinus pennsylvanica*

Leaf: Compound opposite, deciduous, 5–9 leaflets, either a fine-toothed or toothless

Margin: The green ash often has a large unattractive growth at the ends of small branches called an insect gall

Bark: Gray or brown with deep furrows often appearing diamond-shaped

Fruit: Green samara that turns brown when mature

Magickal Properties and Lore: Ash is part of the Druidic fairy triad consisting of oak, ash, and thorn and is sacred to the Druids. Ash wood makes a great wand and can absorb sickness. Used for healing, love, and protection, the ash represents the World Tree, Yggdrasil, or the Tree of Life. Leaves placed under a pillow are said to bring prophetic dreams, and snakes fear the ash tree. You can burn ash to attract prosperity or carry the leaves to attract love. Rub a needle over a wart three times and then stick the needle into an ash tree to heal the wart. The blue and white ash trees share the same magickal properties as the green.

Practical Uses: Ash wood was used by the Celts to make mighty spears, and maypoles were often made of ash. Baseball bats are commonly made from ash wood.

Medicinal Properties: The bark of ash can be used to make an infusion for a mild laxative. The leaves and bark may also be used to reduce fever and treat kidney and urinary infections.

— ASPEN, QUAKING —

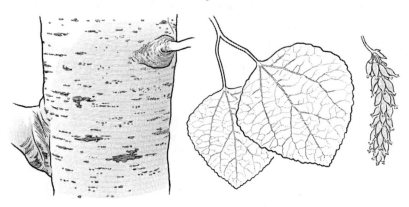

Other Names: Whispering tree, trembling aspen, mountain aspen, popple, white poplar, alamo blanco, and golden aspen. It is the most distributed tree in North America.

Number of Species: 3—quaking, bigtooth, European, and several varieties

Family: Salicaceae

Genus/Species: *Populus tremuloides*

Leaf: Simple alternate, deciduous, sharp point, fine-toothed margin, dark green above, and dull below

Bark: Smooth and greenish-white or cream colored

Fruit: Tiny green capsules that open and release seeds

Magickal Properties and Lore: Use wood for protection against thieves, past-life regression, and to ward off evil spirits. Some mythology claims that the wood Jesus was crucified upon was aspen as this tree represents life, death, and resurrection; it is short lived but reproduces itself easily and quickly. Use for love, victory, joy, peace, and to calm anxiety. The message of aspen is to face our doubts, fears, and to release the old to welcome the new. Aspen wood makes a great wand in symbol of not only communicating with nature spirits, but also communication with the higher self. Keep aspen wood or a sigil of the tree near the bed to generate greater control of your dreams, but be warned, it may induce fearful dreams so that you can learn to face your fears.

Practical Uses: Wood is light in weight and used for boxes, crates, wall panels, matches, and sometimes books, printing paper, and furniture.

Medicinal Properties: Bark and leaves can relieve pains such as a headache and contain the chemical used to make aspirin—hence the name. Leaves and leaf buds may treat burns, aches, and swelling in the joints.

— BEECH, AMERICAN —

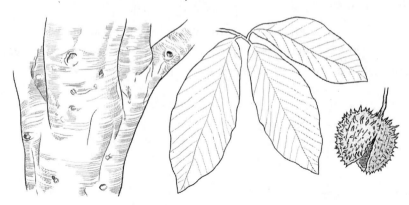

Other Names: Bok, boke, buche, faggio, fago, faya, haya, hetre, phagos, and "Queen of the Woods"

Number of Species: 10

Family: Fagaceae

Genus/Species: *Fagus grandifolia*

Leaf: Simple alternate, deciduous, oval shaped 2–5 inches in length with a long-pointed tip, darker green above and lighter below, 9–15 pairs of veins, toothed margins, buds are long and sharp

Bark: Smooth and light gray

Fruit: Reddish-brown capsule growing in pairs that release a nut. Beechnuts provide nourishment to many animals and humans, as they are rich in minerals, starch, and protein.

Magickal Properties and Lore: Wood may grant wishes. Carve your desire onto the wood and then bury it. Carry the wood or leaves to balance emotional overreactions, discover lost wisdom and knowledge, and increase creative abilities such as writing, poetry, and communication. Used for divination, understanding, and good luck. The wood makes a great wand for communicating with nature spirits, the higher self, and the divine. The essence of beech can help boost confidence, hope, and optimism.

Practical Uses: Wood is valuable and has been used for furniture and flooring. Nuts can be roasted and used in bread. Wood chips are often used to flavor many beers.

Medicinal Properties: Beech can be used for healing as it has astringent, antiseptic, and disinfectant properties. Can be used to treat eczema, skin disorders, and scabs.

— BEECH, EUROPEAN —

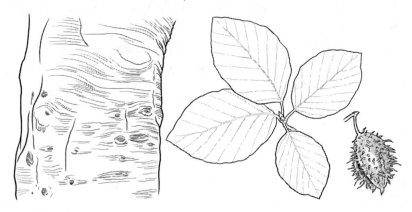

Other Names: Copper beech, common beech, purple beech, bok, boke, bu-che, faggio, fago, faya, haya, hetre, phagos, and "Queen of the Woods"

Number of Species: 10

Family: Fagaceae

Genus/Species: *Fagus sylvatica*

Leaf: Simple alternate leaf, toothless margins, deciduous, green to purple in color, 6–7 veins on each side, sharp pointed buds

Bark: Smooth and light gray, trunk resembles an elephant's foot

Fruit: Reddish-brown capsule growing in pairs that release a nut. Beechnuts provide nourishment to many animals and humans, as they are rich in minerals, starch, and protein.

Magickal Properties and Lore: Wood may grant wishes by carving your wish onto the wood and then burying it. Carry the wood or leaves to balance emotional overreactions, discover lost wisdom and knowledge, and to increase creative abilities such as writing, poetry, and communication. Used for divination, understanding, and good luck. The wood makes a great wand for communicating with nature spirits, the higher self, and the divine. The essence of beech may help to boost confidence, hope, and optimism.

Practical Uses: Wood is valuable and has been used for furniture and flooring. Nuts can be roasted and used in bread. Wood chips are often used to flavor many beers.

Medicinal Properties: Beech can be used for healing as it has astringent, antiseptic, and disinfectant properties. Can be used to treat eczema, skin disorders, and scabs.

— BIRCH, GRAY —

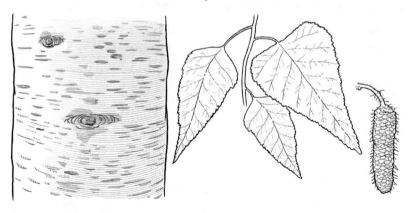

Other Names: Grey birch, old field birch, poverty birch, poplar birch, wire birch, "Lady of the Woods," beith, *beithe* (Celtic), beth, berke, birka

Number of Species: About 60

Family: Betulaceae

Genus/Species: *Betula populifolia*

Leaf: Simple alternate, deciduous, triangular leaf base with an elongated pointed (acuminate) tip 2–3 inches long, dark green above and paler below with a coarse margin. This tree is fairly resistant to the bronze birch borer. Stems are thin and reddish-brown or slightly gray in color.

Bark: Grayish-white, smooth, with black triangular patches. Bark is not quite as white as the paper birch and generally has three trunks.

Fruit: Small nutlet with a single cone-like catkin

Magickal Properties and Lore: Peace, love, balance, new beginnings, purification, sacrifice for a greater cause, protection, magick, birth, life, death, and renewal. Sacred to the Goddess in general, especially Freya, and it has been said that causing harm to this tree will provoke the anger of the Goddess. The wood makes a great wand and can aid with opening communication with the Goddess, but make sure you have permission from the tree and the Goddess first. The essence of birch will help to bring peace, calm the nerves, reduce anxiety, and help one remain calm.

Practical Uses: Wood has been used for fuel, boats, canoes, paper, shoes, and roof tiles. Sap can be used to make a natural shampoo.

Medicinal Properties: Tea from the leaves stimulates the gall bladder, kidneys and liver and makes a good antiseptic mouthwash. Leaves help to relieve rheumatism and gout. Sap of the birch tree can cleanse the blood, balance metabolism, and relieve eczema and psoriasis. Leaves can be added to a salad to provide much nutrition.

—— BIRCH, PAPER ——

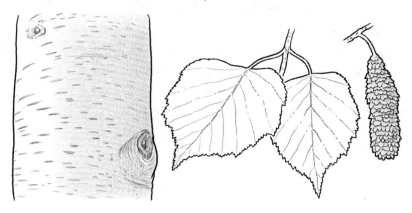

Other Names: "Lady of the Woods," beith, *beithe* (Celtic), beth, berke, birka, white birch, canoe birch

Number of Species: About 60

Family: Betulaceae

Genus/Species: *Betula papyrifera*

Leaf: Simple alternate, deciduous, triangular to oval, 2–4 inches long, toothed margin with pointed tip, darker green above and paler below

Bark: Smooth, white, sometimes peels off in curled sheets and displays horizontal lines, single trunk

Fruit: Small nutlet with catkins growing in threes

Magickal Properties and Lore: Peace, love, balance, new beginnings, purification, sacrifice for a greater cause, protection, magick, birth, life, death, and renewal. Sacred to the Goddess in general, especially Freya, and it has been said that causing harm to this tree will provoke the anger of the Goddess. The wood makes a great wand and can aid with opening communication with the Goddess, but make sure you have permission from the tree and the Goddess first. The essence of birch will help to bring peace, calm the nerves, reduce anxiety, and help one remain calm.

Practical Uses: Wood has been used for fuel, boats, canoes, paper, shoes, and roof tiles. Sap can be used to make a natural shampoo.

Medicinal Properties: Tea from the leaves stimulates the gall bladder, kidneys and liver and makes a good antiseptic mouthwash. Leaves help to relieve rheumatism and grout. Sap of the birch tree can cleanse the blood, balance metabolism, and can relieve eczema and psoriasis. Leaves can be added to a salad to provide much nutrition.

— BIRCH, RIVER —

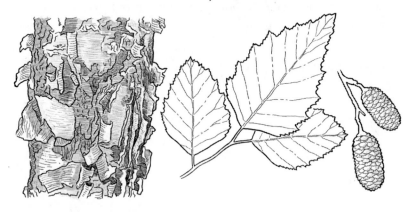

Other Names: "Lady of the Woods," beith, *beithe* (Celtic), beth, berke, birka, red birch, black birch

Number of Species: About 60

Family: Betulaceae

Genus/Species: *Betula nigra*

Leaf: Simple alternate, deciduous, 2–3 inches long, toothed margin, darker green above and paler below

Bark: Reddish-brown and gray, curly, shaggy, and flaky

Fruit: Small nutlet with 1–3 cone-like catkins

Magickal Properties and Lore: Peace, love, balance, new beginnings, purification, sacrifice for a greater cause, protection, magick, birth, life, death, and renewal. Sacred to the Goddess in general, especially Freya, and it has been said that causing harm to this tree will provoke the anger of the Goddess. The wood makes a great wand and can aid with opening communication with the Goddess, but make sure you have permission from the tree and the Goddess first. The essence of birch will help to bring peace, calm the nerves, reduce anxiety, and help one remain calm.

Practical Uses: Wood has been used for fuel, boats, canoes, paper, shoes, and roof tiles. Sap can be used to make a natural shampoo.

Medicinal Properties: Tea from the leaves stimulates the gall bladder, kidneys and liver and makes a good antiseptic mouthwash. Leaves help to relieve rheumatism and grout. Sap of the birch tree can cleanse the blood, balance metabolism, and can relieve eczema and psoriasis. Leaves can be added to a salad to provide much nutrition.

— BIRCH, YELLOW —

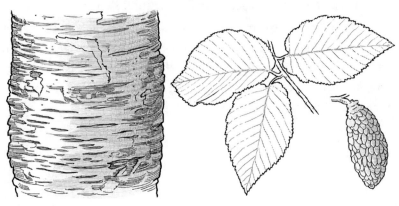

Other Names: "Lady of the Woods," beith, *beithe* (Celtic), beth, berke, birka, swamp birch

Number of Species: About 60

Family: Betulaceae

Genus/Species: *Betula alleghaniensis*

Leaf: Simple alternate, deciduous, 3–5 inches long, pointed tip with toothed margin

Bark: Yellow to bronze in color with darker horizontal lines and curls in papery scales. Scratch the bark of a living stem and you will smell "winter green." You can chew on it as a natural breath freshener.

Fruit: Small nutlet with a cone-like catkin

Magickal Properties and Lore: Peace, love, balance, new beginnings, purification, sacrifice for a greater cause, protection, magick, birth, life, death, and renewal. Sacred to the Goddess in general, especially Freya, and it has been said that causing harm to this tree will provoke the anger of the Goddess. The wood makes a great wand and can aid with opening communication with the Goddess, but make sure you have permission from the tree and the Goddess first. The essence of birch will help to bring peace, calm the nerves, reduce anxiety, and help one remain calm.

Practical Uses: Wood has been used for fuel, boats, canoes, paper, shoes, and roof tiles. Sap can be used to make a natural shampoo.

Medicinal Properties: Tea from the leaves stimulates the gall bladder, kidneys and liver and makes a good antiseptic mouthwash. Leaves help to relieve rheumatism and grout. Sap of the birch tree can cleanse the blood, balance metabolism, and can relieve eczema and psoriasis. Leaves can be added to a salad to provide much nutrition.

— BLACK GUM —

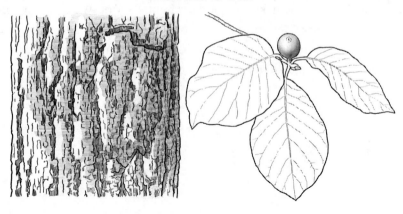

Other Names: Black tupelo, tupelo, sour gum, pepperidge

Number of Species: 5

Family: Nyssaceae

Genus/Species: *Nyssa sylvatica*

Leaf: Simple alternate, deciduous, 2–5 inches long, shiny green above, paler and hairy below, clustered at the end of branch, leaves leave a scar on the twig when pulled off

Bark: Light to dark gray, flaky with thick irregular ridges and furrows

Fruit: Drupes—blue-black fleshy berries when mature and contains one seed, edible

Magickal Properties and Lore: Resistance, strength, standing your ground, love, and health.

Practical Uses: Provides food for birds and mammals, used by bees to make wild honey. Considered a great shade tree.

Medicinal Properties: Fruit is high in fiber, fat, calcium, and phosphorous.

—— BOXELDER ——

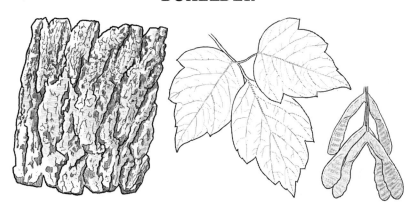

Other Names: Ash leaf maple, manitoba, maple ash, black ash, cut-leaf maple, sugar ash, three-leaved maple, and elf maple. This is not an ash nor an elder tree. It is a maple.

Number of Species: About 125 species of maple

Family: Sapindaceae (the soapberries). The maples were formerly classified as Aceraceae.

Genus/Species: *Acer negundo*

Leaf: Compound opposite, deciduous, 4–9 inches long, 3–5 leaflets, generally 3-lobed, irregular toothed margin

Bark: Light gray to brown, wavy and deeply furrowed

Fruit: Green winged seeds (samara) in pairs 1–2 inches long

Magickal Properties and Lore: Love, romance, knowledge, communication, money and finances, cleansing, protection from evil, sacred to fire and water elementals. Wands are good for spiritual healing.

Practical Uses: Food source for birds and mammals. Wood is good for carving.

Medicinal Properties: Sap can be boiled into maple syrup containing sugars, potassium, calcium, magnesium, vitamin A, B2, B5, B6, folic acid, niacin, biotin, and proteins.

— BUCKEYE, OHIO —

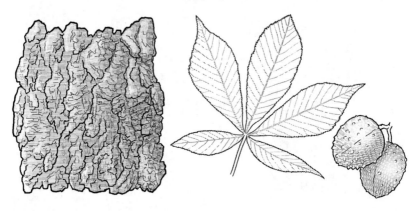

Other Names: Fetid buckeye, American buckeye, stinking buckeye, often confused with horsechestnut

Number of Species: 13–19

Family: Hippocastanaceae

Genus/Species: *Aesculus glabra*

Leaf: Palmate compound opposite, deciduous, 5–15 inches long with 5–7 leaflets, each leaflet 3–5 inches long, fine irregular teeth, lack a leaflet stalk. A simple way to distinguish the Ohio buckeye from a horsechestnut is by examining the buds. The Ohio buckeye produces a large, papery bud while the buds of a horsechestnut are very sticky to the touch

Bark: Gray to brown with scaly patches and furrows

Fruit: Yellow to light brown, spiny capsules, often grow in clusters, poisonous. The nuts contained within the fruit, called buckeyes, are dark brown and glossy when mature

Magickal Properties and Lore: Divination, luck, and financial matters. Carry the seed of a buckeye (brown and shiny) to attract money, especially when wrapped with a dollar bill. Native Americans thought the seed of the tree looks like the eye of a male deer, a buck, hence the name. Due to the fact that the buckeye is toxic and its seed grows in a semihard protective outer casing that is typically covered with small spikes, the buckeye can also be used for protection and magickal defense.

Practical Uses: Wood is light and good for carving and whittling. Fruit contains tannic acid and is poisonous to birds, animals, and humans. The Native Americans had a way of extracting the poisonous acid and roasting and mashing to create a meal; however, this is not suggested.

Medicinal Properties: Buckeye is toxic and contains tannic acid and therefore not recommended for medicinal purposes; however, it has historically been used as a sedative and for relieving constipation, coughs, arthritis, and rheumatism.

— BUCKTHORN, COMMON —

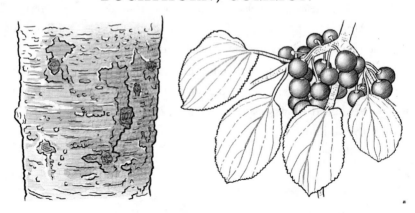

Other Names: European buckthorn, common buckthorn, purging buck-thorn

Number of Species: About 100 species of small trees and shrubs

Family: Rhamnaceae

Genus/Species: *Rhamnus cathartica*

Leaf: Simple opposite or alternate, deciduous, oval-shaped, not to be confused with dogwood, 1–3 inches long, fine-toothed margin, pointed tip, 3–5 pairs of veins that are slightly curved and indented

Bark: Gray with horizontal markings, scaly, with tiny thorns or spines on the stems

Fruit: Dark blue to black when mature and growing in clusters. Each fruit contains 3–4 seeds.

Magickal Properties and Lore: Protection, exorcisms, legal matters, luck. Branches may be placed over doors and windows to ward off evil and negativity. Carry wood to win favor in court or to draw good luck.

Practical Uses: This tree is considered invasive and can quickly overtake and kill other plants nearby.

Medicinal Properties: Berries cause diarrhea and therefore can be used as a laxative. Berries remain on the tree throughout the winter and are used as a food source for birds. Fruit contains vitamins, minerals, and fatty acids with antioxidants. The bark can increase bile secretion and treatment of rheumatism and hepatitis. There are many precautions concerning the use of this tree for medicinal reasons, so always consult a physician first.

— CATALPA, NORTHERN —

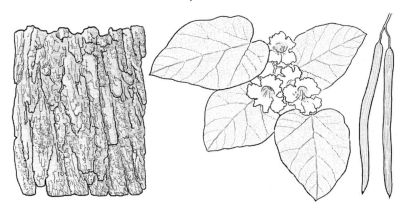

Other Names: Indian bean, bean tree, catawba, cigar tree, hardy catalpa, Western catalpa, hardy catalpa, fish-bait tree

Number of Species: 2 main species in North America and possibly 12 in all

Family: Bignoniaceae

Genus: *Catalpa* speciosa

Leaf: Simple opposite, deciduous, large heart-shaped leaves 5–12 inches long, pointed tip, toothless margin, dull green above and paler below with soft hairs

Bark: Gray to brown with deep furrows and ridges

Fruit: Long capsules resembling beans, 8–18 inches in length, which turn brown when mature and split into 2 parts

Magickal Properties and Lore: Healing, love, and spirit communication. Wood can be used to make a wonderful wand but is very soft and easily broken.

Practical Uses: Wood is soft, excellent for carving, and sometimes used for furniture, cabinets, and boats. Can be used as an ornamental tree due to its large, beautiful, white flowers in the spring and its impressively large leaves and seed pods.

Medicinal Properties: Bark has been used to treat snakebites, coughs, and asthma and as an antiseptic and laxative. Leaves can be used to treat minor wounds and cuts. The roots are very poisonous.

— CEDAR, RED —

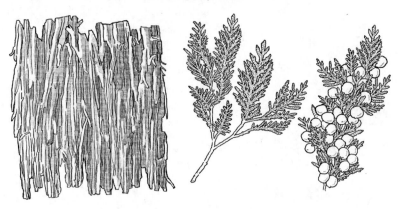

Other Names: Cedar, Eastern red cedar, pencil cedar, chansha, Eastern juniper, or red juniper. This tree is not actually a cedar but is a juniper. It is commonly labeled as a cedar and the two are very similar in appearance

Number of Species: 60–70 species of juniper

Family: Cupressaceae

Genus/Species: *Juniperus virginiana*

Leaf: Scaly needles, evergreen, 1–2 inches in length that overlap each other, sharply pointed, dark green

Bark: Red-brown to gray, peels with age in long, thin, vertical strips

Fruit: Berry-like blue cones with a white powdery surface containing 1–2 seeds

Magickal Properties and Lore: Cleansing, purification, general magick, financial concerns, endurance, immortality, love, protection from negativity, evil, and theft. The scent relieves stress and anxiety. Burn the wood or dried leaves to clear past karma if one has learned his or her lessons, burn to open communication with the spirit world or to send wishes up to the spirit world or to make an offering to local nature spirits. It has been said that King Solomon's temple was built of cedar wood from the forests of Lebanon. The wood makes a good wand or staff to protect from evil and to balance emotion with mind and spirit.

Practical Uses: Food source for many birds. Wood is used in furniture such as storage chests for its wonderful scent. The pointed needles can irritate the skin. The wood is said to resist insects and decay.

Medicinal Properties: Berries strengthen the nervous system and increase appetite while aiding digestion. Tea made from the berries makes a great urinary antiseptic, can settle an upset stomach, and treats coughs and colds.

— CHERRY, BLACK —

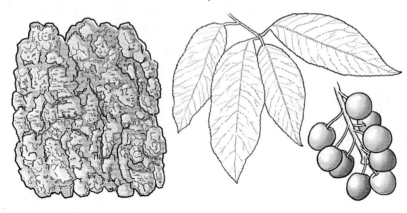

Other Names: Wild cherry, wild black cherry, rum cherry, mountain cherry

Number of Species: Over 400 species of prunus

Family: Rosaceae

Genus/Species: *Prunus serotina*

Leaf: Simple alternate, deciduous, 2–6 inches long with curved tip, fine-toothed margin, dark and shiny green above, paler below

Bark: Young bark is red to brown, smooth, and displays horizontal lines, while the bark of the mature tree is gray to brown and scaly.

Fruit: Red to dark blue-black when mature, grows in clusters, edible

Magickal Properties and Lore: Purity, love, divination, beauty, inspiration, marriage, and is sacred to the Goddess. The message of the cherry tree is insight and new beginnings. The spirit of cherry may help awaken your faith in the divine and to shed your own personal ego that could be holding you back from spiritual growth. Good for shadow work.

Practical Uses: Important source of food for birds and many animals. Cherry trees have ornamental value due to their beautiful spring flowers and attractive bark. Used for making jams, wines, and flavoring.

Medicinal Properties: Bark and roots can be used to treat coughs, bronchitis, heart and stomach troubles, fever, and high blood pressure. Eating cherries not only tastes good but can extend lifespan.

— CHERRY, PIN —

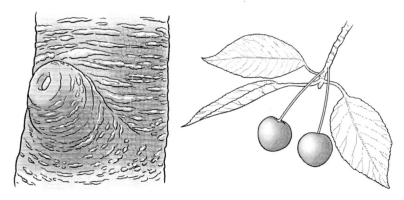

Other Names: Wild red cherry, fire cherry, and bird cherry. Often confused with the similar choke cherry.

Number of Species: Over 400 species of prunus

Family: Rosaceae

Genus/Species: *Prunus pensylvanica*

Leaf: Simple, alternate, deciduous, 2–5 inches long, oval-shaped with curved pointed tip, fine-toothed margin, dark and shiny green above, paler below, and two small glands near the petiole

Bark: Gray to black, smooth with orange to brown lines called lenticels, and sometimes scaly with age

Fruit: Bright red cherries (drupes) when mature, very edible

Magickal Properties and Lore: Purity, love, divination, beauty, inspiration, marriage, and is sacred to the Goddess. The message of the cherry tree is insight and new beginnings. The spirit of cherry may help awaken your faith in the divine and to shed your own personal ego that could be holding you back from true spiritual growth. Good for shadow work.

Practical Uses: Important source of food for birds and many animals. Cherry trees have ornamental value due to their beautiful spring flowers and attractive bark. Used for making jams, wines, and flavoring.

Medicinal Properties: Bark and roots can be used to treat coughs, bronchitis, heart and stomach troubles, fever, and high blood pressure. Eating cherries not only tastes good but can extend the lifespan.

— CHESTNUT, AMERICAN —

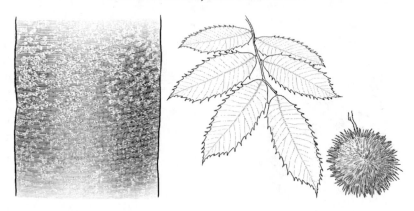

Other Names: Bread tree, dwarf chestnut, sweet chestnut. This tree should not be confused with horsechestnut or chinquapin oak. It is unlikely that you will encounter an American chestnut in the wild. The American chestnuts have largely been wiped out due to chestnut blight. An alternative is the Chinese chestnut, which has been planted to replace it due to its resistance to chestnut blight. The Chinese chestnut has the same magickal properties of the American chestnut.

Number of Species: 5–9

Family: Fagaceae

Genus/Species: *Castanea dentata*

Leaf: Simple alternate, deciduous, 6–12 inches long, unique sharp teeth that extend past the leaf margin resembling a saw. Veins are usually parallel and straight

Bark: Bark of young trees is smooth and dark brown to red or gray. Bark of older trees becomes thick and deeply furrowed.

Fruit: Spiny, bur-like green nut that turns brown when mature, very edible

Magickal Properties and Lore: Love magick, protection, fertility, success, healing, and excellent for grounding and centering. Wands made of chestnut wood are good for healing and general ritual purposes. Create a sigil of chestnut and carry it to promote fertility.

Practical Uses: This tree provides the nuts referred to in the classic Yule-tide/Christmas carol, "The Christmas Song." This tree was once very abundant and quite tall, but was nearly wiped out by a fungal disease called chestnut blight. It was a very common tree in the ancient world. The leaves are quite attractive and could be used as an ornamental tree if not for the fact that they are more of a memory or a legend than an abundant tree. There is, however, a current attempt to reintroduce them back into the wild. If you encounter a chestnut tree, it is probably the Chinese chestnut that looks virtually identical.

Medicinal Properties: Nuts are used as a food source for animals and humans. They are high in starch and carbohydrates, provide a small amount of protein, vitamin C, phosphate, iron, sodium, and are gluten-free. Nuts can be roasted, toasted, grilled, steamed, boiled, and eaten raw if peeled or made into flour, hence the name "bread tree."

— CHESTNUT, CHINESE —

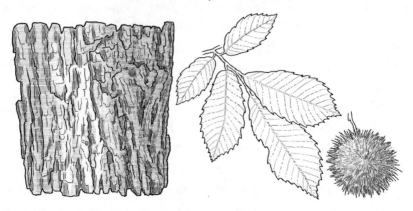

Other Names: Chestnut, bread tree

Number of Species: 5–9

Family: Fagaceae

Genus/Species: *Castanea mollisima*

Leaf: Simple alternate, deciduous, 3–6 inches long, ovate to oblong, sharp narrow teeth with tips pointing forward. The base of the leaf where it attaches is wider than the American chestnut and the twigs and buds are fuzzier. The leaves are a bit smaller than American chestnut.

Bark: Dark brown to gray and deeply fissured when mature. The ridges interlace with one another to form a diamond pattern

Fruit: Spiny, bur-like, green nut that turns brown when mature. Each pod contains 2–3 shiny brown nuts and is very edible. Be careful when handling, as they are very sharp and splintery.

Magickal Properties and Lore: Love magick, protection, fertility, success, healing, and excellent for grounding and centering. Wands made of chestnut wood are good for healing and general ritual purpose. Create a sigil of chestnut and carry it to promote fertility. This was a very common tree in the ancient world and possibly referred to in the Old Testament of the Bible.

Practical Uses: Nuts and leaves are similar to those of American chestnut. Nuts are used as a food source for animals and humans. This tree has been planted to replace the American chestnut because of its resistance to chestnut blight that basically wiped out the American chestnut tree. The Chinese chestnut is valued for its fruits and has ornamental value.

Medicinal Properties: Nuts are used as a food source for animals and humans. They are high in starch and carbohydrates, provide a small amount of protein, vitamin C, phosphate, iron, sodium, and are gluten-free. Nuts can be roasted, toasted, grilled, steamed, boiled, and eaten raw if peeled,or made into flour, hence the name "bread tree."

— CORK TREE, AMUR —

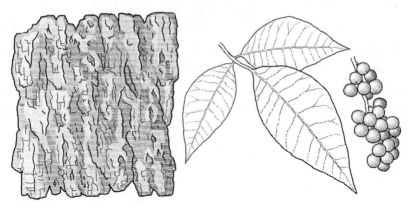

Other Names: Cork tree

Number of Species: About 10 species

Family: Rutaceae

Genus/Species: *Phellodendron amurense*

Leaf: Compound opposite, 5–11 leaflets, each leaf being 10–15 long on a mature tree, dark green and deciduous

Bark: Gray, ridged, and furrowed, soft to the touch like a cork

Fruit: Small fruits grow in clusters, each resembling a pea, green when young and blue-black when mature

Magickal Properties and Lore: Health, healing, gentleness, forgiveness, compassion, empathy, persistence, sight, clarity, and leadership

Practical Uses: Bark has been harvested in Russia to produce cork. This tree has ornamental value for its yellow colors in the fall, its yellow-green flowers, its beautiful and unusual bark, and its good shade.

Medicinal Properties: Used in China as medicine for pain relief, meningitis, pneumonia, and tuberculosis. Tree is invasive but provides food for wildlife, as its fruit is high in sugars. Bark can be used for its antibacterial, antirheumatic, and diuretic properties while also helping to heal skin disorders. May be used as eyewash, treating urinary infections, vaginal infections, diarrhea, boils, and abscesses, lowering fever, and reducing blood pressure and sugar levels.

— COTTONWOOD, EASTERN —

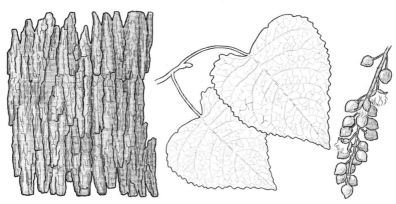

Other Names: Southern cottonwood, Carolina poplar, Eastern poplar, Alamo tree, necklace poplar.

Number of Species: 3–6

Family: Salicaceae

Genus/Species: *Populus deltoides*

Leaf: Simple alternate, deciduous, heart-shaped or triangular, 3–6 inches long, course-toothed margin, shiny green and waxy with a long leaf stalk

Bark: Gray and rough with deep furrows

Fruit: Catkin-like, about 4 inches long with several tiny capsules that split into 3 or 4 parts and release seeds that float on the wind resembling cotton

Magickal Properties and Lore: Honesty, humility, connecting with the divine. The essence of cottonwood can be used to aid in divination and meditation. This tree was considered sacred to some Native Americans. If you have ever stood beneath a cottonwood tree in the late spring when it releases its seeds into the air, then you know that they resemble very large, cottony fluff balls that glide across the air similarly to dandelion seeds but on a larger scale. If you stand beneath a large cottonwood during this time, you will see the ground is covered in white and it appears as almost like snow in the spring. It is absolutely fantastical and almost like a childhood fairy tale. Just like making a wish on a seeded dandelion and then blowing the seeds into the air, use the cottonwood seeds for similar air magick.

Practical Uses: Some Native American tribes used the leaves to make toy tipis and moccasins. Trunk was used to make poles as a center for ceremonies. This tree is not generally considered to have landscape value.

Medicinal Properties: Leaves are anti-inflammatory and can be made into a decoction to treat bruises, insect bites, and minor wounds. The bark and leaves as a decoction can treat snakebites. Bark used as a tea can treat scurvy and is a pain-reliever like aspirin for it contains salicin.

— CRABAPPLE —

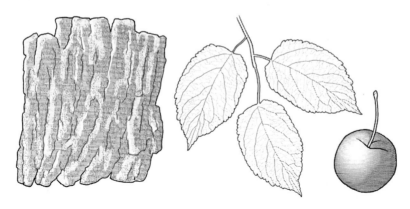

Other Names: Crabapple, wild apple, Adam's pink flowering crabapple, Adam's apple, and *queirt* (Celtic)

Number of Species: Over 35 species of apple trees and 7,500 varieties

Family: Rosaceae

Genus: *Malus*

Note: Due to the fact that there are more varieties and cultivars of crabapple than can possibly be included here, I am simply presenting the crabapple in general.

Leaf: There are many variations of the crabapple, but most leaves are simple, alternate, oval-shaped, with toothed margins, and generally not longer than 3 inches. Flowers can be white, pink, or red and often have five petals. Crabapples are always deciduous.

Bark: Brown or gray and somewhat rough on older trees

Fruit: Red, edible though tart and bitter, diameter of all crabapples is less than 2 inches

Magickal Properties and Lore: Same as apple. In fact, all apples that one finds in the supermarket such as red delicious, golden delicious, granny smith etc., owe their existence to the crabapple. Health, healing, fertility, love, youth, passion, immortality, food for honoring the dead, magickal and otherworld journeys. Can be used for protection on the astral plane such as in dreams, and the wood makes a great wand. Blossoms can be added to love sachets or used in a ritual bath for purification. Cut an apple in half and share with a love interest, and if cut in half horizontally at the middle, one can see a five-pointed star. Plant an apple tree to honor the Goddess. Apple trees are known to be very friendly.

Practical Uses: Crabapples are an important source of food for birds and other wildlife. The trees have ornamental value for their beautiful spring flowers and colorful fruits in the late summer and fall. Fruit is edible but mostly used for making cider, jellies, juices, or flavoring. and It is a source of pectin and can be used as a laxative. Crabapples are a good source of vitamin C and fiber and contain small amounts of iron, calcium, and vitamin A.

—— CYPRESS, BALD ——

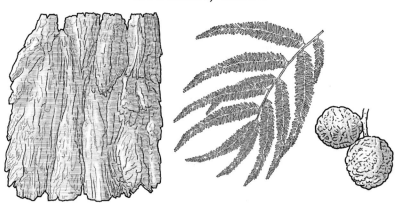

Other Names: Common bald cypress, Southern cypress, white cypress, red cypress, and swamp cypress. It is called "bald" because it drops its leaves in the fall while other types of cypress trees are evergreen. It was sometimes called the "tree of death" in the ancient world.

Number of Species: 3 species of bald cypress, 16 species of the family Taxodiaceae, and over 140 species in the cypress family

Family: Taxodiaceae—now included in the family Cupressaceae (cypress)

Genus/Species: *Taxodium distichum*

Leaf: Deciduous conifer with single needles growing in two rows on the twig, pointed tip, and is feather-like

Bark: Brown to gray with fibers that peel off in strips

Fruit: Green cone that turns brown when mature, either single cones or small clusters near the end of the branch

Magickal Properties and Lore: Healing, longevity, protection. Wood, when carried, prolongs life and makes a good wand for healing and clearing an area. Burned leaves are said to welcome the spirits. A wand of bald cypress, juniper, or any other cypress can also be used for rituals regarding financial matters. Cypress can be used at times of crisis and grief, such as death, to bring comfort and ease of mind and heart.

Practical Uses: Wood is resistant to decay, insects, and water and has been used to build boats and bridges. This tree can live hundreds and hundreds of years. Egyptians used cypress wood to make coffins.

Medicinal Properties: The resin in the cones of the tree have analgesic properties and can be used to treat burns and minor wounds. It is said that the Aztecs used the resin from the tree for this very purpose.

— DOGWOOD, CORNELIAN CHERRY —

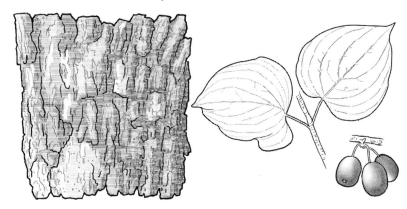

Other Names: Boxwood, budwood, European cornel, hound's tree, and flowering dogwood

Number of Species: 30–60

Family: Cornaceae

Genus/Species: *Cornus mas*

Leaf: Simple opposite, deciduous, ovate to oblong, dark green, 2 to 5 inches long, and produces yellow flowers in the spring

Bark: Gray to reddish brown, scaly, and curling in patches

Fruit: Bright red in late summer, oblong, and edible

Magickal Properties and Lore: Wishes, defense, protection, love. Helps to keep and preserve secrets. The leaves and wood can be used to craft protection amulets. It has been said that gathering a small amount of the sap on the eve of the summer solstice. Rubbing it on a cloth and carrying it daily will grant any wish. Place a dogwood leaf in a journal, a book, or anything that you want to keep private.

Practical Uses: Fruit is used to make jams and can be made into a sauce similar to cranberry if pitted and cooked with sugar. Wood is very dense and will sink in water. This wood has been used to make weapons in earlier times such as spears, and the bark can be used to make red dye.

Medicinal Properties: The fruit is nutritious and can be used to treat fevers, bowel problems, and heart diseases. Flowers have been used to treat diarrhea.

— DOGWOOD, WHITE FLOWERING —

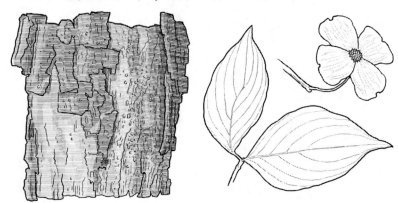

Other Names: Eastern flowering dogwood, flowering dogwood

Number of Species: 30–60

Family: Cornaceae

Genus/Species: *Cornus florida*

Leaf: Simple opposite, deciduous, 2–6 inches long, ovular shape, pointed tip, smooth toothless margin, deep green above and paler below

Bark: Red to brown, sometimes gray, and splits into small square sections

Fruit: Green drupes that turn red when mature, containing 1–2 seeds

Practical Uses: Fruit is used to make jams and can be made into a sauce similar to cranberry if pitted and cooked with sugar. Wood is very dense and will sink in water. This wood has been used to make weapons in earlier times such as spears, and the bark can be used to make red dye.

Medicinal Properties: The fruit is nutritious and can be used to treat fevers, bowel problems, and heart diseases. Flowers have been used to treat diarrhea.

— ELDER —

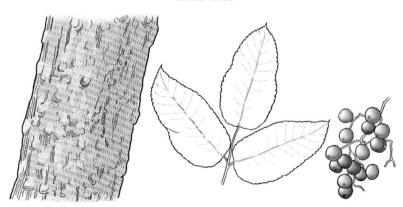

Other Names: Elderberry, common elder, sweet elder, tree of doom, American elder, fairy tree, bat tree, old lady, holle, eldrum, pipe tree, and many more. This tree is a close relative of European elder.

Number of Species: 20–30

Family: Caprifoliaceae but sometimes classified as Adoxaceae

Genus: *Sambucus canadensis*

Leaf: Opposite, deciduous, pinnately compound, 3–11 leaflets but generally 7, each leaflet being 2–6 inches long, oblong, with serrated (sharply toothed) margins. White flowers in the spring grow in bunches.

Bark: Light gray to brown, smooth when young, rough and fissured with age

Fruit: Red when unripe, and purple-black when mature, growing in clusters. Seeds of the berries and unripe berries are toxic and may cause vomiting and nausea. Leaves, twigs, and roots are also toxic so handle with care (use gloves).

Magickal Properties and Lore: Forgiveness, regeneration, stability, protection, healing, prosperity, exorcisms, sleep, burial rites. The wood can make a powerful wand, but precautions must be made due to its toxicity. Hang branches and twigs over doors and windows to ward evil and negative energies, carry the berries for the same purpose. It has been said that Judas of the Bible hung himself on his tree, although that is not a known fact. This tree is sacred to the Goddess and it is mentioned in the Wiccan Rede: "Elder be the Lady's tree, burn it not or cursed you be!"

Practical Uses: Branches have spongy pith that is easily hollowed out, so they have been used to make pipes, dart shooters, and even straws. Ripe berries are used to make jellies and wine.

Medicinal Properties: There are numerous medicinal properties of elder and most parts can be used but take precaution and never use any part without the instruction of a professional due to the fact that all parts contain small amounts of cyanide. Leaves can be used to treat headaches, bruises, and sprains. Flowers can be used to soothe the sinuses and reduce hay fever. Ripe berries have antiviral properties and strengthen the immune system. Fumes of the wood are toxic. Again, never consume unripe berries.

— ELM, AMERICAN —

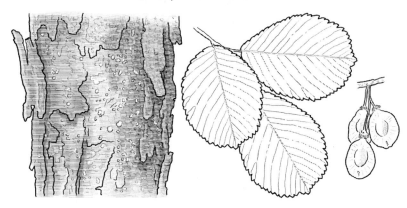

Other Names: White elm, gray elm, water elm, swamp elm, elven tree, survivor tree, and the goddess tree

Number of Species: About 18

Family: Ulmaceae

Genus/Species: *Ulmus americana*

Leaf: Simple alternate, deciduous, 3–6 inches long, 12–18 pairs of veins, pointed tip, double toothed margin, rough and scratchy to the touch

Bark: Gray when mature, brown to gray when young, deeply furrowed and scaly

Fruit: Samaras, flat green disk that turns golden yellow to tan when mature and contains the seed, ovular to round, and about half an inch in diameter

Magickal Properties and Lore: Said to protect from lightning when nearby and loved by nature spirits. The wood attracts love when carried and may enhance intuition and trust. Meditating beneath an elm will help develop spirit communication and strengthen one's rapport with nature. Leaves can be used for divination by rubbing and then placing them under or near your pillow to provoke prophetic dreams. Essence of elm balances the heart chakra, stimulates the mind, guards the third eye, and increases psychic abilities. Elm can guide the souls of the departed to the next life when placed near tombstones or burial sites; consider doing this for your pets as well as loved ones.

Practical Uses: Elm was almost wiped out in the 1970's by Dutch elm disease but is making a comeback. Plant an elm tree and be blessed. Wood has been used for furniture, coffins, and more. The ancient Greeks used elm for temple doors and posts, Minoans made chariot wheels from elm wood.

Medicinal Properties: Leaves are rich in protein, minerals, and starch. Infusions from elm roots can treat colds, coughs, fever, internal bleeding, and diarrhea and can be applied on wounds to promote healing.

—— ELM, ENGLISH ——

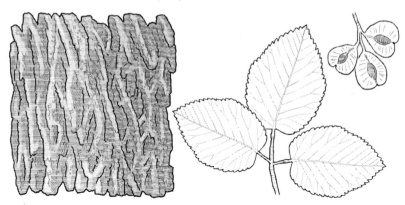

Other Names: Common elm, elven tree, atinian elm, and the goddess tree

Number of Species: About 18

Family: Ulmaceae

Genus/Species: *Ulmus procera*

Leaf: Simple alternate, deciduous, dark green, oval to oblong, 2–5 inches long, double toothed and course, rough and scratchy to the touch

Bark: Gray and deeply furrowed

Fruit: Small winged seeds (samara), tan or light brown when mature

Magickal Properties and Lore: Said to protect from lightning when nearby and loved by nature spirits. The wood attracts love when carried and enhances intuition and trust. Meditating beneath an elm will help develop spirit communication and strengthen one's rapport with nature. Leaves can be used for divination by rubbing and then placing them under or near your pillow to provoke prophetic dreams. Essence of elm balances the heart chakra, stimulates the mind, guards the third eye and increases psychic abilities. Elm can guide the souls of the departed to the next life when placed near tombstones or burial sites; consider doing this for your pets as well as loved ones.

Practical Uses: Elm was almost wiped out in the 1970's by Dutch elm disease but is making a comeback. Plant an elm tree and be blessed. Wood has been used for furniture, coffins, and more. The ancient Greeks used elm for temple doors and posts, Minoans made chariot wheels from elm wood.

Medicinal Properties: Leaves are rich in protein, minerals, and starch. Infusions from elm roots can treat colds, coughs, fever, internal bleeding, and diarrhea, and can be applied on wounds to promote healing.

— FIR, DOUGLAS —

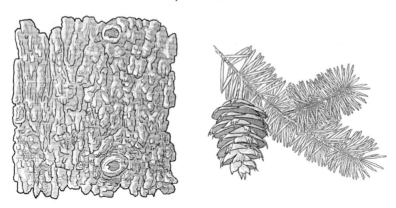

Other Names: Douglas tree, Oregon pine, yellow spruce, red spruce, Douglas spruce, or *ailm* (Celtic), often confused with spruce, although they are related and similar. This is not a true fir

Number of Species: About six species, but this is controversial. Two varieties are recognized. There are 40 species of true firs.

Family: Pinaceae

Genus/Species: *Pseudotsuga menziestii*

Leaf (Needle): Evergreen, coniferous, needle-like leaves, flat and soft to the touch, 2–4 centimeters long, growing in a spiral pattern and slightly twisted at the base

Bark: Gray, thick, and furrowed

Fruit: Seed cones, 5–8 centimeters long. This tree is dependent on forest fires for survival and reproduction.

Magickal Properties and Lore: Immortality, endurance, strength, passion, rebirth, protection, youth, purification, and healing. Can represent the World Tree and help to understand our connection to the divine.

Practical Uses: Wood can withstand heavy weight and has been used for building boats and furniture. This tree is often used as a Christmas or Yule tree. It is an important source of food for animals and birds. The bark can be used to make brown dye, and the inner bark can be made into a meal for bread-making.

Medicinal Properties: Resin from the trunk can be used as an antiseptic for treating coughs, sore throats, and respiratory infections. A decoction of the buds can treat venereal diseases, the sprouts can be used for colds, and the twigs can be used as an infusion to treat bladder and kidney problems. The needles contain vitamin C.

— FIR, WHITE —

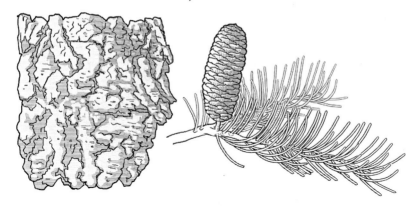

Other Names: Colorado white fir, concolor fir, silver fir, mountain white fir, and *ailm* (Celtic)

Number of Species: About 40 species of fir

Family: Pinaceae

Genus/Species: *Abies concolor*

Leaf (Needle): Evergreen, coniferous, needle-like and flat, 2–3 inches long and curved upward, green to blue in color, pointy tip, grows in a spiral arrangement, and shows two white lines underneath. Fir and spruce are very closely related; one difference is that the cones of the fir grow above the stems and the cones of the spruce point down and below the stems. Fir needles tend to be a bit softer to the touch than those of the spruce, and if you carefully pluck out a single needle from a spruce, you will find a small woody stub at the base that is absent on the fir

Bark: Somewhat smooth when young and becomes thick and furrowed with age, grayish white in color

Fruit: Cones are brown when mature, 4–5 inches in length

Magickal Properties and Lore: Immortality, endurance, strength, passion, rebirth, protection, youth, purification, and healing. Can represent the World Tree and help us understand our connection to the divine.

Practical Uses: Wood is soft and sometimes used for paper and cheap construction. Often used as a Christmas or Yule tree and has ornamental value due to its attractive appearance.

Medicinal Properties: This tree is toxic and may cause skin problems or symptoms that appear similar to eczema or dermatitis, so be careful when touching it. Resin from the trunk can be used as an antiseptic for treating coughs, sore throats, and respiratory infections. Extracts from the bark can fight tumors. The resin has been used as a filling for tooth decay, and there are many other medicinal benefits, but due its toxicity, please don't use without professional counsel and much research.

—— FRINGE TREE ——

art to come

Other Names: Old-man's beard, graybeard tree, poison ash, white fringe-tree, snowflower, and snowdrop tree

Number of Species: About 80

Family: Oleaceae

Genus/Species: *Chionanthus virginicus*

Leaf: Simple opposite, deciduous, narrow and oblong, 3–8 inches long, smooth margin, shiny green above, paler and slightly hairy below. White, feathery flowers in the spring.

Bark: Brown with a tint of reddish scales. This is a small tree.

Fruit: Dark blue or purple when mature and droops like grape clusters, usually containing one seed. Not edible for humans.

Magickal Properties and Lore: Healing, grounding, relaxation, focusing on goals. Visualize yourself as the fringe tree to move about unnoticed.

Practical Uses: This tree has ornamental value due to its beautiful flowers and because of its small size. It makes a great border tree. The fruits are a valuable source of food for birds and wildlife.

Medicinal Properties: There are many medicinal properties such as treating asthma, coughs, bladder conditions, and possibly cancer. Always research first and refer to a licensed doctor.

— GINKGO —

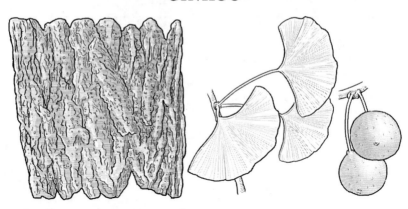

Other Names: maidenhair tree, grandfather-grandchild tree

Number of Species: Only 1 has survived to our present day, but this tree is one of the oldest living trees in the world.

Family: Ginkgoace

Genus/Species: Ginkgo biloba

Leaf: Simple alternate, deciduous, 1–3 inches long with 2 lobes, hence the term biloba, leaf resembles a fan and lacks a midrib, very easy to identify

Bark: Gray, rough, and very furrowed when mature

Fruit: Yellow to green, thick and fleshy coat when ripe. It is edible but avoid contact with the seeds. It has been called the grandfather-grandchild tree because it takes three generations of growth before the tree can produce fruit.

Magickal Properties and Lore: All-Purpose. Use for ancestor communication, memory, concentration, meditation, survival, endurance, sex, love, desire, to draw money, enhance beauty, youth, and healing. Four ginkgo trees survived the release of the atomic bomb on Hiroshima in 1945 and still live today. Burn the wood to ward off evil and negative energies. Place leaves or bark on the magickal altar for such things or store leaves in a spirit bag while meditating to remember past lives. You may also try placing the leaves under your pillow to induce dreams of past lives and of the future or simply carry the leaves with you after charging them for a specific intent. Just make sure to contact the tree first, give it thanks, and reveal your intention or desire before using. Never manipulate the will of another!

Practical Uses: Nuts are eaten in Asia, but seeds must be handled with caution as they contain oil similar to poison ivy or poison oak. Ginkgo has great landscape value due to its unique leaves and bright yellow color in the fall. The tree does well in the city and is quite adaptable. However, buyer must be warned that the female tree produces very foul-smelling fruits that remind one of rotting cheese.

Medicinal Properties: There are many medicinal properties, such as treating asthma, coughs, bladder conditions, and possibly cancer. Research first.

— GOLDEN RAIN TREE —

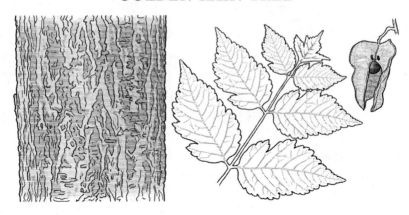

Other Names: China tree, varnish tree, pride of India, Chinese flame tree, flame gold, and others

Number of Species: 3

Family: Sapindaceae

Genus/Species: *Koelreuteria paniculata*

Leaf: Compound alternate, deciduous, pinnate arrangement, 6–18 inches long with 7–15 leaflets, each leaflet 1–4 inches long. Yellow flowers with 4 petals bloom in early July.

Bark: Light gray to brown, rough and furrowed with age

Fruit: Papery capsule about 2 inches long containing the seed and turning brown when mature

Magickal Properties and Lore: Leave this tree in peace if you encounter it. Give it a blessing of love and the nature spirits shall bless you in return.

Practical Uses: The flowers can be used to make yellow dye. This tree makes for a very beautiful showpiece and features very unique leaves. The yellow flowers of this tree bloom in the summer rather than in the spring and the tree is quite pleasing to the eye.

Medicinal Properties: There are not many known medicinal uses for this tree.

— HACKBERRY —

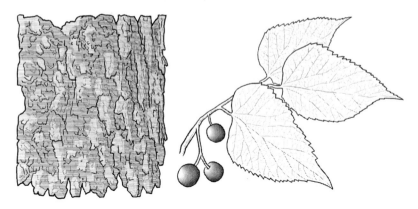

Other Names: Common hackberry, hack tree, sugarberry, northern hackberry, beaver wood, and lotus berry

Number of Species: 60 or more

Family: Ulmaceae

Genus/Species: *Celtis occidentalis*

Leaf: Simple alternate, deciduous, ovate growing in two rows, each leaf being 2–4 inches long, pointed tip, sharp teeth, leaves often bear round galls caused by plant lice, dark green above, paler below. Stems are a bit furry and grow in a zig-zag pattern.

Bark: Light brown to gray, covered with narrow corky ridges

Fruit: The small green drooping berries turn purple when mature and taste similar to prunes. They are sweet and edible when ripe and contain one seed. Birds love them.

Magickal Properties and Lore: Protection, wards against evil and negative energies. This tree is sacred to nature spirits. The older wood is not good for making a wand as it tends to rot. Consider using young specimens.

Practical Uses: Fruit of the hackberry is very loved by many birds and provides a great source of food. Older wood is soft and rots quickly, but has been used for furniture, boxes, plywood, and crates.

Medicinal Properties: The bark has been used to induce abortions and cure venereal diseases. Leaves and bark can be used as an astringent, to aid diarrhea, and has other uses as well. Do not use if pregnant. The berries have some, but little, nutritional value.

— HAWTHORN, ENGLISH —

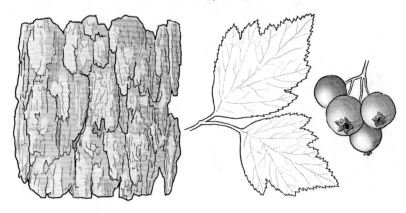

Other Names: *Huath* (Celtic), cheese tree, bread tree, hagthorn, maybush, maythorn, mayflower, haw, thornapple, midland hawthorn, woodland hawthorn

Number of Species: Over 1,000

Family: Rosaceae

Genus/Species: *Crataegus laevigata*

Leaf: Simple alternate, deciduous, dark green, round to ovate, 2–3 inches long, sharp teeth. Flowers are white to pink with 5 petals.

Bark: Gray to brown, scaly like apple, 1-inch-long thorns grow on the branches

Fruit: Orange to deep red apple-like berries that grow in clusters and are edible

Magickal Properties and Lore: Protection, cleansing, purity, fertility. Essence of hawthorn cleanses negativity and opens the heart to love, compassion, and forgiveness. Flowers have been used to decorate the maypole, and it is said that hawthorn protects the vicinity in which it grows from evil spirits and lightning. Carry any part of this tree to promote happiness. Hawthorn is sacred to the fairies and nature spirits, and is one part of the fairy triad: oak, ash, and thorn. However, on a divinatory level, this tree can be a warning of the end of something to come, such as the death card in the tarot, but promises a new beginning to follow.

Practical Uses: Fruits provide nourishment for much wildlife. Birds love to build their nests in hawthorn trees as the thorns provide extra protection. Hawthorns are often used to create natural fences and boundaries. Berries are used to make jellies and wine.

Medicinal Properties: The flowers and berries help to normalize blood pressure and can treat heart disorders. Hawthorn can help circulation and balance blood pressure in less than a minute when used as a tonic or as a tea made from the flowers.

— HAWTHORN, WASHINGTON —

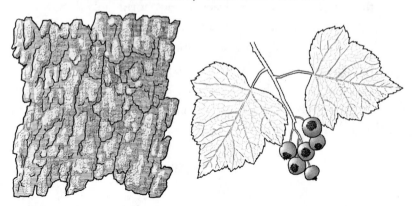

Other Names: *Huath* (Celtic), cheese tree, bread tree, hagthorn, maybush, maythorn, mayflower, haw, thorn apple, Washington thorn

Number of Species: Over 1,000

Family: Rosaceae

Genus/Species: *Crataegus phaenopyrum*

Leaf: Simple alternate, deciduous, 1–3 inches long, deep green, serrated margins, white flowers with five petals

Bark: Gray to brown, scaly like apple tree bark, thorns of 1–3 inches on stems

Fruit: Orange to deep red apple-like berries that grow in clusters. Edible

Magickal Properties and Lore: Protection, cleansing, purity, fertility. Essence of hawthorn cleanses negativity and opens the heart to love, compassion, and forgiveness. Flowers have been used to decorate the maypole, and it is said that this tree protects the nearby area from evil spirits and lightning. Carry any part of this tree to promote happiness. Hawthorn is sacred to the fairies and nature spirits, and is one part of the fairy triad: oak, ash, and thorn. However, on a divinatory level, this tree can be a warning of the end of something to come, such as the death card in the tarot, but promises a new beginning to follow.

Practical Uses: Fruits provide nourishment for much wildlife. Birds love to build their nests in hawthorn trees as the thorns provide extra protection. Hawthorns are often used to create natural fences and boundaries. Berries are used to make jellies and wine.

Medicinal Properties: The flowers and berries help to normalize blood pressure and can treat heart disorders. Hawthorn can help circulation and balance blood pressure in less than a minute when used as a tonic or as a tea made from the flowers.

— HEMLOCK, CANADIAN —

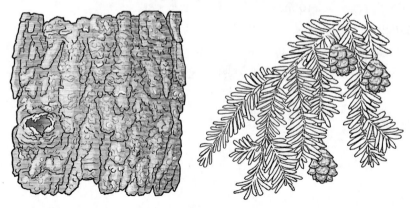

Other Names: Eastern hemlock, *pruche du Canada* (French), hemlock spruce. Do not confuse the name with the poisonous hemlock plant as the two are not related.

Number of Species: About 10

Family: Pinaceae

Genus/Species: *Tsuga canadensis*

Leaf: Single needles, evergreen, and 1 inch long, growing in 2 rows. Each needle is flat, soft, and yellow to green in color above with 2 parallel white lines below

Bark: Dark brown to gray with deep grooves, scaly and fissured. The trunk is generally straight.

Fruit: Brown cones when mature, round to ovate and ½ to 1 inch long hanging down

Magickal Properties and Lore: Protection, survival, immortality, and healing

Practical Uses: The wood is soft and used for crates, construction, and railroad ties. Makes a great hedge tree as long as it is not close to busy city streets where the roads are heavily salted in the winter.

Medicinal Properties: Bark is rich in tannic acid. Inner bark has been used for treating eczema and burns. Canadian hemlock is rich in vitamin C and has antibacterial properties.

— HICKORY, BITTERNUT —

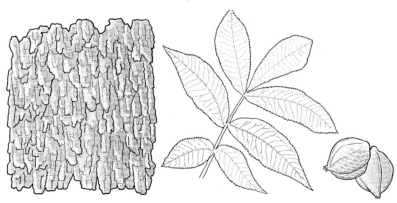

Other Names: Hickory, swamp hickory, and bitter pecan

Number of Species: 17–19 in the United States, Canada, and Mexico

Family: Juglandaceae

Genus/Species: Caryacordiformis

Leaf: Pinnately compound, alternate (though appears as opposite without a close look), deciduous. Leaves are 6–10 inches long with 7–11 leaflets; each leaflet being 3–6 inches long with pointed tips, fine-toothed margins and attached directly to the central stalk (a sessile).

Bark: Gray, cracked, and scaly, but smoother than many other hickories

Fruit: Green when young, brown when mature round nut covered with small hairs and a pointed tip. Too bitter to eat.

Magickal Properties and Lore: Good luck, legal matters, victories, flexibility, hidden messages, persistence, new possibilities and goals. Hang a fallen branch of hickory over your door to prevent legal troubles. Meditate under a hickory to receive unknown answers. Wood makes a very powerful wand.

Practical Uses: Seeds provide nourishment to wildlife. Hickory wood is very hard and strong and is therefore used for lumber, furniture, ladders, tool handles, brooms, dowel rods, and more. Also used for smoking meats or charcoal to add wonderful flavor to a meal.

Medicinal Properties: The inner bark and leaves can be used as a laxative and is good for sores, diarrhea, rheumatism, and colitis.

— HICKORY, SHELLBARK —

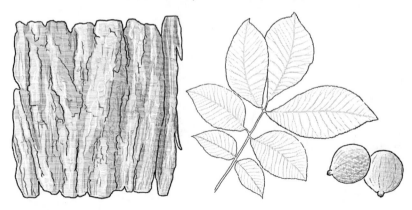

Other Names: Hickory, king nut, big-leaf hickory, big shellbark, Western shellbark, bottom shellbark, and thick shellbark

Number of Species: 17–19 in the United States, Canada, and Mexico

Family: Juglandaceae

Genus/Species: *Carya laciniosa*

Leaf: Pinnately compound alternate, deciduous, 10–24 inches long, 7 leaflets and rarely 9, fine-toothed margin, shiny green above, paler below, and covered with soft hairs

Bark: Gray, rough and shaggy with age, usually peeling in long strips

Fruit: Green, dark brown when mature, round, splits into 4 sections, sweet and edible

Magickal Properties and Lore: Good luck, legal matters, victories, flexibility, hidden messages, persistence, new possibilities and goals. Hang a fallen branch of hickory over your door to prevent legal troubles. Meditate under a hickory to receive unknown answers. Wood makes a wonderful wand.

Practical Uses: Seeds provide nourishment to wildlife. Hickory wood is very hard and strong and is therefore used for lumber, furniture, ladders, tool handles, brooms, dowel rods, and more. Also used for smoking meats or charcoal to add wonderful flavor to a meal. Inner bark can be used to make a yellow dye.

Medicinal Properties: The inner bark and leaves can be used as a laxative and is good for sores, diarrhea, rheumatism, and colitis. Due to its rich supply of magnesium, it can help with heart function.

— HOLLY, AMERICAN —

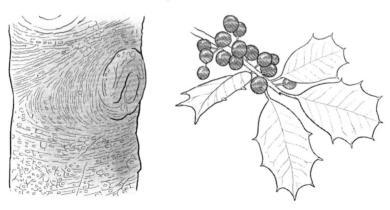

Other Names: *Tinne* (Celtic), bat's wing, wool of bat, Christ's thorn, holy tree, hulm, white holly

Number of Species: 400

Family: Aquifoliaceae

Genus/Species: *Ilex opaca*

Leaf: Simple alternate, evergreen, 1–4 inches long, sharp pointed spiky tips on the margin, green to white flowers

Bark: Light gray and smooth

Fruit: Small red berries containing 4 seeds persisting into the winter, poisonous

Magickal Properties and Lore: Creativity, luck, dream magick, spiritual warfare, protection, eternal life, stimulates the heart chakra, expression of emotion, love; overcoming anger, hate, and jealousy. Opens communication with nature spirits and angels. Place 9 holly leaves under your pillow to receive prophetic dreams. This wood makes a great wand or staff. The word holly comes from the Anglo-Saxon word *holegn* and the Old German word *hulius*, meaning holy. Per some mythology commonly celebrated by many Pagans, each year on the winter and summer solstice, the oak and the holly kings battle. On the winter solstice, giving rise to returning sun and spring, the oak king rules until the summer solstice, when the holly king attains victory. Deck the halls with boughs of holly!

Practical Uses: Provides food for birds; used for hedges; wood is good for carving. Native American Seminole tribes made arrows from the wood.

Medicinal Properties: Berries are poisonous and should never be used without consulting a professional. Some Native Americans made a drink from the leaves to be consumed in the morning like coffee. Leaves can reduce fever and to treat bronchitis and arthritis.

—— HOPTREE ——

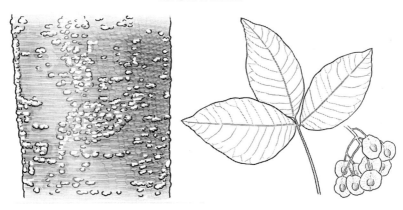

Other Names: Common hop tree, three-leaved hop tree, wafer ash, stinking ash, and water ash (though not a true ash tree)

Number of Species: At least 4

Family: Rutaceae

Genus/Species: *Ptelea trifoliata*

Leaf: Compound alternate, deciduous, 4–7 inches long with 3 leaflets, each being 2–4 inches long, smooth toothless margin, wider in the middle with pointed tips. Attaches directly to the central stalk and has a citrus scent when crushed.

Bark: Reddish brown to gray, smooth with horizontal lines

Fruit: Flat, green, wafer-like disks called samaras that turn yellow to brown when mature

Magickal Properties and Lore: Healing, sleep, dreams, and communication with the divine. Sleep with the dried seeds under your pillow to grant a good night of slumber and rest. Some Native Americans considered this tree a sacred medicine tree.

Practical Uses: Seeds have been used to brew beer as a substitute for actual hops.

Medicinal Properties: Some Native Americans used the bark of the roots to increase the potency of other herbal medicines. Leaves can be used to treat wounds and intestinal worms.

— HORNBEAM, AMERICAN —

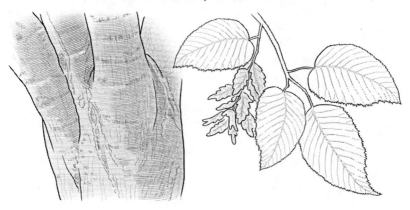

Other Names: Blue beech, water beech, ironwood (although not actually ironwood), and musclewood

Number of Species: About 30

Family: Betulaceae

Genus/Species: *Carpinus caroliniana*

Leaf: Simple alternate, deciduous, 2–5 inches long, light green, ovate; fine, sharp, saw-toothed margins with pointed tip. The buds of the American hornbeam are straight, and the tree is generally smaller than the European hornbeam.

Bark: Blue-gray to gray and smooth like the bark of beech trees

Fruit: Small nutlets that grow within a green papery pod-like cluster (samara). Seeds are edible when cooked, although not very tasty.

Magickal Properties and Lore: Safety, guarding, shielding, protection, trust, strength, durability, persistence, achieving goals, healing, sight, spirit vision, and intuition. Sit for a spell beneath this tree or smell the leaves to relieve stress and anxiety. This tree is one that represents both the Green Man and the wisdom of the Goddess.

Practical Uses: The name hornbeam is derived from "horn" to represent strength, durability, might, toughness, and the lord of the wild, the god of the hunt, or the horned one. The word "beam" stands for tree or wood. The wood is tough and hard, used for drumsticks and tool handles. The leaves, twigs, and fruit provide food for much wildlife. This is another understory tree, meaning that it often grows under the shade or umbrella of older and taller trees.

Medicinal Properties: Can be used to treat wounds, some eye conditions, and urinary problems.

— HORNBEAM, EUROPEAN —

art to come

Other Names: Common hornbeam

Number of Species: About 30

Family: Betulaceae

Genus/Species: Carpinusbetulus

Leaf: Simple alternate, deciduous, 2–5 inches long, light green, ovate; fine, sharp, saw-toothed margin with pointed tip. The buds of the European hornbeam are curved, and this tree is a bit larger than the American hornbeam.

Bark: Gray to greenish gray and smooth

Fruit: Small nutlets that grow within a green, papery, pod-like cluster (samara)

Magickal Properties and Lore: Safety, guarding, shielding, protection, trust, strength, durability, persistence, achieving goals, healing, sight, and intuition. Sit for a spell beneath this tree or smell the leaves to relieve stress and anxiety. This tree is one that represents both the Green Man and the wisdom of the Goddess.

Practical Uses: The name hornbeam is derived from "horn" to represent strength, durability, might, toughness, and the lord of the wild, the god of the hunt, or the horned one. The word "beam" stands for tree or wood. The wood is tough and hard, used for drumsticks and tool handles. The leaves, twigs, and fruit provide food for much wildlife. This is another understory tree, meaning that it often grows under the shade or umbrella of older and taller trees. This tree is also excellent as a landscape tree.

Medicinal Properties: Can be used to treat wounds, some eye conditions, and urinary problems.

— HORSECHESTNUT, COMMON —

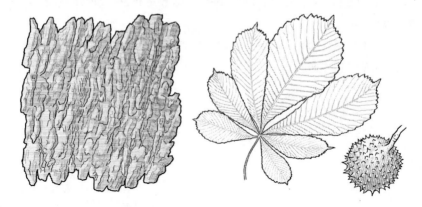

Other Names: European horsechestnut, buckeye, and conker tree

Number of Species: 13–19

Family: Hippocastanaceae

Genus/Species: *Aesculus hippocastanum*

Leaf: Palmate compound opposite, deciduous, 5–10 inches long with 7 leaflets (though sometimes 5 or 9) each leaflet being 4–10 inches in length and all forming around a center point. Leaflets have a sharp-toothed margin, dull green above and paler and hairy below. White-clustered, erect flowers reach toward the sun in the spring. The buds are sticky to the touch as opposed to the non-sticky, papery buds of the Ohio buckeye.

Bark: Dark brown to gray with scales and furrows when mature. Smooth when young

Fruit: Thick green-yellow capsules, 2–3 inches in diameter, covered by small spikes that contain at least one seed and are virtually identical to a buckeye. These seeds are called buckeyes or conkers. Children in Britain and Ireland play a game called "conkers" using these seeds. Poisonous and not edible if eaten raw

Magickal Properties and Lore: Divination, luck, patience, and financial matters. Carry the seed of a buckeye (brown and shiny) to attract money, especially when wrapped with a dollar bill. Native Americans thought the seed of the tree looks like the eye of a male deer, a buck, hence one name of the seed. The essence of the leaves and flowers can ease the mind and enhance intuition. Carry the seed to ward off rheumatism, arthritis, and backaches.

Practical Uses: Seeds have been used to treat coughs for horses. The flower buds can be used as a substitute for hops in beer brewing. The seeds contain a soap-like juice, which can be used to wash clothing.

Medicinal Properties: Aesculin can be extracted from the leaves and bark to protect skin. Ointments, creams, and tinctures can be made from the seeds to treat hemorrhoids and varicose veins.

— IRONWOOD —

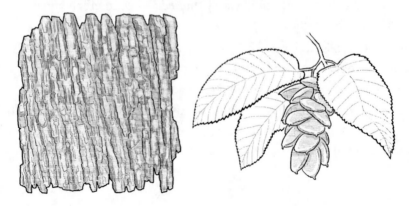

Other Names: American hophornbeam, hophornbeam, Eastern hophornbeam, hardhack, lever wood

Number of Species: At least 3

Family: Betulaceae

Genus/Species: *Ostrya virginiana*

Leaf: Simple alternate, 2–5 inches long, ovate, double-toothed margin like the teeth of a saw, pointed tip, and furry to the touch

Bark: Gray with scaly ridges that spiral vertically up and down the trunk

Fruit: Cone-like clusters grow down resembling hops and contain flat nutlets within, light green when young and tan when mature

Magickal Properties and Lore: Trust, silence, shielding, safety, security, new beginnings, humility, community, and unity. Sit beneath this tree to rediscover yourself.

Practical Uses: This tree is often found growing beneath the shade of taller trees, and for this reason they are referred to as understory trees. The wood is strong and heavy, used for making tool handles, tent stakes, and fence posts. The fruit and flowers provide nourishment for much wildlife. It is commonly called hophornbeam because the fruit clusters resemble hops.

Medicinal Properties: Leaves are high in calcium. Can be used to cleanse the blood and as a treatment for fever, coughs, kidney and stomach problems, rheumatism, and nerves. Sometimes used as a temporary relief for toothaches.

— KATSURATREE —

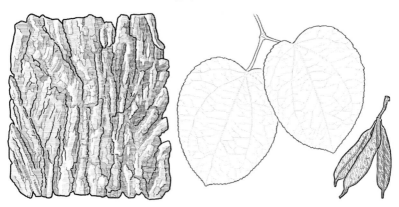

Other Names: Japanese katsura tree, morioka tree, amazing grace

Number of Species: 2

Family: Cercidiphyllaceae

Genus/Species: *Cercidiphyllum japonicum*

Leaf: Simple opposite, deciduous, 2- to 4-inch-long heart-shaped to ovular leaves with an almost smooth margin and pointed tips, red flowers and red stems

Bark: Gray to brown, shaggy and peeling. Tree shape is like a pyramid and has a dense crown.

Fruit: Clusters of 2–4 small winged pods (samara)

Magickal Properties and Lore: Love, beauty, blood, healing and calming sensitive emotions, communication with ancestors and the divine. Burn the leaves to produce a scent like cotton candy or sugar. This essence will help to open and heal the heart chakra.

Practical Uses: Katsura is an ornamental tree planted for its beauty. Wood has been used to make some board games, furniture, and boxes.

Medicinal Properties: There are no known medicinal properties.

— KENTUCKY COFFEE TREE —

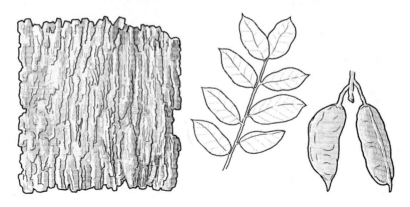

Other Names: Coffee tree, naked branch, and chicot

Number of Species: 3

Family: Fabaceae

Genus/Species: *Gymnocladus dioicus*

Leaf: Twice compound (bipinnate) alternate, deciduous, 12–36 inches long with up to 70 leaflets, each leaflet being about 2 inches long, toothless margin. Flowers are white with 4–5 petals. The leaves of this tree bloom late, and after the initial planting, this tree appears dead and leafless for about 6 months, hence the name the naked branch.

Bark: Gray, deeply furrowed and peeling with age, though smooth and brown when young

Fruit: Green pods with a leathery texture turning red to brown when mature, 4–10 inches long and containing 6–9 dark brown seeds in each pod. Raw seeds are poisonous and not edible.

Magickal Properties and Lore: Shadow work, truth, learning to face death and to embrace the next life. It is sacred to nature spirits. The message of this tree is to discover the hidden magick that resides within you.

Practical Uses: The seeds are bitter and rarely eaten by wildlife. Carpenters and cabinetmakers use the wood of this tree. The seeds have been roasted and used as a substitute for coffee, although it does not contain caffeine. Some Native American tribes roasted these seeds and ate them like nuts.

Medicinal Properties: Used to relieve constipation and coughs.

— LARCH —

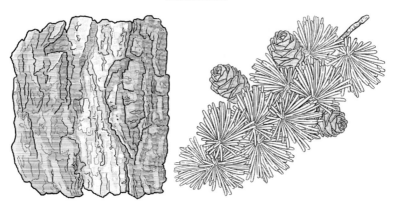

Other Names: Tamarack, Eastern larch, and American larch

Number of Species: 10

Family: Pinaceae

Genus/Species: Larixlaricina

Leaf: Clustered needles, deciduous conifer, needle clusters grow on the twigs, and each cluster contains 12–30 needles, each being ¾–1¼ inches long, pointy but soft to the touch, light green in color. This tree sheds its leaves in the fall.

Bark: Reddish brown with flaky scales

Fruit: Brown round cone, ½ an inch to 1 inch in diameter

Magickal Properties and Lore: Binding, uniting, protection, strength, endurance, death and rebirth, resistance, renewal, survival, healing, self-esteem, overcoming obstacles, and achieving goals. The essence of this tree will help to balance the throat and heart chakras. This tree is sacred to nature spirits and other world entities that take residence nearby so approach with respect and love as they, in turn, guide and protect animals and humans. Larch is also very sacred to the God, or the Green Man, of Pagan beliefs. Carry the leaves, cones, or bark to ward off psychic attack.

Practical Uses: Wood is both fire resistant and waterproof. Resin can be used to waterproof roofs, boats, and more. This tree has ornamental value.

Medicinal Properties: Used to treat some skin conditions such as psoriasis and eczema. Ancient Europeans and Native Americans have used the needles and bark to treat colds, coughs, urinary infections, and bronchitis.

— LINDEN, AMERICAN —

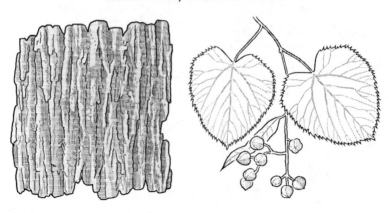

Other Names: Basswood, American basswood, bee tree, and lime tree

Number of Species: About 30–40 species

Family: Tiliaceae

Genus/Species: *Tilia americana*

Leaf: Simple alternate, deciduous, ovate to heart-shaped, 5–7 inches long, very sharp-toothed margin, pointed tip. Flowers are yellow with 5 petals.

Bark: Gray, deeply fissured and scaly with age, though smooth when young. The inner bark is fibrous and paper-like.

Fruit: Round green nut-like fruits with 1–3 seeds, turning yellow when mature, hanging in clusters from a leaf-like wing and covered with very tiny hairs

Magickal Properties and Lore: Mercy, victory in legal battles, luck, healing, peace, love, sleep, dreams, freedom, immortality, and protection. Hang branches, dried leaves, or bark over the door to protect the home. Linden is sacred to Freya, Frigga, Mary, Jesus, Thor, and Phylira. The message of this tree is to never give up on your dreams.

Practical Uses: The wood is soft and great for carving, used to make yardsticks, and Native Americans have used the inner bark to weave baskets, ropes, and floor mats. Bees gather pollen from the flowers to make honey, and this honey is considered superior in taste and of very high quality. The leaves are sometimes used in salads.

Medicinal Properties: Flowers as a tea are beneficial for the blood and can be used to lower cholesterol and high blood pressure. It can be used to soothe diarrhea, clear the sinuses, promote sleep, and soothe inflammations and burns.

— LINDEN, LITTLE LEAF —

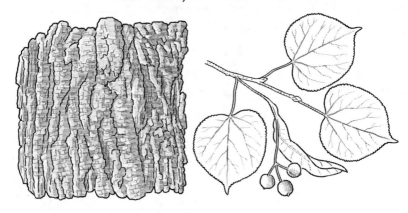

Other Names: Small leaf linden, small-leaved lime

Number of Species: About 30–40 species

Family: Tiliaceae

Genus/Species: *Tilia cordata*

Leaf: Simple alternate, deciduous, ovate to heart-shaped, 2–4 inches long, dark green and shiny above, paler below, sharp-toothed margin with pointed tips

Bark: Gray to brown and furrowed, inner bark is fibrous

Fruit: Round green nut-like fruits with 1–3 seeds, turning yellow when mature, hanging in clusters from a leaf-like wing and covered with very tiny hairs

Magickal Properties and Lore: Mercy, victory in legal battles, luck, healing, peace, love, sleep, dreams, freedom, immortality, and protection. Hang branches, dried leaves, or bark over the door to protect the home. Linden is sacred to Freya, Frigga, Mary, Jesus, Thor, and Phylira. The message of this tree is to never give up on your dreams.

Practical Uses: The wood is soft and great for carving, used to make yardsticks, and Native Americans have used the inner bark to weave baskets, ropes, and floor mats. Bees gather pollen from the flowers to make honey, and this honey is considered superior in taste and of very high quality. The leaves are sometimes used in salads.

Medicinal Properties: Flowers as a tea are beneficial for the blood and can be used to lower cholesterol and high blood pressure. It can be used to soothe diarrhea, clear the sinuses, promote sleep, and soothe inflammations and burns.

— LINDEN, SILVER —

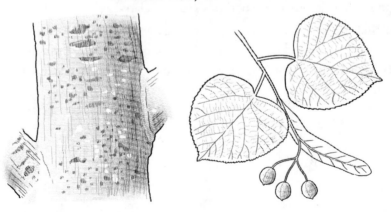

Other Names: Silver lime tree

Number of Species: About 30–40 species

Family: Tiliaceae

Genus/Species: *Tilia tomentosa*

Leaf: Simple alternate, deciduous, 2–5 inches long, dark green above, white or silver-like below, sharp-toothed margin, round to heart-shaped

Bark: Light gray and smooth

Fruit: Small round to oval nutlet

Magickal Properties and Lore: Mercy, victory in legal battles, luck, healing, peace, love, sleep, dreams, freedom, immortality, and protection. Hang branches, dried leaves, or bark over the door to protect the home. Linden is sacred to Freya, Frigga, Mary, Jesus, Thor, and Phylira. The message of this tree is to never give up on your dreams.

Practical Uses: The wood is soft and great for carving, used to make yardsticks, and Native Americans have used the inner bark to weave baskets, ropes, and floor mats. Bees gather pollen from the flowers to make honey, and this honey is considered superior in taste and of very high quality. The leaves are sometimes used in salads.

Medicinal Properties: Flowers as a tea are beneficial for the blood and can be used to lower cholesterol and high blood pressure. It can be used to soothe diarrhea, clear the sinuses, promote sleep, and soothe inflammations and burns.

— LOCUST, HONEY —

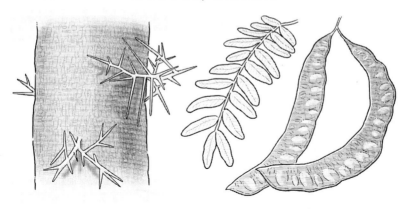

Other Names: Locust

Number of Species: 2 species of honey locust, and about 15 species of locust

Family: Fabaceae

Genus/Species: *Gelditsia triacanthos*

Leaf: Twice compound alternate, pinnate, deciduous, 12–24 inches long with 14–30 leaflets, each leaflet being about 1 inch long, ovate to elliptical, and smooth

Bark: Gray to brown to almost black, fissured and scaly, covered with long sharp thorns, although there does exist a very common thornless variety, which is the one you will most likely encounter (*Gledistia triacanthos* var. *inermis*).

Fruit: Flat dark brown curved pods, 6–16 inches long, containing many beanlike seeds. The pulp that grows within these pods is edible as opposed to the toxic black locust.

Magickal Properties and Lore: Protection, family matters, love, healing, defense, strength, endurance, and passion. This wood makes for an incredibly powerful and reliable wand.

Practical Uses: Much wildlife finds nourishment from the sweet honey-like pods of this tree. The sweet pulp within the pods has been used by some Native Americans as a source of food and can be used to brew beer. The wood is very strong and resistant to rot. It has been used for making boats, fence posts, flooring, and furniture.

Medicinal Properties: Extracts of honey locust have been discovered to have anticancer properties. Can be used to treat rheumatism.

— MAACKIA, AMUR —

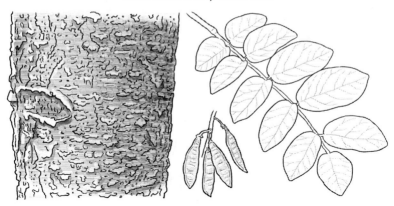

Other Names: Maackia, sometimes called Chinese maackia

Number of Species: 11

Family: Fabaceae or sometimes Leguminosae

Genus/Species: *Maackia amurensis*

Leaf: Compound alternate, deciduous, dark green leaves when mature, 5–8 inches long with 5–11 leaflets, each leaflet being 2–4 inches long and toothless

Bark: Orange to brown, shiny, and peels with age

Fruit: Small, flat brown pods that point upwards are 2–4 inches long when mature

Magickal Properties and Lore: Love, beauty, optimism, positive outlooks, and resisting negativity

Practical Uses: This is a small tree and great for planting as a lawn decoration or shade tree and has ornamental value for its summer flowers. It is resistant to pests and diseases.

Medicinal Properties: None known.

— MAPLE, JAPANESE —

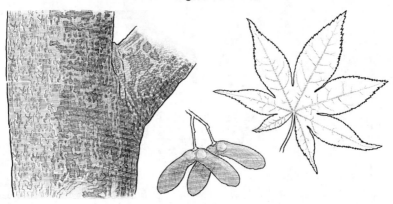

Other Names: Smooth Japanese maple. Native to Japan, China, and Korea but has been imported and loved for its beauty. There are many varieties and cultivars.

Number of Species: About 125 species of maple

Family: Sapindaceae (the soapberries) and formerly classified as Aceraceae

Genus/Species: *Acer palmatum*

Leaf: Lobed palmate opposite, deciduous, 5–9 pointed lobes with sharp teeth, colors vary from green to red

Bark: Gray-brown and smooth

Fruit: Winged fruits (samara) usually in pairs. Wings are green to red in color.

Magickal Properties and Lore: Love, generosity, protection from negative entities, health, healing, finances, longevity, balancing the masculine and feminine, intuition, and creativity. It has been said that the famous Trojan horse was made from maple wood. Maple can be used to make a very powerful wand. Place fresh leaves on an altar to add an additional boost for love magick.

Practical Uses: This tree has incredible ornamental value but is not good for producing maple syrup.

Medicinal Properties: Many parts can be used to treat eye and liver diseases. It is an anti-inflammatory. Consult a professional before using.

— MAPLE, NORWAY —

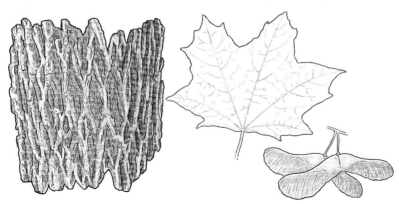

Other Names: Common Norway maple

Number of Species: About 125 species of maple

Family: Sapindaceae (the soapberries) and formerly classified as Aceraceae

Genus/Species: *Acer platanoides*

Leaf: Simple lobed opposite, deciduous, 4–7 inches long, palmately shaped, pointed tips and teeth, dark green above and lighter below, generally with 5 lobes but sometimes 3–7. This tree is easily confused with sugar maple. Gently pluck a leaf stem from the base of the twig and look to see if it produces a milky white sap. If it does, it is a Norway maple. The sugar maple will produce a clear sap. In addition, the Norway maple is not known for having good fall color.

Bark: Gray to brown, smooth when young, deeply furrowed with rough vertical ridges when aged

Fruit: 1–2–inch-long pairs of flat winged seeds (samara)

Magickal Properties and Lore: Love, generosity, protection from negative entities, health, healing, finances, longevity, balancing the masculine and feminine, intuition, and creativity. It has been said that the famous Trojan horse was made from maple wood. Maple can be used to make a very powerful wand. Place fresh leaves on an altar to add an additional boost for love magick.

Practical Uses: Maple wood is tough and good for high quality carvings and has been used to make musical instruments. Some Native have used maple wood to make paddles, oars, and baskets. The sap is used to produce maple syrup, but it takes about 40 gallons of sap to make 1 gallon of syrup. For this reason, true maple syrup can be costly but well worth the price.

Medicinal Properties: Maple syrup contains balanced sugars, potassium, vitamins A, B2, B5, B6, folic acid, biotin, niacin, and protein. Although all maple trees can produce maple syrup, the sugar maple tree is generally the only one used. The inner bark and leaves are good for the liver, the spleen, and the entire body. The Norway maple is one of the most pest and disease resistant species of maple.

— MAPLE, CRIMSON KING NORWAY —

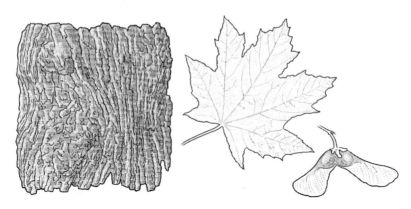

Other Names: Crimson king. This variety of the Norway maple shares most of the same characteristics as the green Norway maple. The main difference is the color of the leaves.

Number of Species: About 125 species of maple

Family: Sapindaceae (the soapberries) and formerly classified as Aceraceae

Genus/Species: *Acer platanoides*

Leaf: Simple lobed opposite, deciduous, 4–7 inches long, palmately shaped, pointed tips and teeth, red to purple in color, generally with 5 lobes but sometimes 3–7

Bark: Gray-brown, smooth when young, deeply furrowed with vertical ridges when aged

Fruit: 1- to 2-inch-long pairs of flat winged seeds (samara)

Magickal Properties and Lore: Love, generosity, protection from negative entities, health, healing, finances, longevity, balancing the masculine and feminine, intuition, and creativity. It has been said that the famous Trojan horse was made from maple wood. Maple can be used to make a very powerful wand. Place fresh leaves on an altar to add an additional boost for love magick.

Practical Uses: Maple wood is tough and good for high quality carvings and has been used to make musical instruments. Some Native Americans have used maple wood to make paddles, oars, and baskets. The sap is used to produce maple syrup, but it takes about 40 gallons of sap to make one gallon of syrup. For this reason, true maple syrup can be costly but well worth the price.

Medicinal Properties: Maple syrup contains balanced sugars, potassium, vitamins A, B2, B5, B6, folic acid, biotin, niacin, and protein. Although all maple trees can produce maple syrup, the sugar maple tree is generally the only one used. The inner bark and leaves are good for the liver, the spleen, and the entire body. The Norway maple is one of the most pest and disease resistant species of maple.

— MAPLE, RED —

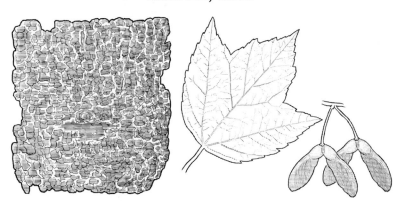

Other Names: Swamp maple, scarlet maple, water maple

Number of Species: About 125 species of maple

Family: Sapindaceae (the soapberries) and formerly classified as Aceraceae

Genus/Species: *Acer rubrum*

Leaf: Simple lobed opposite, deciduous, 2–4 inches long with 3 lobes (rarely 5), double-toothed margins. Stalks are red and there is a part of this tree that is red for most of the year. Red maple has great fall color.

Bark: Smooth and gray in color with irregular cracks

Fruit: A pair of red winged seeds up to an inch long (samara)

Magickal Properties and Lore: Love, generosity, protection from negative entities, health, healing, finances, longevity, balancing the masculine and feminine, intuition, and creativity. It has been said that the famous Trojan horse was made from maple wood. Maple can be used to make a very powerful wand. Place fresh leaves or seeds (samaras) on an altar to add an additional boost for love magick.

Practical Uses: Maple wood is tough and good for high quality carvings and has been used to make musical instruments. Some Native Americans have used maple wood to make paddles, oars, and baskets. The sap is used to produce maple syrup, but it takes about 40 gallons of sap to make one gallon of syrup. For this reason, true maple syrup can be costly but well worth the price.

Medicinal Properties: Maple syrup contains balanced sugars, potassium, vitamins A, B2, B5, B6, folic acid, biotin, niacin, and protein. Although all maple trees can produce maple syrup, the sugar maple tree is generally the only one used. The inner bark and leaves are good for the liver, the spleen, and the entire body.

— MAPLE, SILVER —

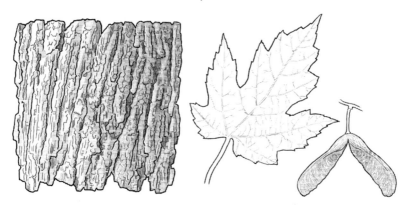

Other Names: Silverleaf maple, soft maple, white maple, river maple

Number of Species: About 125

Family: Sapindaceae (the soapberries) and formerly classified as Aceraceae

Genus/Species: *Acer saccharinum*

Leaf: Simple lobed opposite, deciduous, 4–6 inches long with 5–7 lobes, pointed tips, double-toothed margin, dull green above and silver to white below. This maple doesn't give a spectacular show of colors in the fall but sometimes turns yellow.

Bark: Gray, furrowed, and peeling with age, but smooth and silver when young

Fruit: A pair of winged seeds, 1–3 inches long (samara).

Magickal Properties and Lore: Love, generosity, protection from negative entities, health, healing, finances, longevity, balancing the masculine and feminine, intuition, and creativity. It has been said that the famous Trojan horse was made from maple wood. Maple can be used to make a very powerful wand. Place fresh leaves on an altar to add an additional boost for love magick.

Practical Uses: Maple wood is tough and good for high quality carvings and has been used to make musical instruments. Some Native Americans have used maple wood to make paddles, oars, and baskets. The sap is used to produce maple syrup, but it takes about 40 gallons of sap to make one gallon of syrup. For this reason, true maple syrup can be costly but well worth the price.

Medicinal Properties: Maple syrup contains balanced sugars, potassium, vitamins A, B2, B5, B6, folic acid, biotin, niacin, and protein. Although all maple trees can produce maple syrup, the sugar maple tree is generally the only one used. The inner bark and leaves are good for the liver, the spleen, and the entire body.

— MAPLE, SUGAR —

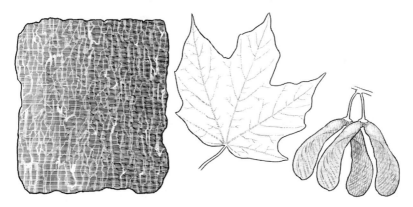

Other Names: Hard maple, rock maple

Number of Species: About 125

Family: Sapindaceae (the soapberries) and formerly classified as Aceraceae

Genus/Species: *Acer saccharum*

Leaf: Simple lobed opposite, deciduous, 3–6 inches long with 5 lobes, pointed tips, light to medium green above and paler below. Sugar maple is easily confused with Norway maple. Gently pluck a leaf stem from the base of the twig and if it has a clear sap it is sugar maple. Norway maple will produce a milky-white sap. Sugar maple is known for its beautiful and glorious red-orange fall colors.

Bark: Gray and furrowed with scaly ridges when mature, smooth and darker when young, resembling black maple

Fruit: Pair of winged seeds up to 2 inches long (samara)

Magickal Properties and Lore: Love, generosity, protection from negative entities, health, healing, finances, longevity, balancing the masculine and feminine, intuition, and creativity. It as been said that the famous Trojan horse was made from maple wood. Maple can be used to make a very powerful wand. Place fresh leaves (especially those that have turned red/orange in the fall) on an altar to add an additional boost for love magick.

Practical Uses: Maple wood is tough and good for high quality carvings and has been used to make musical instruments. Some Native Americans have used maple wood to make paddles, oars, and baskets. The sap is used to produce maple syrup, but it takes about 40 gallons of sap to make one gallon of syrup. For this reason, true maple syrup can be costly but well worth the price.

Medicinal Properties: Maple syrup contains balanced sugars, potassium, vitamins A, B2, B5, B6, folic acid, biotin, niacin, and protein. Although all maple trees can produce maple syrup, the sugar maple tree is generally the only one used. The inner bark and leaves are good for the liver, the spleen, and the entire body.

— MIMOSA —

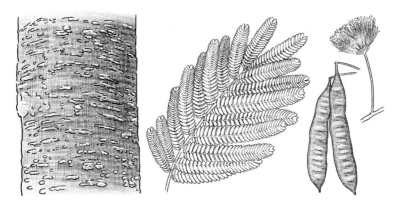

Other Names: Silk-tree, powderpuff tree, Persian acacia, Persian silk, albizzia, and pink siris

Number of Species: About 400 species

Family: Fabaceae

Genus/Species: *Albizia julibrissin*

Leaf: Twice compound pinnate, deciduous, 6–20 inches long resembling fern leaves with 5–12 pairs of leaflets, each leaflet with 15–30 smaller ovate individual toothless leaflets, very beautiful clusters of pink puffy flowers. These leaflets fold up at night and during rain.

Bark: Brown to gray, almost smooth

Fruit: Bean-like pods, 5–8 inches long, pointed and flat

Magickal Properties and Lore: Protection, health, love, purification, and prophetic dreams. Carry leaves or flowers to invite love, scatter leaves and flowers or burn the dried leaves to purify an area. Place leaves under pillow to induce prophetic dreams or crush dried leaves and add to bath water to break a curse. This tree supports the idea that plants have a nervous system, since some mimosa varieties will close their leaflets when touched by human hands.

Practical Uses: Flowers provide nectar for bees, butterflies, and hummingbirds.

Medicinal Properties: Bark can be used as an antidepressant and for calming nerves and anxiety. Tea can be used as a sedative.

— MULBERRY —

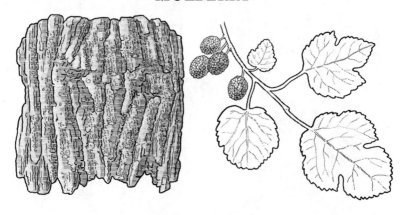

Other Names: There are 3 common types of mulberry: red mulberry, white mulberry, and black mulberry.

Number of Species: 7

Family: Moraceae

Genus: *Morus*

Leaf: Simple alternate, deciduous, ovate to lobed, 2–5 inches long, course toothed margin, shiny green above, and leaks a milky sap when cut

Bark: Gray to brown and deeply furrowed with age

Fruit: White to red to black. Colors are dark when mature and resemble raspberries and consist of many one-seeded fruits. Very edible and delicious

Magickal Properties and Lore: Protection, strength, and willpower. The wood can be used to protect against evil, negative energies, and psychic attack, and a powerful wand can be made from it for very reasons. Place a mulberry leaf near a crib to protect babies. In some Chinese traditions, the World Tree is depicted as a mulberry.

Practical Uses: Fruit provides nourishment for much wildlife and is used to make jellies, jams, and pies. Some Native Americans used mulberry fruit to make preserves, cakes, and beverages.

Medicinal Properties: Black mulberry fruits can be used to ease sore throats and coughs. Mulberry fruit can nourish the blood, is beneficial to the kidneys, and can possibly prevent premature graying of the hair. The fruit consists mostly of water, which is beneficial for hydration of the body, some carbohydrates, and a small amount of natural fats, fiber, and other minerals.

— OAK, BUR —

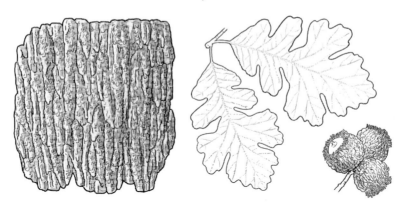

Other Names: *Duir* (Celtic), blue oak, mossy oak, mossycup oak

Number of Species: Over 600

Family: Fagaceae

Genus/Species: *Quercus macrocarpa*

Leaf: Simple lobed alternate, deciduous, 4–12 inches long with 7–9 round lobes, smooth margin, and shiny dark green in color. The shape of the leaf resembles a cello or a bass, twigs are covered with corky ridges

Bark: Dark gray and deeply furrowed with many scales and ridges

Fruit: Brown acorns when mature, 1–2 inches long and covered with hairy burs. All acorns are true nuts and quite edible, but they must be shelled first, just like removing the peanut from its shell. Also, the tannin must be leached out first. I suggest watching videos on YouTube for tutorials. The process is quite simple but time-consuming.

Magickal Properties and Lore: Power, rulership, might, protection, health, healing, money, fertility, luck, and victory in war and battles. The oak, however, is a tree of peace and harmony. Oak was considered sacred to the Druids and other ancient Europeans. Twigs of oak can be brought into the home to ward evil. Acorns can be placed in windowsills to protect from lightning and can be carried to attract good luck. The wood makes a powerful wand or staff. Many ancient Celts and Europeans associated the oak with deities of weather, especially the gods of thunder and lightning.

Practical Uses: Oak acorns provide nourishment to many birds, animals, and humans; however, acorns contain tannin (tannic acid) and this can be toxic in large amounts, causing pain in the stomach, thirst, severe diarrhea, and excessive urination. The tannin can be boiled out, but it is, like with all plants, best that you consult a professional first before using any plant for medicinal purposes. Bur oak is a member of the white oak group and has thick corky bark, which enables it to endure fires. As a helpful tip, white oaks have rounded lobes and red oaks have pointed lobes.

—— OAK, CHINQUAPIN ——

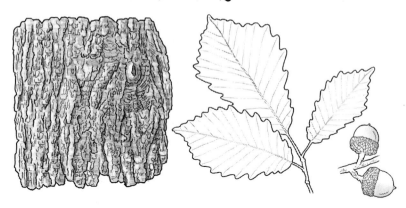

Other Names: *Duir* (Celtic), chinkapin oak, yellow oak, yellow chestnut oak, and rock oak

Number of Species: Over 600

Family: Fagaceae

Genus/Species: *Quercus muehlenbergii*

Leaf: Simple, alternate, oblong, deciduous, 4–7 inches long, rich dark green color above, lighter below, and a very course toothed margin like a saw. This tree does not provide color in the fall.

Bark: Light gray color, flaky and rough

Fruit: Small wide acorn up to an inch in length. The cap covers the top half of the nut.

All acorns are true nuts and quite edible, but they must be shelled first, just like removing a peanut its shell. Also, the tannin must be leached out first. I suggest watching videos on YouTube for tutorials. The process is quite simple but time-consuming.

Magickal Properties and Lore: Power, rulership, might, protection, health, healing, money, fertility, luck, and victory in war and battles. The oak, however, is a tree of peace and harmony. Oak was considered sacred to the Druids and some ancient Europeans. Twigs of oak can be brought into the home to ward evil. Acorns can be placed in windowsills to protect from lightning and can be carried to attract good luck. The wood makes a powerful wand or staff. Many ancient Celts and Europeans associated the oak with deities of weather, especially the gods of thunder and lightning.

Practical Uses: Oak acorns provide nourishment to many birds, animals, and humans; however, acorns contain tannin (tannic acid), and this can be toxic in large amounts causing pain in the stomach, thirst, severe diarrhea, and excessive urination. The tannin can be boiled out, but it is, like with all plants, best that you consult a professional first before using any plant for medicinal purposes.

— OAK, PIN —

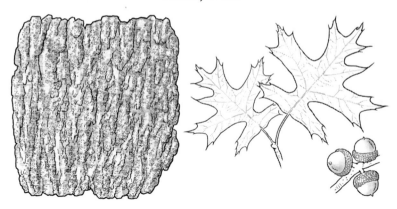

Other Names: *Duir* (Celtic), Spanish oak, swamp oak

Number of Species: Over 600

Family: Fagaceae

Genus/Species: *Quercus palustris*

Leaf: Simple lobed alternate, deciduous, 3–5 inches long, 5–7 lobes with pointed tips, elliptic to ovate in shape, dark green above and slightly paler below. This tree may have a red-orange fall color or possibly a yellow to brown color, but it tends to hold those leaves into the winter season.

Bark: Gray to brown, hard, smooth when young, shallow furrows and ridges when older

Fruit: Brown acorns when mature, about a half inch in length, cap covers upper part of the nut. All acorns are true nuts and quite edible, but they must be shelled first, just like removing the peanut its shell. Also, the tannin must be leached out first. I suggest watching videos on YouTube for tutorials. The process is quite simple but time-consuming.

Magickal Properties and Lore: Power, rulership, might, protection, health, healing, money, fertility, luck, and victory in war and battles. The oak, however, is a tree of peace and harmony. Oak was considered sacred to the Druids and some ancient Europeans. Twigs of oak can be brought into the home to ward evil. Acorns can be placed in windowsills to protect from lightning and can be carried to attract good luck. The wood makes a powerful wand or staff. Many ancient Celts and Europeans as-

sociated the oak with deities of weather, especially the gods of thunder and lightning.

Practical Uses: Oak acorns provide nourishment to many birds, animals, and humans; however, acorns contain tannin (tannic acid), and this can be toxic in large amounts causing pain in the stomach, thirst, severe diarrhea, and excessive urination. The tannin can be boiled out, but it is, like with all plants, best that you consult a professional first before using any plant for medicinal purposes.

— OAK, RED —

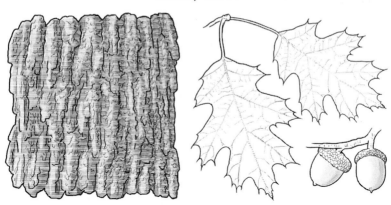

Other Names: *Duir* (Celtic), nuttall oak, gray oak, champion oak, and Northern red oak

Number of Species: Over 600

Family: Fagaceae

Genus/Species: *Quercus rubra*

Leaf: Simple lobed alternate, deciduous, 4 to 9 inches long, 4–6 inches wide 7 to 11 lobes with pointed tips. Dark green color above and paler with a yellowish tint below. The leaves are larger than the scarlet oak. Buds are red, pointy, and resemble an egg.

Bark: Gray and smooth when young and deeply furrowed with age

Fruit: Brown acorns when mature, cap covers the top quarter of the nut. All acorns are true nuts and quite edible, but they must be shelled first, just like removing a peanut from its shell. Also, the tannin must be leached out first. I suggest watching videos on YouTube for tutorials. The process is quite simple but time-consuming.

Magickal Properties and Lore: Power, rulership, might, protection, health, healing, money, fertility, luck, and victory in war and battles. The oak, however, is a tree of peace and harmony. Oak was considered sacred to the Druids and some ancient Europeans. Twigs of oak can be brought into the home to ward evil. Acorns can be placed in windowsills to protect from lightning and can be carried to attract good luck. The wood makes a powerful wand or staff. Many ancient Celts and Europeans as-

sociated the oak with deities of weather, especially the gods of thunder and lightning.

Practical Uses: Oak acorns in general provide nourishment to many birds, animals, and humans; however acorns contain tannin, (tannic acid) and this can be toxic in large amounts causing pain in the stomach, thirst, severe diarrhea, and excessive urination. The tannin can be boiled out, but it is, like with all plants, best that you consult a professional first before using any plant for medicinal purposes. The acorns of this particular oak are not so loved by wildlife, as they are bitter. The wood is used for flooring and furniture and is considered valuable.

— OAK, SCARLET —

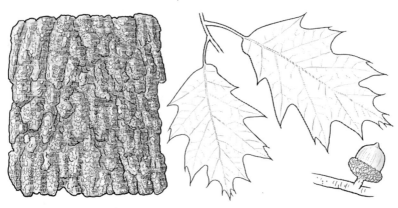

Other Names: *Duir* (Celtic), sometimes called red oak and mistaken for black or pin oak

Number of Species: Over 600

Family: Fagaceae

Genus/Species: *Quercus coccinea*

Leaf: Simple lobed alternate, deciduous, 3–7 inches in length with 5–7 pointed lobes, dark green above and paler below. Leaves turn scarlet red in the fall. Buds are white and fuzzy.

Bark: Dark gray and deeply furrowed with age. Inner bark has a reddish color.

Fruit: Brown acorn when mature, up to an inch in length, the cap can cover up to half the top portion of the nut. All acorns are true nuts and quite edible, but they must be shelled first, just like removing a peanut from its shell. Also, the tannin must be leached out first. I suggest watching videos on YouTube for tutorials. The process is quite simple but time-consuming.

Magickal Properties and Lore: Power, rulership, might, protection, health, healing, money, fertility, luck, and victory in war and battles. The oak, however, is a tree of peace and harmony. Oak was considered sacred to the Druids and some ancient Europeans. Twigs of oak can be brought into the home to ward evil. Acorns can be placed in windowsills to protect from lightning and can be carried to attract luck. The wood makes a powerful wand or staff. Many ancient Celts and Europeans associated the oak with deities of weather, especially the gods of thunder and lightning.

Practical Uses: The wood is often marketed as red oak, but is lesser quality and weaker. Acorns in general provide nourishment to many birds, animals, and humans; however, they contain tannic acid, and this can be toxic in large amounts, causing pain in the stomach, thirst, severe diarrhea, and excessive urination. The tannin can be boiled out, but it is, like with all plants, best that you consult a professional first before using any plant for medicinal purposes.

— OAK, SHINGLE —

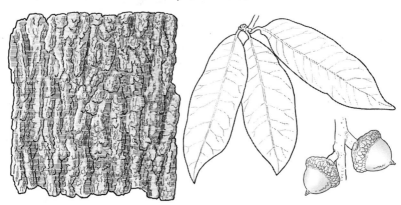

Other Names: *Duir* (Celtic), Jove's nuts, often mistaken for laurel oak

Number of Species: Over 600

Family: Fagaceae

Genus/Species: *Quercus imbricaria*

Leaf: Simple alternate, deciduous, 3–6 inches in length, oblong, smooth lobeless margin, dark green above, and lighter below with small soft hairs, usually pointed at the end

Bark: Brown to gray, smooth when young, furrowed and scaly with age

Fruit: Brown acorns when mature, almost round, grow single or in pairs. All acorns are true nuts and quite edible, but they must be shelled first, just like removing a peanut from the shell. Also, the tannin must be leached out first. I suggest watching videos on YouTube for tutorials. The process is quite simple but time-consuming.

Magickal Properties and Lore: Power, rulership, might, protection, health, healing, money, fertility, luck, and victory in war and battles. The oak, however, is a tree of peace and harmony. Oak was considered sacred to the Druids and some ancient Europeans. Twigs of oak can be brought into the home to ward evil. Acorns can be placed in windowsills to protect from lightning and can be carried to attract good luck. The wood makes a powerful wand or staff. Many ancient Celts and Europeans associated the Oak with deities of weather, especially the gods of thunder and lightning.

Practical Uses: Oak acorns provide nourishment to many birds, animals, and humans; however, acorns contain tannin (tannic acid) and this can be toxic in large amounts causing pain in the stomach, thirst, severe diarrhea, and excessive urination. The tannin can be boiled out, but it is, like with all plants, best that you consult a professional first before using any plant for medicinal purposes. Early American settlers made roof shingles from the wood, hence the name.

—— OAK, WHITE ——

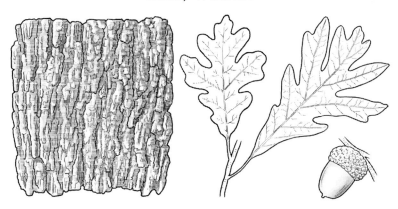

Other Names: *Duir* (Celtic), stave oak, Eastern oak. It is the state tree of Illinois.

Number of Species: Over 600

Family: Fagaceae

Genus/Species: *Quercus alba*

Leaf: Simple lobed alternate, deciduous, 4–9 inches in length, 5–9 round slender lobes that almost come to a point, toothless margin, bright green above and paler below

Bark: Gray, furrowed, and scaly with age

Fruit: Brown acorn when mature, up to an inch and a half long, cap covers the upper third of the nut. All acorns are true nuts and quite edible, but they must be shelled first, just like removing a peanut from the shell. Also, the tannin must be leached out first. I suggest watching videos on YouTube for tutorials. The process is quite simple but time-consuming.

Magickal Properties and Lore: Power, rulership, might, protection, health, healing, money, fertility, luck, and victory in war and battles. The oak, however, is a tree of peace and harmony. Oak was considered sacred to the Druids and some ancient Europeans. Twigs of oak can be brought into the home to ward evil. Acorns can be placed in windowsills to protect from lightning and can be carried to attract good luck. The wood makes a powerful wand or staff. Many ancient Celts and Europeans as-

sociated the oak with deities of weather, especially the gods of thunder and lightning.

Practical Uses: Very valuable high-grade wood. Oak acorns provide nourishment to many birds, animals, and humans; however, acorns contain tannin (tannic acid) and this can be toxic in large amounts causing pain in the stomach, thirst, severe diarrhea, and excessive urination. The tannin can be boiled out, but it is, like with all plants, best that you consult a professional first before using any plant for medicinal purposes.

—— OSAGE ORANGE ——

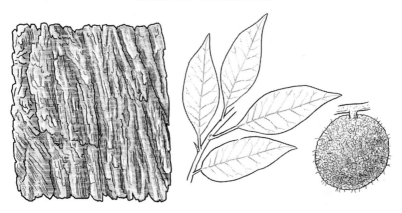

Other Names: Hedge-apple, horse apple, bodark, bodock, bowwood, and *bois d'arc* (French)

Number of Species: 1

Family: Moraceae

Genus/Species: *Maclura pomifera*

Leaf: Simple alternate, deciduous, 2–5 inches in length, ovate with a long and pointed tip, toothless margin, bright green above and paler below. Leaves contain a milky sap. Thorns grow upon the twigs.

Bark: Brown to gray, deeply furrowed with wavy vertical ridges, inner bark is orange

Fruit: Very large round light green fleshy ball, 3–6 inches in width, creamy white sap and contains many brown seeds

Magickal Properties and Lore: Protection, endurance, and fertility. Place the fruit under your bed or in a window to repel spiders and unwanted insects such as mosquitoes, roaches, and ticks. The fruit contains elemol, which is just as effective for repelling insects as deet. The wood is hard and decay-resistant and can be a very effective wand.

Practical Uses: The Osage Amer-Indians used this wood to make bows and other weapons. This tree, because of its thorns, used to be planted in rows to serve as a natural fence before barbed wire came into being. The inner bark can be used to make yellow dye. Use the fruits as a natural insect repellent.

—— PAWPAW ——

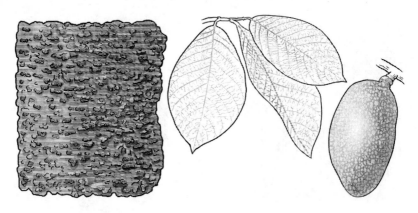

Other Names: Wild banana, poor man's banana, prairie banana, false banana, Indian banana, and custard apple

Number of Species: More than 2,000

Family: Annonaceae

Genus/Species: *Asimina triloba*

Leaf: Simple alternate, deciduous, large ovate leaves, 6–12 inches in length, toothless margin with a short-pointed tip, greener above and paler below

Bark: Gray to brown, smooth, and with tiny bumps

Fruit: Yellowish brown large fleshy fruits when mature, 3–5 inches in length, soft, and edible. Tastes like a combination of a pear and banana.

Magickal Properties and Lore: Love, fertility, and protection. Carry the seeds to attract love and good luck.

Practical Uses: Fruit provides nourishment to wildlife and humans. Early settlers and Native Americans valued this fruit for nourishment. They are sometimes used to make juice, wine, bread, pie, and ice cream. The leaves and bark contain natural insecticides and the inner bark was used by Native Americans to make rope and fishing nets.

Medicinal Properties: The fruit provides a higher level of protein than most other fruits and contains more vitamins, minerals, calories, and amino acids than apples, grapes, and peaches.

— PEACH —

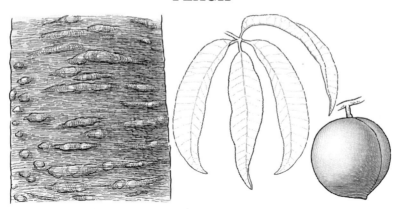

Other Names: Persian apple and stone fruit

Number of Species: About 430 species of prunus

Family: Rosaceae

Genus/Species: *Prunus persica*

Leaf: Simple alternate, deciduous, dark green glossy leaves, 3–6 inches in length, narrow and oblong with a fine-toothed margin and curvy pointed tip

Bark: Reddish brown, smooth and thin, but may become fissured with age

Fruit: Round, yellow to orange fruits, 2–3 inches in diameter, fleshy and covered with tiny hairs. Each fruit contains a stoned pit with a seed, sweet and edible

Magickal Properties and Lore: Exorcisms, love, longevity, immortality, fertility, and wisdom. Share the fruit with a loved one. Place the wood in an area to drive away negative energies and evil spirits. Carry the wood to increase longevity. Wood makes a powerful wand or staff.

Practical Uses: Peaches provide nourishment to both humans and wildlife. The peach and the nectarine are nearly identical in all ways and the only difference is that the peach is covered with tiny hairs and the nectarine has a smooth hairless surface.

Medicinal Properties: The leaves can be used as a laxative, relaxant, and sedative; as an aid with stomach, bladder, and uterine problems; to expel worms; and as a potent remedy for morning sickness during pregnancy. Peaches provide many vitamins and nutrients.

— PEAR, COMMON —

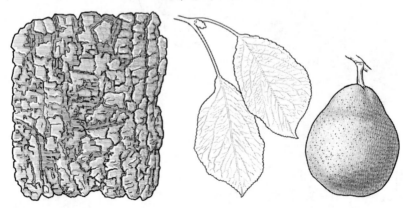

Other Names: European pear

Number of Species: About 20 and more than 3,000 varieties

Family: Rosaceae

Genus/Species: *Pyrus communis*

Leaf: Simple alternate, deciduous, 1–4 inches in length, ovate to elliptical in shape, fine-toothed margin, short pointed tips, shiny green above and paler below

Bark: Brown to gray, smooth when young, becoming scaly with age

Fruit: Pears are generally 2–4 inches in length, green to brown skin, sweet and edible

Magickal Properties and Lore: Love, fertility, lust, health, and fortune. It has been said that witches used to dance beneath a pear tree to promote fertility and fortune. The wood makes an excellent may branch and a wonderful wand. Sacred to Hera, Venus, Freya, and Aphrodite.

Practical Uses: Pears are an important source of food for wildlife and humans. The wood has been used to make musical instruments.

Medicinal Properties: The bark can be used to treat bruises and sprains. Pears contain fiber and many vitamins and minerals such as A, B, C, potassium, iron, and calcium. Pear can help treat chest colds and urinary conditions.

— PECAN —

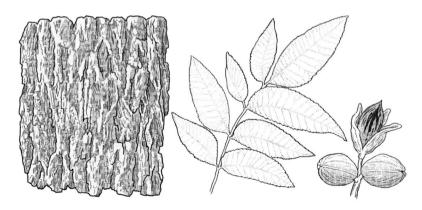

Other Names: Sweet pecan

Number of Species: 60

Family: Juglandaceae

Genus/Species: *Carya illinoinensis*

Leaf: Pinnately compound alternate, deciduous, 12–20 inches in length with 9–17 curved leaflets, each leaflet being 2–7 inches long with pointed tips and fine-toothed margins. Yellowish green above and paler below

Bark: Gray, thick, furrowed and ridged with age

Fruit: Clusters of brown nuts when ripe, each nut 1–2 inches in length, oblong, and edible

Magickal Properties and Lore: Money, prosperity, employment, and stability. Carry the shells of the nut during an interview or with you to work to help ensure future employment and to attract money. The wood makes a great wand.

Practical Uses: Pecans are an important source of food for humans and many animals. The wood has been used to make furniture, flooring, and charcoal. The pecan is one of the most commercially valuable trees in North America.

Medicinal Properties: Pecans provide protein, unsaturated fats, antioxidants, and can reduce cholesterol levels if eaten in small amounts.

— PERSIMMON —

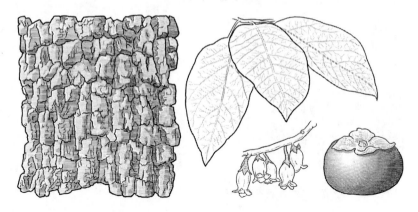

Other Names: Common persimmon, sugar plum, simmon, and possum-wood

Number of Species: About 400 throughout the world

Family: Ebenaceae

Genus/Species: *Diospyros virginiana*

Leaf: Simple alternate, deciduous, 2–6 inches in length, ovate to oblong with pointed tips and toothless margin, dark green above and lighter below. The springtime brings white bell-shaped flowers.

Bark: Brown to dark gray almost black, thick, and deeply furrowed into shapes resembling squares

Fruit: Round fleshy berries 1–2 inches in length and width, yellow-orange to brown and edible when mature, smooth skin, and contain many brown seeds. The fruit needs to be harvested after the first frost.

Magickal Properties and Lore: Health and good luck. Burry the immature green fruits or the leaves near your home to attract good luck. This tree is sacred to Zeus; hence the scientific name *Diospyros*, which means the fruit of the god Zeus.

Practical Uses: The fruit is a valuable source of nourishment for many animals, birds, and humans. It has been used to make cakes, bread, pudding, and alcoholic beverages. The wood is used in furniture and to make the heads of golf clubs.

Medicinal Properties: Native Americans once made bread from the fruit and dried them like prunes in order to store them. They also made a decoction from the tree to treat bloody stool. The leaves are high in vitamin C and the bark can be boiled into water to use as a mouthwash.

—— PINE, AUSTRIAN ——

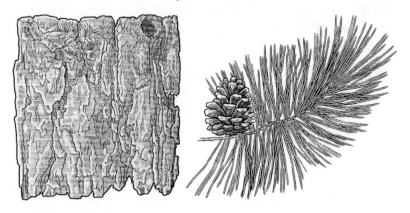

Other Names: European black pine, sometimes mistaken for red pine or scotch pine

Number of Species: Over 90 species of coniferous evergreen trees

Family: Pinaceae

Genus/Species: *Pinus nigra*

Needle: Clustered pokey needles grow in pairs, but these pairs do not twist around each other at the base like those of the Scotch pine, 3–6 inches in length, 2 needles per cluster, dark green, and pointed. The needles of the Austrian pine do not break evenly when bent.

Bark: Brown and gray, very scaly. Branches are reddish in color.

Cones: Brown cones when mature, 1–3 inches in length. Each scale of the cone ends with a sharp pointed tip and contains two seeds per scale.

Magickal Properties and Lore: Protection, spell breaking, longevity, purification, fertility, exorcisms, healing, money. Pine is an all-purpose magickal tree. Carry pinecones to increase longevity and fertility. Burn needles to purify and cleanse an area of unwanted negative energies, or spread the needles on the ground to ward off evil spirits. Burn the needles to break or reverse a curse or spell. Place a pine branch over or near the bed to ward off sickness and bad dreams. Carry or burn the sawdust for any of the above. Essence of pine is relaxing and will ease stress and tension, promote insight and intuition, and develop self-confidence. Pinewood makes a great wand or staff.

Practical Uses: Pines are an important and valued source of timber and many species produce edible seeds (or nuts) that can be eaten raw or roasted into breads or cakes.

Medicinal Properties: Pine nuts provide potassium, magnesium, carotene, and vitamin E. Needles can be used for teas, ointments, or bath water to soothe coughs, congestion, breathing, circulation, or as a disinfectant or diuretic.

— PINE, SCOTCH —

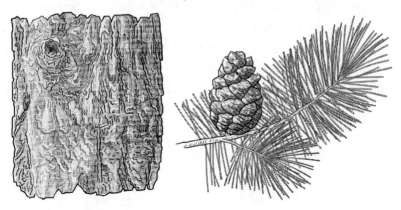

Other Names: Scots pine

Number of Species: Over 90 species of coniferous evergreen trees

Family: Pinaceae

Genus/Species: *Pinus sylvestris*

Needle: Clustered needles, two needles per cluster that twist around each other at the base, each being 1–3 inches in length and pointed tips. The needles of the Scotch pine are shorter than those of the Austrian pine and have a blue tint.

Bark: Orange brown to gray and scaly. The inner bark is reddish orange in color.

Cones: Brown cones, ovate, 1–3 inches in length, and usually grow in clusters of 2–3 cones pointing back toward the branch

Magickal Properties and Lore: Protection, spell breaking, longevity, purification, fertility, exorcisms, healing, money. Pine is an all-purpose magickal tree. Carry pinecones to increase longevity and fertility. Burn needles to purify and cleanse an area of unwanted negative energies, or spread the needles on the ground to ward off evil spirits. Burn the needles to break or reverse a curse or spell. Place a pine branch over or near the bed to ward off sickness and bad dreams. Carry or burn the sawdust for any of the above. Essence of pine is relaxing and will ease stress and tension, promote insight and intuition, and develop self-confidence. Pinewood makes a great wand or staff.

Practical Uses: The Scotch pine is one of the most popular evergreen used for Christmas trees. Pines are an important and valued source of timber and many species produce edible seed (or nuts) that can be eaten raw or roasted into breads or cakes.

Medicinal Properties: Pine nuts provide potassium, magnesium, carotene, and vitamin E. Needles can be used for teas, ointments, or bath water to soothe coughs, congestion, breathing, circulation, or as a disinfectant or diuretic.

—— PINE, WHITE ——

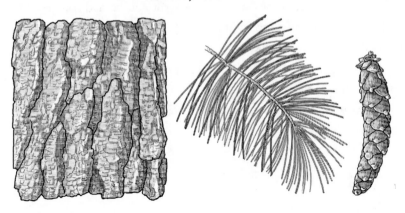

Other Names: Soft pine, Eastern white pine, Northern white pine, and Weymouth pine

Number of Species: Over 90 species of coniferous evergreen trees

Family: Pinaceae

Genus/Species: *Pinus strobus*

Needle: Clusters of needles with 5 per cluster, each needle 3–5 inches in length. The needles of white pines are very soft to the touch and flexible.

Bark: Gray to brown, smooth when young and furrowed with age.

Cones: Brown when mature, long and curved, 4–8 inches in length with pointed white tips

Magickal Properties and Lore: Protection, spell breaking, longevity, purification, fertility, exorcisms, healing, money. Pine is an all-purpose magickal tree. Carry pinecones to increase longevity and fertility. Burn needles to purify and cleanse an area of unwanted negative energies, or spread the needles on the ground to ward off evil spirits. Burn the needles to break or reverse a curse or spell. Place a pine branch over or near the bed to ward off sickness and bad dreams. Carry or burn the sawdust for any of the above. Essence of pine is relaxing and will ease stress and tension, promote insight and intuition, and develop self-confidence. Pinewood makes a great wand or staff.

Practical Uses: The white pine is a favorite nesting tree for bald eagles. Pines are an important and valued source of timber and many species produce edible seed (or nuts) that can be eaten raw or roasted into breads or cakes.

Medicinal Properties: Pine nuts provide potassium, magnesium, carotene, and vitamin E. Needles can be used for teas, ointments, or bath water to soothe coughs, congestion, breathing, circulation, or as a disinfectant or diuretic.

—— PLUM, AMERICAN ——

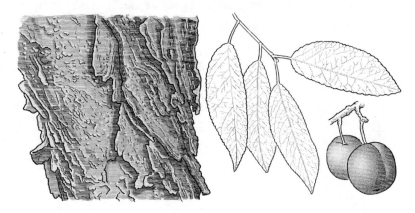

Other Names: Wild plum, red plum, August plum, hog plum, and river plum

Number of Species: About 430

Family: Rosaceae

Genus/Species: *Prunus americana*

Leaf: Simple alternate, deciduous, ovate, 2–5 inches in length, double-toothed margin, pointed tip, and dark green in color

Bark: Reddish brown to gray and scaly with sharp thorns

Fruit: Round fleshy plums about an inch wide, red to purple when mature, edible, and containing one seed

Magickal Properties and Lore: Love, healing, protection, purification. Hang twigs or branches over a door or place them in a room to ward off negative energies and spirits. Share the fruit with a loved one to strengthen the relationship. Some Native Americans used the wood to fashion prayer sticks in effort to petition to the gods a healing request for a sick person.

Practical Uses: Plums are an important source of food for wildlife and humans. Plums can be eaten raw and have been used for jams, jellies, and preserves. The roots can be used to make red dye.

Medicinal Properties: The inner bark can be boiled and gargled to help cure mouth sores. Fruits contain many vitamins and minerals and can assist with weight loss, heart problems, can be used to treat diabetes, to promote healthy bones and combat osteoporosis, reduce anxiety, and may even have anticancer properties. Note that these benefits apply strictly to the fruit and not to store-bought plum juices, because these juices usually contain a high amount of sugar and little fruit.

— POPLAR, BLACK —

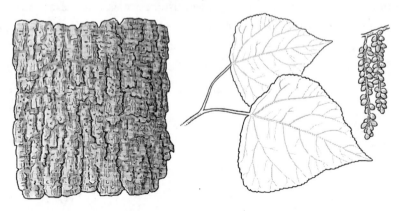

Other Names: Lombardy poplar, Italian poplar

Number of Species: 35

Family: Salicaceae

Genus/Species: *Populus nigra*

Leaf: Simple alternate, deciduous, triangular to ovate shaped, 2–4 inches in lengths and generally wider than long, fine toothed margin, pointed tip, darker green above and paler below. This tree grows in a columnar form.

Bark: Gray and furrowed with dark patches lower down and smoother higher up

Fruit: Small capsules containing many seeds

Magickal Properties and Lore: Money, security, relief, healing, protection, astral projection, goals, perseverance. Carry the leaves or buds to attract money. The leaves can be made into an ointment to promote astral projection. Plant a poplar tree with a goal in mind, and as the tree grows, so will your goal manifest. Place a branch near the bed to induce inspirational dreams. The wood makes a great wand.

Practical Uses: Black poplar trees were once used to build homes due to their resistance to fire. The leaves of the poplar are a popular source of food for livestock. Wood has been used to make matches and packing boxes.

Medicinal Properties: The bark contains salicylic acid that is used as an anti-inflammatory and analgesic. Buds are used to treat chest, kidney, and prostate problems. The bark can be used externally to treat rashes, burns, wounds, and eczema. Leaves, bark, and buds can help pain, diarrhea, hay fever, liver troubles, the influenza, and more.

— POPLAR, WHITE —

Other Names: Silver poplar, silver leaf poplar, abele, European white poplar

Number of Species: 35

Family: Salicaceae

Genus/Species: *Populus alba*

Leaf: Lobed alternate, deciduous, resembling a maple leaf, 2–5 inches in length, and 3–5 pointed lobes, smooth rounded teeth, light green above and silver-white below

Bark: White to gray, often with diamond shaped markings, rough and furrowed at the base and smoother higher up

Fruit: Egg-shaped capsules 2–3 inches in length containing many seeds, which float on the wind like cotton

Magickal Properties and Lore: Money, security, relief, healing, protection, astral projection, goals, perseverance. Carry the leaves or buds to attract money. The leaves can be made into an ointment to promote astral projection. Plant a poplar tree with a goal in mind, and as the tree grows, so will your goal manifest. Place a branch near the bed to induce inspirational dreams. The wood makes a great wand.

Practical Uses: The leaves of the poplar are a popular source of food for livestock. Wood has been used to make matches and packing boxes.

Medicinal Properties: The bark contains salicylic acid that can be used as an anti-inflammatory and analgesic (pain relief). Buds are used to treat chest, kidney, and prostate problems. The bark can be used externally to treat rashes, burns, wounds, and eczema. Leaves, bark, and buds can help pain, diarrhea, hay fever, liver troubles, the influenza, and more.

— REDBUD, EASTERN —

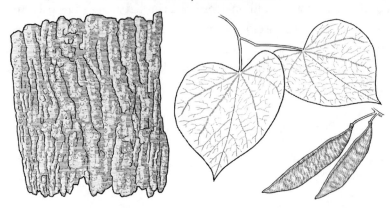

Other Names: Judas tree, American redbud, love tree

Number of Species: About 10

Family: Fabaceae

Genus/Species: *Cercis canadensis*

Leaf: Simple alternate, deciduous, heart-shaped leaves 2–6 inches in length, toothless margin, pointed tips, dark shiny green in color. Fragrant pink flowers bloom early in the spring.

Bark: Reddish brown to gray, smooth when young and becoming furrowed and scaly with age

Fruit: Clusters of green pods turning reddish brown when mature, 2–4 inches in length with pointed tips at each end, edible

Magickal Properties and Lore: Creativity, intuition, health, and love. Meditate under or near a redbud to bring inspiration and creativity or sleep with the leaves near your pillow. Legend says that Judas hung himself on a relative of this tree after betraying Jesus; however, I find this to be very unlikely considering the fact that redbuds are small trees and I doubt they could support the weight of a grown man. This by no means taints the magickal properties of this beautiful tree.

Practical Uses: A valuable source of food for humans and other wildlife. Bees often use the flowers of this tree for nectar. Native Americans used the flowers and pods as a source of food. Flowers and buds are sometimes added to salads, breads, and pancakes. The pods may be eaten raw, sautéed, or boiled. The twigs, when boiled in water, can make yellow dye. This tree has ornamental value due to its beautiful spring flowers and heart-shaped leaves.

Medicinal Properties: Flowers and buds are a good source of vitamin C. May treat coughs, congestion, and fevers.

— REDWOOD, DAWN —

Other Names: Water fir, water larch, Shui Shan, and often mistaken for bald cypress. It is considered to be critically endangered.

Number of Species: 3

Family: Once considered to belong to the Taxodiaceae family but now considered as belonging to the Cupressaceae (cypress) family.

Genus/Species: *Metasequoia glyptostroboides*

Leaf: Compound opposite needles. This tree is a deciduous conifer. Needles are oppositely attached in pairs, pinnate; each needle is about an inch long and bright green to yellow green in color. An easy way to distinguish this tree from the bald cypress is that the bald cypress leaves are alternately attached while those of the dawn redwood are oppositely attached

Bark: Orange to reddish brown and peeling in vertical strips

Fruit: Round cones, green when young becoming brown when mature, about an inch across

Magickal Properties and Lore: Protection, balance, ancestor magick, longevity, and healing. This tree symbolizes our connection to the worlds above, below, and connects our past, present, and future. This tree has many magickal properties, but due to it being endangered, I do not recommend using it for anything other than propagation.

Practical Uses: Redwood trees are fire resistant and have been used to make railroad ties and frames for buildings. The dawn redwood is a living fossil and was once thought to be extinct. The redwoods are amongst the oldest living trees on earth.

Medicinal Properties: The sap contains tannic acid, which helps in the process of healing.

—— ROWAN ——

Other Names: Mountain ash (although not a true ash), *Luis* (Celtic), wittern, wiggen, witch wood, wichen, witch bane, quick beam, quick bane, delight of the eye, and Thor's helper

Number of Species: 85

Family: Rosaceae

Genus/Species: *Sorbus aucuparia*

Leaf: Compound alternate, deciduous, 4–8 inches in length with 9–17 leaflets, and each leaflet being 1–2 inches long, ovate, with fine-toothed margins

Bark: Gray and smooth with horizontal lines

Fruit: Clusters of orange to red berry-like fruits containing 1 or 2 black seeds

Magickal Properties and Lore: Protection, power, exorcisms, discovering secret knowledge, psychic ability, healing, divination, and success. Rowan is another all-purpose magickal tree. Use wood, leaves, or berries to add an extra boost to all spell work. Hang twigs or branches over a door to ward off negative and harmful energies or to break curses. Place twigs near the bed to repel nightmares and to induce peaceful sleep. The flower essence can cleanse and protect the aura. Wood can make a very powerful wand, staff, or dowsing rod.

Practical Uses: Rowan wood is hard and has been used to make spinning wheels, tool handles, and stakes. The berries are an important source of nourishment for birds and other wildlife and can be boiled to make jams, jellies, and wine.

Medicinal Properties: Rowan can be used to cleanse the blood, strengthen the immune system, combat some forms of cancer, and is high in vitamin C. The bark can be used externally to treat cuts, sores, and skin problems.

—— RUBBER TREE ——

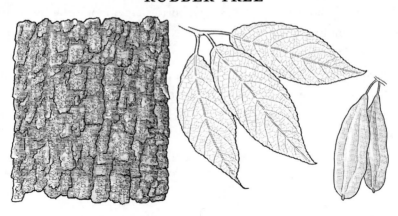

Other Names: Hardy rubber tree, Chinese rubber tree, hard rubber tree, and Gutta-Percha tree. Do not confuse rubber tree with rubber plant as the two are sometimes mislabeled on some internet sources.

Number of Species: 1

Family: Eucommiaceae

Genus/Species: *Eucommia ulmoides*

Leaf: Simple alternate, deciduous, ovate, up to 8 inches in length, fine-toothed margin. When a leaf is slowly pulled apart, one will notice a sticky latex binding.

Bark: Gray to brown and deeply fissured

Fruit: Clusters of green to yellowish winged pods containing one seed (samaras).

Magickal Properties and Lore: Can be used for strength, healing, recovery, discovering hidden and secret mysteries, survival, invisibility, and union.

Practical Uses: Rubber trees make excellent shade trees and have ornamental value for their beautiful deep shiny green foliage in the summer. If the leaves are torn horizontally, small almost invisible strands of latex exude from the veins, which become like rubber and hold the torn parts together. This tree is the only surviving species in the family and is often considered as a living fossil.

Medicinal Properties: The bark of the rubber tree is very valued in Chinese healing medicine and used for high blood pressure, arthritis, diabetes, and heart problems.

— SASSAFRAS —

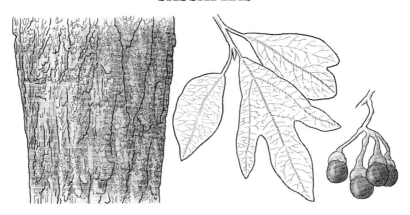

Other Names: Ague tree, saxifrax, cinnamon wood, white sassafras, red sassafras, silky sassafras, and saloip

Number of Species: 3

Family: Lauraceae

Genus/Species: *Sassafras albidum*

Leaf: Simple or lobed alternate, deciduous, 3–5 inches in length, elliptical, 1–3 lobes, smooth margin, shiny green above, paler and hairy below. The lobed leaves often resemble mittens.

Bark: Brown to gray, deeply furrowed and thick with age. The wood is very soft and breaks easily.

Fruit: Blue to black drupes

Magickal Properties and Lore: Money and healing. Carry the leaves or wood chippings in the wallet or purse to attract money. Use dried leaves or bark in healing spells or sachets. The essence of the leaves and bark can be used for aromatherapy to promote healing and peace.

Practical Uses: The sassafras is a valuable source of food for wildlife and has ornamental value for its interestingly shaped leaves and colored fruits. The crushed leaves and twigs emit a spicy fragrance, and the roots are used to make perfumed soaps, tea, and the flavor of root beer.

Medicinal Properties: The root bark was once used as a cure-all for many diseases and ailments. The sassafras is a stimulant, diaphoretic, and a diuretic. A tea made from sassafras can cleanse the blood and relieve gas, kidney, bladder, chest, and throat troubles. The oil of sassafras is excellent to ease toothaches.

—— SERVICEBERRY ——

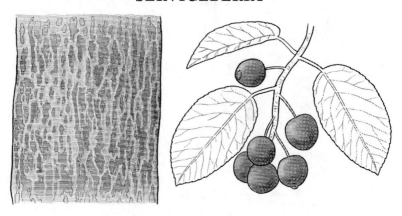

Other Names: Juneberry, shadbush, shadblow, downy serviceberry, common serviceberry, servicetree, and Sarvis-tree

Number of Species: About 20

Family: Rosaceae

Genus/Species: *Amelanchier arborea*

Leaf: Simple alternate, deciduous, 1–4 inches in length, ovate or elliptical, pointed tip, fine-toothed margin, dull green above and paler below

Bark: Light gray, smooth when young, furrowed and ridged with age

Fruit: Round red to purple edible berries containing several seeds, edible

Magickal Properties and Lore: Love, merriment, and well-being

Practical Uses: Valuable source of food for birds and humans. The berries have been used to make pies, jams, breads, and can be eaten raw. The taste is similar to blueberries. The wood has been used for tool handles and fishing rods.

Medicinal Properties: Used to treat diarrhea and is an anthelmintic (used to treat parasitic worms).

— SPRUCE, BLUE —

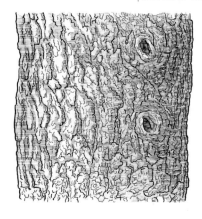 

Other Names: Colorado blue spruce, silver spruce, or peace tree. The spruce is closely related to the fir

Number of Species: 35 species of coniferous evergreen trees

Family: Pinaceae

Genus/Species: *Picea pungens* f. *glauca*

Needle: Single needles up to 1 inch in length, sharp and stiff to the touch, blue to silvery green in color. If a single needle is carefully pulled from the stem, one will find a brown woody base.

Bark: Brown to gray and deeply furrowed

Cones: Cones grow either single or in clusters, each being 2–4 inches in length, and hang down from the boughs.

Magickal Properties and Lore: Protection, dreams, intuition, spirit communication, immortality, and connecting with the divine. The spruce loves human contact and is very willing to protect and guard a home or property from negative energies so long as you, from time to time, take a moment to tell the tree that you love it and give it thanks. The spruce is very talkative if you are open to listen. Plant one near your home or place the wood indoors to ward off negativity. In the Slavic tradition, the goddess of the woods inhabits the spruce/fir trees and the king of the woods (also known as the Green Man) resides in the oldest living specimen in the region. The Nordic rune that represents protection, called algiz, just so happens to resemble the pattern of the outer parts of the branches.

Practical Uses: The spruce and fir are often used as Christmas trees. Native Americans have used parts of the spruce/fir for bedding, ropes, toys, paddles, tent frames, roofing, and cabins. Spruce is considered as one of the best woods for making musical instruments.

Medicinal Properties: Seeds (nuts) can be eaten raw or cooked as an emergency source of food and contain vitamin C and fats. Likely you would not enjoy the flavor, but you can use them as a survival food if you ever find yourself in such a predicament. Note that some people may be allergic.

— SPRUCE, NORWAY —

Other Names: European spruce

Number of Species: 35 species of coniferous evergreen trees

Family: Pinaceae

Genus/Species: *Picea abies*

Needle: Single needles grow up to 1 inch in length, stiff, pointed, and sharp to the touch, slightly curved, shiny green in color with white lines along the central vein. Pull a single needle from the stem and you will find a small, brown, papery base.

Bark: Reddish brown to gray and scaly.

Cone: Long brown cones, 2–7 inches in length, hanging down from the boughs. The Norway spruce produces the largest cones of all spruce trees.

Magickal Properties and Lore: Protection, dreams, intuition, spirit communication, immortality, and connecting with the divine. The spruce loves human contact and is very willing to protect and guard a home or property from negative energies so long as you, from time to time, take a moment to tell the tree that you love it and give it thanks. The spruce is very talkative if you are open to listen. Plant one near your home or place the wood indoors to ward off negativity. In the Slavic tradition, the goddess of the woods inhabits the spruce/fir trees and the king of the woods (also known as the Green Man) resides in the oldest living specimen in the region. The Nordic rune that represents protection, called

Algiz, just so happens to resemble the pattern of the outer parts of the branches.

Practical Uses: The spruce and fir are often used as Christmas trees. Native Americans have used parts of the spruce/fir for bedding, ropes, toys, paddles, tent frames, roofing, and cabins. Spruce is considered as one of the best woods for making musical instruments.

Medicinal Properties: Seeds (nuts) can be eaten raw or cooked as an emergency source of food and contain vitamin C and fats. Likely you would not enjoy the flavor, but you can use them as a survival food if you ever find yourself in such a predicament. Note that some people may be allergic.

— SUMAC, STAGHORN —

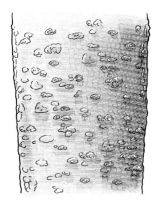 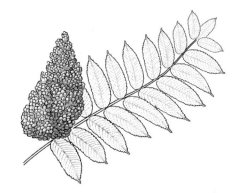

Other Names: Velvet tree, vinegar tree, closely related to the smooth sumac, which lacks hairs below the leaflets

Number of Species: About 250

Family: Anacardiaceae

Genus/Species: *Rhus typhina*

Leaf: Pinnately compound alternate, deciduous, 12–24 inches in length with 12–31 leaflets (often 19), each leaflet being 2–4 inches long, fine-toothed margins, dark green with small red hairs below, and attached directly to the stalk

Bark: Brown to gray and fairly smooth to slightly scaly

Fruit: Red fuzzy drupes that grow in cone shaped clusters

Magickal Properties and Lore: Healing, love, matters of the heart, learning, and also binding, banishing, cursing, and curse breaking, as it is associated with the planet Saturn.

Practical Uses: Valuable source of food for animals and birds but best not to plant one in your yard or especially near the foundation of a building as they are rather invasive and hard to get rid of. The crushed fruit can be used to make a lemonade-like drink, but be extremely cautious that you do not mistake this sumac for the poison sumac, which has the same oils as poison oak and poison ivy. The bark, leaves, wood, and fruit can be boiled to make a natural black dye or ink.

Medicinal Properties: Some Native Americans used parts of this tree to make a tea or gargle for easing sore throats.

— SWEETGUM —

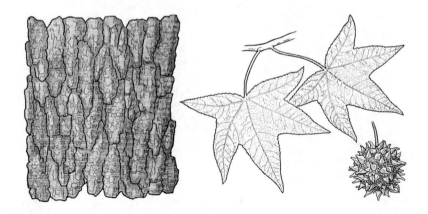

Other Names: American sweetgum, red gum, sap gum

Number of Species: About 25 genera and 100 species

Family: Hamamelidacea

Genus/Species: *Liquidambar styraciflua*

Leaf: Lobed alternate, deciduous, 3–6 inches in length with 5–7 pointed lobes, fine-toothed margins, shiny dark green above, and lighter below. Sometimes this tree is mistaken for a maple due to the shape of the leaf, however the leaf of the sweetgum resembles a five-pointed star whereas most maples do not.

Bark: Brown to gray, scaly, and deeply furrowed

Fruit: Round green clusters turning brown when mature with many small, prickly, pointed spikes containing many flat, winged seeds

Magickal Properties and Lore: Protection, connecting with the elementals, with spirit, and developing wisdom. Place leaves of mature fruits in an area you wish to clear of negative energies or use as a correspondence on the altar to increase the power of your working. The wood is very good for crafting a wand.

Practical Uses: Seeds are a source of nourishment for some birds and animals. The hard and heavy wood is used for furniture, barrels, cabinets, boxes, and plywood. The gum is used for some medicinal properties but better known for the production of chewing gum.

Medicinal Properties: Antiseptic properties that can treat minor cuts and wounds, a diuretic, used to treat rheumatism, coughs, congestion, sore throats, and has sedative properties.

— SYCAMORE —

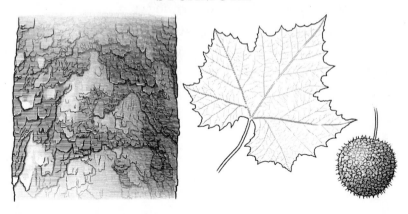

Other Names: American sycamore, buttonball tree, buttonwood, American plane tree, and ghost tree

Number of Species: 7–10

Family: Platanaceae

Genus/Species: *Platanus occidentalis*

Leaf: Simple lobed alternate, deciduous, 4–8 inches in length and width, triangular in shape, 3–5 pointed lobes, toothed margin, bright green above and paler beneath

Bark: Grayish white, thin, fairly smooth, and peeling off in flaky sections. The lower bark is often darker than the upper bark.

Fruit: Round, brown, aggregate fruits, generally 1 inch in diameter and very dense

Magickal Properties and Lore: Beauty, new beginnings, love, empathy, intuition, healing atrophy, opens spirit communication, humility, and inspiration. This tree is associated with the element of water and can be used as a powerful assistant regarding shadow magick. The sycamore was a very sacred tree to the ancient Egyptians and the goddess Hathor. The wood can be used to create a very powerful staff or wand used for invoking the divine. It has been said that where one finds a sycamore tree, one will find a source of nourishment whether it be food, water, or of a spiritual nature nearby.

Practical Uses: The wood has been used for furniture, flooring, particle-board, and pulpwood. Some older sycamore trees have hollowed trunks that provide shelter and refuge to wildlife. To needlessly cut down a sycamore could bring karmic and spiritual retribution so be warned. The tree has ornamental value for its beautiful, unique bark.

Medicinal Properties: Can be used to treat minor cuts and wounds due to its astringent properties.

—— TREE OF HEAVEN ——

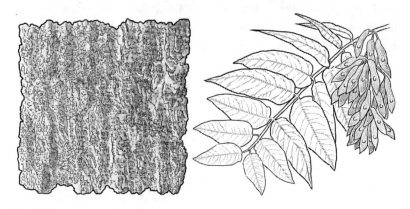

Other Names: Ailanthus, ghetto-tree, and stink-tree

Number of Species: 150

Family: Simaroubacea

Genus/Species: *Ailanthus altissima*

Leaf: Pinnately compound alternate, deciduous, 12–24 inches in length with 13–25 leaflets, each leaflet being 3–5 inches long, ovately shaped, margins have very few teeth, pointed tips, green above and paler below

Bark: Brown to gray, smooth when young and becoming rough and fissured with age

Fruit: Samaras (winged fruits) about 1 and a half inch in length, reddish-green to reddish-brown

Magickal Properties and Lore: Properties are controversial. The flowers grow with five petals and can be used as a correspondence for Goddess, elemental, and spirit workings. Several parts of this tree emit a foul odor and can be used for driving out unwanted energies and for bindings or banishments. The wood grows very straight and may be tempting to use for a wand or staff, but is easily broken and not recommended for this purpose.

Practical Uses: This is a very invasive tree and should not be planted in locations where other trees grow because they quickly take over. Tree of heaven has been planted for shade and ornamental purposes due to its incredibly rapid growth and beauty. It is sometimes used to feed silk-worms.

Medicinal Properties: In traditional Chinese medicine, this tree has been for used for many purposes such as treating mental illness, boils, itches, and balding. The roots are poisonous.

—— TULIP TREE ——

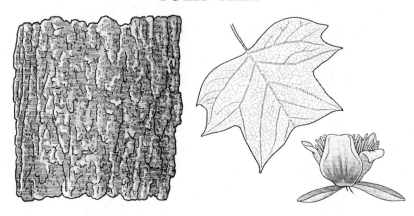

Other Names: Tulip magnolia, whitewood, and often called yellow poplar or tulip poplar, but this tree is not a true poplar

Number of Species: 2

Family: Magnoliaceae

Genus/Species: *Liriodendron tulipfera*

Leaf: Simple lobed alternate, deciduous, 3–6 inches in length, each leaf is very uniquely shaped with 4–6 pointed lobes, smooth toothless margin, shiny green above and paler below. The yellow flowers resemble a tulip and usually have an orange base.

Bark: Brown to gray and deeply furrowed

Fruit: Aggregate fruits are 2–3 inches in length, light brown when mature, cone-shaped, and grow upright on the branches

Magickal Properties and Lore: Love, youth, energy, vibrance, healing, and matters of the heart

Practical Uses: The wood has been used to make canoes, toys, pulpwood, furniture, cabinets, crates, and musical instruments.

Medicinal Properties: Some Native Americans consumed the root bark to rid the body of worms. Other parts, such as the leaves, bark, and branches, are used to reduce fever and promote urination. The inner bark is a powerful aid for treating problems with the heart, the nervous system, and the digestive system.

— WALNUT, BLACK —

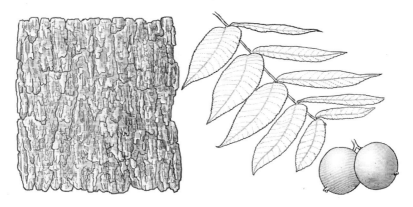

Other Names: English walnut, walnoot, and tree of evil

Number of Species: 40–60

Family: Juglandaceae

Genus/Species: *Juglans nigra*

Leaf: Pinnate compound alternate, deciduous, 12–24 inches in length with 15–23 leaflets, each leaflet being 2–5 inches long, pointed tips and fine-toothed margins

Bark: Brown to dark gray with rough narrow ridges

Fruit: Round brown nuts when mature, 1–2 inches in length and edible

Magickal Properties and Lore: Health, confidence, intellectual development, and wish fulfillment. Give a walnut to a friend or loved one to promote the manifestation of his or her goals and realistic wishes. Carry the wood to strengthen the heart or carry the leaves to ease one through times of a broken heart or stressful situations. This wood makes a great wand or staff. It has been said that walnut wood can attract lightning so do not carry it during a storm, but do think about the sacred symbolism in this regard. The wood is very sacred to the Goddess and may not be abused without facing the consequence.

Practical Uses: Walnut is an important source of food for wildlife. The wood is a highly valued commercial source for manufacturing furniture and cabinets. The ancient Romans used walnut to make wine and natural dyes.

Medicinal Properties: Walnuts provide potassium, protein, and folic acids. The nuts and leaves help to strengthen the immune system, promote blood circulation, easing colds, coughs, constipation, bladder stones, kidney ailments, acne, skin conditions, and swollen glands.

—— WILLOW, WEEPING ——

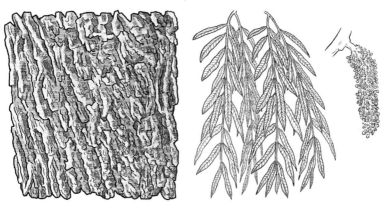

Other Names: Chinese willow, golden willow, Babylon weeping willow, osier, *saille* (Celtic), swamp willow, gooding willow, saugh tree, tree of enchantment, withe, withy, and witches' aspirin

Number of Species: More than 300

Family: Salicaceae

Genus/Species: *Salix babylonica*

Leaf: Simple alternate, deciduous, long narrow leaves are 2–4 inches in length with fine-toothed margins, pointed tips, bright green to yellow above and almost white below

Bark: Light brown to gray with vertical furrows and ridges

Fruit: Catkin-like capsules about an inch long, which open and release many seeds

Magickal Properties and Lore: Ruled by the moon and the element of water. Used for divination, prophecy, psychic workings, developing intuition, dream magick, love, beauty, death and passing, easing of pain, the sacred feminine, purification, healing, and protection. Carry the leaves to attract love. Willow wood can make a wonderful wand or staff. The leaves, bark, flowers, roots, and branches can be carried or placed in an area to ward off negative and evil energies. All parts can be used in healing spells. The traditional witches' besom has often been made from willow. Many willows are friendly, but some can be cruel and wicked if not approached in a respectful manner.

Practical Uses: This valuable wood is used for furniture, baskets, doors, cabinets, toys, pulpwood, boxes, and much more. Planting a willow helps to prevent nearby soil erosion. Willows love water and thrive near ponds, streams, creeks, lakes, and rivers. In turn, the willow helps to purify the water that nurtures it.

Medicinal Properties: Willow bark contains salicylic acid, which has anti-inflammatory properties and is a natural pain reliever; the main ingredient in aspirin.

—— WITCH HAZEL ——

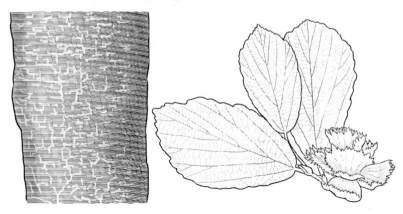

Other Names: Common witch hazel, snapping hazelnut, winter bloom, American witch hazel, spotted alder, and easily mistaken for the common hazel, which is sometimes called Harry Lauder's walking stick. Hazel and witch hazel are different when it comes to scientific classification and medicine, but the magickal properties are shared.

Number of Species: About 100 species worldwide

Family: Hamamelidaceae

Genus/Species: *Hamamelis virginiana*

Leaf: Simple alternate, deciduous, ovate to round in shape, 3–6 inches in length, course toothed margins, round or pointed tips, dark green above and lighter below. Leaves, twigs, and bark are aromatic.

Bark: Light brown to gray, smooth and sometimes scaly

Fruit: Light brown to orange elliptic catkin-like capsules, up to an inch long, and split open when mature to release 1 or 2 black edible seeds

Magickal Properties and Lore: Associated with the sun and the element fire, used for protection, emotional healing, and divination. The wood has been used for crafting dowsing rods to locate local sources of water. Carry the leaves, bark, or twigs to promote the healing of a broken heart, to promote an environment of love and peace, or to protect from harmful energies. The wood can be used to make a very special wand.

Practical Uses: This very small tree or shrub makes an attractive border and has beautiful foliage and flowers.

Medicinal Properties: Leaves and twigs can used to ease aches, swellings, inflammations, and bruises. The Native American Iroquois brewed a tea from the boiled leaves and sweetened the beverage with maple sugar or sap for the simple pleasure of enjoyment.

— YELLOWWOOD —

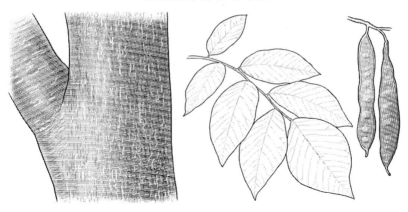

Other Names: Kentucky yellowwood, American yellowwood, gopher wood, and virgilia

Number of Species: 7

Family: Fabaceae

Genus/Species: *Cladrastis kentukea*

Leaf: Pinnately compound alternate, deciduous, 8–12 inches in length with 5–11 ovate leaflets, each leaflet being 2–4 inches long, smooth margins and pointed tips, yellow-green above and paler below

Bark: Gray and very smooth much like the bark of the beech tree

Fruit: Clusters of flat brown pods when mature, 1–4 inches long, and containing 2–6 seeds

Magickal Properties and Lore: Individuality, self-esteem, and nurturing uniqueness. Carry the leaves to help conquer the fear of speaking in public and expressing what is truly on the heart. Once you have done this, return the leaves to the earth. Place the wood or leaves near your bed to enhance self-importance and awakening.

Practical Uses: The majority of trees with compound leaves are oppositely attached, but the yellowwood leaves and leaflets are alternately attached making them very unique. The wood is yellow when freshly cut and can be used to make yellow dye. Yellowwood has ornamental value.

Medicinal Properties: Unknown

—— YEW ——

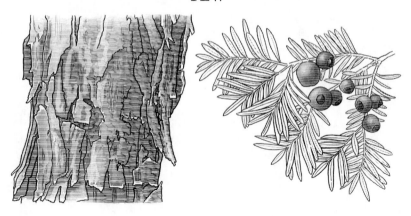

Other Names: *Idhadh* (Celtic), common yew, European yew, English yew, and graveyard tree

Number of Species: 18 species of evergreen trees

Family: Taxaceae

Genus: *Taxus*

Leaf: Needle-like evergreen leaves, up to an inch and a quarter in length, dark green above, paler below with two segments

Bark: Red to brown, scaly and peeling off in vertical strips

Fruit: Beautiful red fleshy berry-like fruits are the only part of this tee that is not poisonous, but the seeds within the fruit are toxic as well.

Magickal Properties and Lore: Death, passing, rebirth, longevity, banishing, binding, and communicating with departed souls. Ruled by Saturn, this tree should never be touched without gloves, as every part is poisonous. It was often planted in ancient Europe near churchyards, cemeteries, and used to mark graves.

Practical Uses: Both the trees and shrubs are used for decorations and borders. Some living specimens of yew are known to have existed for hundreds to thousands of years.

Medicinal Properties: Yews are one of the most toxic plants. Exposure to this tree/shrub can cause heart problems, skin issues, and may even lead to physical death. Please do not touch this tree without great caution. Modern medicine has found that the yew contains powerful properties, which can be safely extracted without causing harm, to the tree, that can fight against cancer. This is a very sacred tree.

Section Three

TREE CORRESPONDENCES WITHIN VARIOUS SPIRITUAL SYSTEMS

Above dry dirt cracked tiny sprouts
South to west and north to east
Children know before learning doubt
The hidden language of hallowed things

Chapter 5
DIVINE CORRESPONDENCES
OF TREES

For the magickal practitioner, there will certainly be times when a basic knowledge of trees and their magickal correspondences will be helpful in ritual, spell craft, healing, divination, growing close to nature, and forming a personal alignment with the divine and archetypal forces of the universe.

For example, there was a time when a former member of the group I practice and study with needed funds to keep his family house. We used the correspondences of the waxing moon on a Thursday to draw in the needed resources and included cedar and olive wood because these woods are associated with Jupiter, which rules over Thursday, and is a good correspondence for drawing in needed funds. The results were amazing. Of course, there was much more to the work than this, but that would be another book regarding ritual magick.

Keep in mind that magick should not be used for greed, to feed one's ego, or to cause harm, because many types of magick can improve your life or destroy it. If ever you are in doubt about the ethical use of magick please meditate, pray, and let spirit take care of the need or goal for you instead of taking things into your own hands.

I will soon be presenting a list of some collected mythological, archetypal, and divine tree associations throughout the ages. Though all trees are sacred, and because there are over eighty thousand species of trees throughout the world (making it impossible to present each one), the following list represents twenty-six common trees shared throughout North America and Europe. The final chapter of this book is a field guide to help correctly identify many of the common trees found throughout North America and Europe, including the taxonomy, lore, medicinal, and magickal properties of each. Regarding deity in relation to the magickal properties of trees, my personal belief is that most gods and goddesses of mythology are but different names, faces, and aspects of the same incomprehensible spirit or source. This may be better understood when we examine the Qabalistic Tree of Life.

I do not claim my viewpoint is the only one worthy of consideration, but I do feel everyone should take his or her time to think about it. I believe that this Great Spirit, this incomprehensible force, has presented itself to the hearts of humankind throughout many cultures and civilizations of the past and continues to do so today—those who have experienced in their heart a connection with the divine and felt inspired to record the experience, wrote texts, sacred scriptures, and what we now call mythology. Although these accounts may have been divinely inspired and sometimes include a measure of historical facts, humans wrote them from personal points of view and individual experiences based on the environment and culture of their time; hence the many different names of god and goddess.

Some may say this view is based on the influence of a dominant monotheistic Judeo-Christian theology and societal upbringing, but I don't necessarily agree. If there truly exist hundreds of gods and goddesses, did they all work together to create the universe? From where did they all come? Are they only archetypes or created thought forms? These are questions that must be left to each individual to ponder. This is the true beauty of the mystery traditions, for only by experiencing them first-hand may we form our own take on what the divine means to us and how we relate to it. For example, I go by the name Gregory, but my family members call me Greg. Many of my Latino friends have given me a different nickname, and in our study group/coven, I sometimes go by my private magickal name. These are four different names and aspects of me, but they all represent different qualities of my whole being. We are different at work than we are with our friends, and different when we are with family, and different again when we are alone, happy, upset, teaching, learning etc. It is likely the same with the divine meanings and names of the many gods and goddesses.

In Norse mythology, the goddess of love, sensuality, springtime, magickal arts, occult knowledge, cats, war, childbirth, death, and sometimes considered as a name given to Mother Earth is called Freya, but in Greek mythology she is similar to Aphrodite. In Roman mythology, she is called Venus, and in other cultures of antiquity she may be Inanna, Ishtar, Asarte, Astra, and the list goes on. These are different names formulated by different cultures and civilizations but could possibly represent the same primordial Goddess. It is likely the same scenario with many other mythical goddesses and gods as well, for many ancient cultures often influenced and borrowed from one another, and each storyteller wrote and taught based on his or her personal subjective view.

If we think about the theory of evolution, which has evidence to support it, while also thinking about the big bang and creation theories, these schools of thought can be joined to form the idea of divine evolution; that is one supreme, unknowable, great creator/initiator birthed everything into being via the process of evolution. I once heard in a documentary (I forget which for I watch many), something along the lines of "God spoke and bang it happened!" This Great Spirit, or all-permeating divine force which we cannot fathom, can be better understood as it filters or breaks itself down into forms of human understanding beginning by dividing into or appearing as male and female—the Goddess and God—and then many different goddesses and gods.

We could also call the big bang theory the "great copulation,"considering the divine union of male and female. A Pagan and mystical concept of spirit, life, love, magick, the universe, and every dimension and realm, can be summed up in the mystery of as above, so below. Below, that is here on earth, it takes a male and female to create life. It is the same in the realm of spirit, above.

If after millions of years there came into existence all the parts needed to create a car, a clock, or a computer, and each part was put into a bag or box, no matter how many trillions of times they are shaken up, the parts would never just happen to fall into place and form a functional mechanism. The human eye is even more complicated. It seems to me that a divine creator is logically responsible for the design, and then used the process of evolution to perfect each part.

Another thing to ponder is the natural phenomenon of the solar eclipse, which is when the moon is aligned in just the right way to block the light of the sun from our view on earth. The sun is four hundred times larger than the moon, and "coincidentally" the moon is exactly four hundred times closer to the earth than is the sun, and therefore they appear to be the same size. This makes a seemingly perfect match. My question is what are the chances that this exact alignment could coincidentally occur unless there were some form of intellectual design? I am not claiming that my viewpoint is the right one for you, but sharing it only as fuel for thought.

I believe that the divine is not separate from its creation. Mankind created the car, but it is the human that drives the car and occupies it. A car has been created and designed but cannot function without a driver. The creator is within and part of its creation. We, and every form of life including trees, are all a part of the divine and the divine is a part of us. As above, so it is below!

In contemporary Paganism, it is common to hear the phrase; "all gods are one god, and all goddesses are one goddess." I largely agree. If civilizations and cultures of the past had embraced this way of thinking as opposed to thoughts such as "my god is greater than your god," or "our god is the only god," many holy wars, homicides, genocides, and individual oppression, suppression, and depression may have been avoided. Yes, this is a book regarding the magick of trees, but to understand the symbolism of the tree requires a certain level of not mere tolerance, but acceptance and welcome of other concepts, beliefs, cultures, and possibilities.

I'm amazed that some of those who claim to be tolerant of other religions, cultures, and viewpoints seem to reject anything that might challenge their own concept of the divine. As a tree grows new branches that reach for the sun, we should rise above the claim to know the only way—because not one of us do. It takes every leaf and bough to complete the whole part.

Whether you subscribe to atheism, monotheism, duotheism, or polytheism is up to you as an individual to decide, and nobody should judge you for it. Besides, in the end, it's all the same. What I can say for certain is that the gods and goddesses of the past and present, whether conceived and created by us or not, are at least universal archetypes; and through the process of worship and prayer over the ages, these aspects or archetypes exist as thought forms via the energies and prayers that have been given to them. They have become a part of our collective unconscious.

26 DIVINE TREE ASSOCIATIONS

Below I have chosen twenty-six trees and have listed many ancient gods, goddesses, and other mythical figures associated with each.

Alder: Daghdha, Bran, Llyr, Lir, Persephone, Demeter, Hecate, Athena, Cronos, Poseidon, Phoroneus

Apple: Aphrodite, Venus, Freya, Frigga, Demeter, Yahweh, Dionysus, Olwen, Apollo, Pomona, Hera, Athena, Zeus, Diana, Iduna, Gaia, Rhiannon, Bes, Ithun, Lugh

Ash: Uranus, Poseidon, Thor, Odin, Woden, Mars, Neptune, Gwydion, Apollo, Daghdha, Lugh, Askr, Mimir, Saturn

Aspen: Daghdha, Hermes, Mercury, Hercules, The Martus (Hindu), Jupiter, Jove, Nun/Nu, Zeus

Birch: Freya, Frigga, Blodeuwedd, Ariadne, Thor, Daghdha, Aphrodite, Venus, Lugh, Lady of the Woods, Cerridwen, Eostre, Astarte, Astra, Ostara, Esther, Ishtar, the White Goddess

Cedar/Juniper: Apollo, Artemis, Daghdha, Jupiter, Zeus, Sezh, used by King Solomon, Persephone, Poseidon, Wotan

Cottonwood: Wakan Tanka, Demeter

Cypress: Hercules, Hecate, Saturn, Cronus/Kronos, Artemis, Aphrodite, Apollo, Mithras, Pluto, Cupid, Jupiter, Zoroaster, Hebe, Astarte

Elder: Venus, Holda, Aphrodite, CailleachBera, the Dryads, all Goddesses

Elm: Odin, Hoenin, Lodr, the Devas

Hawthorn: Hera, Flora, Hymen, Cardea, Maia, Olwen, Daghdha, the White Goddess

Hazel: Thor, Hermes, Mercury, Diana, Artemis, Manannan Mac Lir, Brigid, Eire, Fodhla, Banbha, Danu, Aphrodite, Chandura

Holly: Jesus, Govannon, Daghdha, the Green Man, Odin, Mars, Unicorns

Linden: Venus, Lada, Aphrodite, Virgen Mary, Lipa, Zeus, Philyra

Locust: Ereshkigal, Yahweh

Maple: Moon and love Goddesses, associated with Libra and Virgo

Mulberry: Diana, Minerva, San Ku Fu Jen, the Nymphs

Myrrh: Ra, Marian, Isis, Adonis, Juno, Saturn, Demeter, Hecate, Rhea, Cybele, Jesus, Aphrodite

Oak: Daghdha, Herne, Thor, Jupiter, Rhea, Dianus, Hecate, Pan, Erato, Janus, Zeus, Cybele, Hercules, Jehovah, El, Allah, Brahma, Hades, Horus, Jumala/Ukko, Mars, Pluto, Vishnu

Olive: Athena, Ra, Minerva, Apollo, Irene, Poseidon, Brahma, Ganymede, Indra, Jupiter, Jove, Wotan

Palm: Jesus, Yahweh, Heh, Asar, Osiris, Aset, Isis, Panaiveriyamman, Taalavaasini, Hanuman, Hermes, Mercury

Pine (also Fir and Spruce): Pan, Attis, Dionysus, Astarte, Venus, Cybele, Sylvanus, Poseidon, Asar, Bacchus, Osiris, Boruta and Dziwitza (Slavic), Adonis, Ishtar, Freya, Astra, Aphrodite, the Green Man, Artemis, the Great Spirit

Rowan: Brigid, Brigantia, Thor, Daghdha, the Sacred Eagle, Zeus

Sycamore: Osiris, Isis, Re, Ra, Nut, Hathor

Willow: Hermes, Ceridwen, Hecate, Artemis, Ceres, Persephone, Hera, Mercury, Belil, Belinus, Daghdha, the Green Man, Pluto, Apollo, Orpheus, Circe, Diana, Astarte, Arianrhod, Rhiannon, Osiris, Demeter

Yew (Poisonous): Hecate, Artemis, Cronus/Kronos, Saturn, Banbha

Chapter 6

CALENDAR
CORRESPONDENCES
OF TREES

DAYS OF THE WEEK TREE CORRESPONDENCES

The following list is based on the planetary days of the week as we know them, beginning with an examination of the names of the seven days in other languages, for by knowing these, we may obtain a greater understanding and an easier way to remember the heavenly bodies that energetically influence each day. Included are some of the magickal correspondences and trees associated with each day.

Monday

Heavenly Body: Moon

Ancient Greek: Hemera Selenes

Latin: Dies Lunae

Spanish: Lunes

French: Lundi

Italian: Lunedi

Romanian: Luni

Norse Meaning: Moon's day

Welsh: DyddLlun

Element: water, spirit

Magickal Workings: all purpose, psychic workings, divination, the underworld, spirit communication, discovering hidden knowledge and mysteries, intuition, empathy, dreams, the sacred feminine, and new beginnings

Trees: willow, birch, elder, holly, hazel, apple, sycamore, evergreens, palm, walnut, chestnut, yew, fir, cypress, cedar, laurel, myrtle, cherry, plum, olive, pear, myrrh, mimosa, pawpaw, papaya, and alder

Tuesday

Heavenly Body: Mars

Ancient Greek: Hemera Areos

Latin: Dies Martis

Spanish: Martes

French: Mardi

Italian: Martedi

Romanian: Marti

Norse Meaning: Tyr's day

Welsh: DyddMawrth

Element: fire, air

Magickal Workings: victory, overcoming obstacles and challenges, resolving inner conflicts, arguments and battles, fulfilling goals, legal matters, courage, strength, protection, defense

Trees: alder, vine, cottonwood, oak, hawthorn, yew, hickory, elm, holly, and pine

Wednesday

Heavenly Body: Mercury

Ancient Greek: Hemera Hermou

Latin: Dies Mercurii

Spanish: Miercoles

French: Mercredi

Italian: Mercoledi

Romanian: Miercuri

Norse Meaning: Woden's day

Welsh: DyddMercher

Element: air

Magickal Workings: communication, travel, peace, knowledge, learning, memory, inspiration, and art

Trees: willow (for other world communication), aspen, palm, olive, hazel, linden, mulberry, pecan, pomegranate, ash, and oak

Thursday

Heavenly Body: Jupiter

Ancient Greek: Hemera Dios

Latin: Dies Jovis

Spanish: Jueves

French: Juedi

Italian: Giovedi

Romanian: Joi

Norse Meaning: Thor's day

Welsh: Dydd Lau

Element: earth, fire, spirit

Magickal Workings: prosperity, healing, finances, protection, stability, health, to attract forces, success, beginnings

Trees: cedar, olive, juniper, aspen, cypress, oak, bohdi, chestnut, linden, maple, rowan, sassafras, poplar, and birch

Friday

Heavenly Body: Venus

Ancient Greek: Hemera Aphrodites

Latin: Dies Veneris

Spanish: Viernes

French: Vendredi

Italian: Venerdi

Romanian: Vineri

Norse Meaning: Freya's day

Welsh: DyddGwener

Element: water, spirit

Magickal Working: love of all kinds, health, beauty, passion, forgiveness, divination, shadow work, understanding, empathy, desire, romance, passion, and union

Trees: apple, maple, willow, cherry, myrtle, birch, linden, cedar, apricot, elder, pine, cypress, myrrh, laurel, blackberry, chestnut, lilac, magnolia, mimosa, orange, papaya, pawpaw, peach, pear, and plum

Saturday

Heavenly Body: Saturn

Ancient Greek: Hemera Kronou

Latin: Dies Saturni

Spanish: Sabado

French: Samedi

Italian: Sabato

Romanian: Sambata

Norse Meaning: Saturn's day / Washer's day

Welsh: DyddSadwrn

Element: fire, water, spirit, earth

Magickal Workings: rest, release, banishing, letting go, clearing, cleansing, protection, and exorcisms

Trees: yew, ash, hawthorn, hazel, elder, pomegranate, elm, beech, buckthorn, locust, oak, willow, alder, poplar, rowan, chestnut, lemon, and spruce

Sunday

Heavenly Body: Sun

Ancient Greek: Hemera Helio

Latin: Dies Solis

Spanish: Domingo

French: Dimanche

Italian: Domenica

Romanian: Dumenica

Norse Meaning: Sun's day

Welsh: Dydd Sul

Element: spirit, fire, air

Magickal Workings: family, friends, optimism, power, all-purpose, strength, success, divine masculine, inspiration, protection, clarity, divination, truth, healing, and finances

Trees: oak, holly, aspen, hazel, lemon, orange, rowan, cottonwood, cedar, sycamore, palm, evergreens, ash, apple, plane tree, olive, poplar, laurel, fig, chestnut, and juniper

Chapter 7
CELTIC AND DRUIDIC TREE CORRESPONDENCES

It is generally accepted that the Druids, the once and still highly revered spiritual leaders of the ancient Celtic peoples throughout Europe, considered many trees to be sacred. However, most Druidic beliefs and teachings were passed down in an oratory tradition and very little was written and recorded. What we know of them is a blurred mix of fact, fantasy, theory, speculation, and accounts from their enemies. A fair portion of contemporary attempts to reconstruct the Druidic teachings and practices regarding the sacredness and magick of trees have been derived from Robert Graves' book called *The White Goddess*. Again, as mentioned in chapter one, there is great debate concerning the validity of much of Graves' claims in this classic text, but he based these claims on surviving accounts of Celtic folklore and poetry, biblical mythology, and an in-depth study of other Pagan beliefs and sacred writings. Much of what Graves wrote seems to have had at least a ring of historical accuracy, but was likely written from his own subjective beliefs and experiences. I highly recommend reading the excellent book *Stalking the Goddess* by Mark Carter for a very in-depth examination of Graves' famous work.

One controversy lies within Graves' report of the Celtic tree calendar. This tree calendar may or may not have been used by the Druids, we don't really know, but it does make sense on a certain level regardless. If something works, it does not need to be of ancient origin to use it. As quoted by Christopher Penczak, a prominent author of more than twenty books, witch, Reiki Master, teacher, and magician, regarding Graves' book *The White Goddess*, "It's a poetic work of inspiration with a historic basis."

Before examining this tree calendar, let's begin with a brief look at the well-accepted Celtic tree alphabet called the tree ogham.

THE CELTIC TREE OGHAM

The Celtic tree ogham is a pictorial system of lettering using lines and notches that represent both a letter and a tree. These were often carved into stone or wood to deliver an encrypted message or possibly to charge and imbue an object with specific properties. Therefore, the tree ogham can be used to communicate, to bless and charge magickal tools such as a wand, staff, athame, stones, the besom, talismans, and amulets, and also for divination. A few of the trees included in the tree ogham are not technically trees but shrubs, vines, and bushes that the Celts may have revered as magickal and symbolic on a spiritual level. Below are twenty common characters of the Celtic tree ogham:

Tree: birch
Celtic Name: beith/beithe/beth
Letter: B
Symbolism: new beginnings, self-sacrifice, youth, dedication to the greater good

Tree: rowan (European mountain ash)
Celtic Name: luis
Letter: L
Symbolism: magickal work, protection, warding evil, more effort is needed

Tree: alder

Celtic Name: fearn

Letter: F

Symbolism: facing obstacles, courage, finding strength to face challenges, shielding, defense, protection, and passion

Tree: willow

Celtic Name: sail / saille

Letter: S

Symbolism: new journeys, otherworld contact, confidence in times of doubt, easing pain, water, intuition, vision, emotion, psychic workings, look inward for answers

Tree: ash

Celtic Name: nion

Letter: N

Symbolism: inertia, need to work toward goals, address laziness and procrastination, change of outlook, difficult time at hand, more effort is needed, wisdom, survival

Tree: hawthorn

Celtic Name: huath

Letter: H

Symbolism: unpleasant time ahead, but one that ends well. It may be time to examine your flaws, completion and consequence of past actions, hypocrisy, great success after trials.

Tree: oak

Celtic Name: duir

Letter: D

Symbolism: higher powers at work, time to rest, master your life, leadership, find inner strength, stability, and wisdom

Tree: holly

Celtic Name: tinne

Letter: T

Symbolism: substitution, things may not be as they appear, a middle period between two opposites, a new guide will appear, happiness and joy

Tree: hazel

Celtic Name: coll

Letter: C

Symbolism: end of hardship, death, change, transformation, wisdom, letting go, recovery and healing

Tree: apple

Celtic Name: queirt

Letter: Q

Symbolism: awakening other world senses, protection in spiritual matters, prior work pays off, beauty, love, compassion, and health

Tree/wood: vine (grape)

Celtic Name: muin

Letter: M

Symbolism: hidden knowledge, otherworld help, inspiration, and overcoming adversaries

Tree/wood: ivy

Celtic Name: gort

Letter: G

Symbolism: warnings, time to think twice about current plans, perspectives, emotions, restrictions, patience and determination

Tree/wood: broom, reed

Celtic Name: ngetal

Letter: nG

Symbolism: work not yet completed, need of more work, let go of what is no longer needed, learn from past experiences, health, healing, and growth

Tree/wood: blackthorn

Celtic Name: straiph

Letter: St, Z, or Str

Symbolism: get ready for change; prepare for the new, sudden changes coming, death, and a new door will open

Tree: elder (elderberry). Please do research before using elder, as the red elderberry fruit (seeds only) are poisonous and the wood of elder emits toxic fumes when burned.

Celtic Name: ruis

Letter: R

Symbolism: the sacred, face the truth around you, face the truth of who you really are, time to look in the mirror and examine yourself, transition and change

Tree: fir/pine/spruce

Celtic Name: ailm

Letter: A

Symbolism: experience, wisdom, protection, guidance, mysteries, eternity, achievement, look at your relationships and learn, new realizations coming soon

Tree/wood: furze/gorse

Celtic Name: onn

Letter: O

Symbolism: use time wisely, more information is needed, look forward to what awaits after a hard time, and stand up for new ideas that may not be accepted

Tree/wood: heather

Celtic Name: ur

Letter: U

Symbolism: responsibility, think about what you are doing, prepare for the results of your actions, a new baby or new life, dreams, romance coming

Tree: aspen

Celtic Name: edhadh

Letter: E

Symbolism: spiritual growth and progress, watch your ego, success, victory, time to listen, and protection.

Tree: yew (very toxic wood—be extremely careful)

Celtic Name: idhadh

Letter: I

Symbolism: love, illusion, deception, death, prepare for changes, if using Ogham Sticks perhaps redraw.

The Ogham, when written or inscribed, is traditionally employed vertically but can be used horizontally as well.

THE CELTIC TREE CALENDAR

Birch (Beith, Beithe, Beth) December 24–January 20

Rowan (Luis) January 21–February 17

Ash (Nion) February 18–March 17

Alder (Fearn) March 18–April 14

Willow (Saille) April 15–May 12

Hawthorn (Huath) May 13–June 09

Oak (Duir) June 10–July 07

Holly (Tinne) July 08–August 04

Hazel (Coll) August 05–September 01

Vine (Muin) September 02–September 29

Ivy (Gort) September 30–October 27

Reed (nGetal) October 28–November 24

Elder (Ruis) November 25–December 22

December 23 is not ruled by a tree but is a day of rest and gives meaning to the infamous "year and a day" in Wiccan practice. As previously stated, there is great controversy concerning the above tree calendar, but at the same time, there is a portion of truth to it; it does make sense if you do some research on the meanings of the trees. This topic is too big to go into detail here and many books have been written on the subject, but I do want to point out that using this system in a manner comparable to our modern astrological horoscope may indeed hold some validity as a new system to be worked with and developed.

TREE HOROSCOPE

Many mystics, Pagans, occultists, and astrologers have developed the following tree horoscope based upon the work of Robert Graves and the properties and deeper spiritual meanings of each tree. I personally find this horoscope to be fairly accurate.

Recently we have learned of the suggested "new" horoscope and the signs of many people have changed. There is, however, something wrong with this new system. Based on the zodiac that we all grew up with, I am a Cancer, but the new system states that I am a Gemini. Everything about Cancer is exactly who and what I am, but not Gemini. While there may be a possible thirteenth sign of the zodiac, something is not right here and if the common horoscope is to add the thirteenth sign, then qualities of each sign need to change on a certain level. Instead, why not give the tree horoscope a go? Try it out and give it a chance before accepting or rejecting it. Keep in mind that each of us have both positive and negative aspects, and that we all have shadow areas in our lives to improve as well as traits to be proud of. Be honest with yourself while reading your tree sign and then decide if it is accurate. Also, try it with your friends and loved ones. Interestingly, I tested this based on the birthdays of my cats, and it does match their personalities quite well. If something works, use it!

December 24–January 20
Tree: birch
Ambitious, driven, loyal, and faithful, good leadership skills, able to take charge of situations, hold high ideals, quick-witted, charming, tolerant, and self-sacrificing to help others

January 21–February 17
Tree: rowan (European mountain ash)
Deep thinking, philosophical, a visionary, creative and original, sometimes misunderstood, great inner passion, very influential, able to maintain your cool in a crowd despite your inner passions, artistic, and sometimes unconventional

February 18–March 17
Tree: ash
Imaginative, intuitive, artistic, good communication skills, sometimes moody, enjoys time alone, in touch with inner-self, lover of nature, writ-

ing, poetry, science, and theology. From time to time you are labeled as a recluse but only because you are working toward your goals. You are not concerned with what others think about you.

March 18–April 14

Tree: alder
Fiery passion, a mover and shaker, charming, able to mix with any crowd like a chameleon, easy to get along with, confident, focused, enjoys and needs to play and have a good time, conservative and object to wasting, diplomatic, loyal, courageous, but sometimes overlooks the emotional needs of others

April 15–May 12

Tree: willow
Influenced by the moon, intuitive, flexible, creative, mystical, possess psychic ability, realistic, strong willed, patient, have great potential but sometimes hold back in fear of being obsessive. You often hold your tongue to keep the peace and are sometimes misunderstood because of this.

May 13–June 09

Tree: hawthorn
Wise, spontaneous, and sometimes impatient, fiery and creative on the inside, but calm and cool on the outside. You have a tendency to present yourself differently than you truly are. You are adaptable, have a curious nature, and good listening skills. You have a good sense of humor but don't give yourself enough credit.

June 10–July 07

Tree: oak
Protective, strong, a good spokesperson, you are loving, giving, mighty, confident, optimistic, a good teacher, organized, and in control of your life. Family, heritage, and ancestry are important to you. You are generally responsible, or at least strive to be, and you like to be involved. You are proud but sometimes stubborn.

July 08–August 04

Tree: holly

You are self-confident and make a great leader. You easily overcome challenges and obstacles and are very persistent. You never give up. When faced with challenges and difficult tasks, or failure the first time around, you persevere and work harder to achieve your goals. Some may see you as egotistical, but you are actually just confident and very often misunderstood. You are generous and kind to those that have your trust. You are intelligent and enjoy learning but easily bored and tend to be lazy if not working toward a goal. You are very protective but can be moody, emotional, and overly sensitive.

August 05–September 01

Tree: hazel

Intelligent, organized, and a good multi-tasker, you are a good student. You demonstrate knowledge and easily impress others. You are blessed with the gift of memorization and understand numbers, science, and details. You make your own rules in life and have a tendency to look at life intellectually rather than emotionally.

September 02–September 29

Tree/plant: vine

You are changeable, unpredictable, and sometimes indecisive. You have the ability to see all sides of the story and are empathic. You are sometimes misunderstood and accused of not being loyal, but this is because you see the good in all people. You know what you like, have great taste, and value beauty. You have class and enjoy the company of others who realize this. You are balanced and have potential to achieve your goals. You are not too concerned with what others think about you, but you are critical of yourself. You are a romantic.

September 30–October 27

Tree/plant: ivy

Intelligence, loyalty, and compassion are your greatest attributes. You enjoy helping others and volunteering when time allows. Sometimes you think that life is unfair and struggle with hardships while wondering what you did to deserve this. This could be because you are generally peaceful and spiritual but have the ability to be victorious over all obstacles. You are charming, social, and mostly cheerful.

October 28–November 24

Tree/plant: reed
You seek the truth and hidden meanings of life while taking nothing for granted. You do not easily accept what you are told as fact until you dig into the matter. However, you are sometimes influenced by drama and gossip before doing your own research. You are persuasive and can be manipulative even when you mean no harm. Subconsciously you seek to enlighten others. You can sometimes be stubborn and jealous.

November 25–December 22

Tree: elder
You are a seeker of thrill and pleasure. You value your freedom. You are often misunderstood for speaking your mind a bit too much, but this is because you simply enjoy other people and are willing to share what you see as the honest truth. You can be reclusive from time to time because of being misjudged. You are generous, giving, and helpful but may appear to others as mean. This is upsetting because you were only trying to help by being honest.

December 23

This day is given to the Celtic "year and a day." In a nutshell, it is a magickal day off and a period of rest. This is mostly symbolic in nature.

Chapter 8
THE TREE OF LIFE
AND ASTROLOGICAL
CORRESPONDENCES

THE WORLD TREE

Before we begin to examine the Qabalistic Tree of Life, I would like to briefly mention the World Tree, as the two ideas complement each other. The concept of the World Tree is found across the globe and throughout many cultures of the past and present. Sometimes the World Tree is viewed as a ladder, a mountain, or the axis mundi (world axis or center of the world). If you take a moment to think about the purpose of a ladder, the obvious use is to climb to a higher location that you cannot reach on your own. There are also steps to safely descend back to where you came from.

The World Tree is a symbolic and pictorial representation of life, death, rebirth, and most significantly the bridge between us and the divine. The roots of a tree grow deep beneath the soil and represent the underworld, our ancestors, and our subconscious mind where we can find a deeper connection to all peoples and all times, and sometimes called the collective unconscious or the Akashic records.

The trunk represents our waking or conscious mind, our physical needs, desires, and the survival instinct. The upper boughs and leaves of the tree represent our divine selves and our need or desire to connect with spirit. As a tree reaches up toward the sky to absorb sunlight, so does our spirit long to reach out and embrace the great all, our higher self, and to discover our place in the universe and our relation to the divine. The leaves and boughs also represent the desire of spirit to reach down and into each of us. Additionally, the World Tree represents not only these three realms but all realms and the seven major energy points, or energy wheels of our bodies called the chakras. Both the World Tree and the Tree of Life can be viewed as a way to connect all forms of creation and or existence.

THE TREE OF LIFE

The Qabalistic Tree of Life, while of ancient mystical Judeo/Hebraic origin, is a valuable study and one of great consideration by many mystics, magicians, and occultists. This system may not have anything to do with the Tree of Life mentioned throughout the Bible, but I sometimes wonder.

Per biblical lore, the consumption of the fruit of the Tree of Life grants immortality. By this it seems that to understand, grasp, and embrace this wisdom will grant life after death, or better said, a way to understand that we are immortal beings; for examining the Tree of Life is a way to understand deity, a way to connect with spirit, and a way to understand the passage and filtering down of deity into all life and back to spirit once again. It is a great mystery but can easily be understood by all. I need to point out that the spelling used here, the Qabalistic Tree of Life, is used in reference to the hermetic *qabalah*, which is employed to indicate the use of the Judaic *Kabbalah* as a magickal and occult system often used in ritual magick and is largely astrological in nature. In the Judaic system of the Kabbalah, the ten sephiroth or spheres are used to represent some of the various aspects and personalities of God, while in the Qabalistic system, the ten sephiroth represent ten aspects of the magickal or astral world and have been assigned a planetary body such as the sun, the moon, the earth, and planets. In my own practice, I incorporate both of the above-mentioned systems since I do not separate magick from the divine.

The first time I studied the Qabalistic Tree of Life was in the book called *The Temple of High Witchcraft: Ceremonies, Spheres, and the Witches' Qabalah* by Christopher Penczak, and I highly recommend this work if you are interested in learning more. The Tree of Life referred to here can be viewed as a pictorial and symbolic representation of all the worlds and realms of manifest divinity. This is a huge study, so I will only be presenting a very basic overview.

Each sphere or realm is called a sephira and the combination, the plural form of the sephira, is called the sephiroth (see Figure 1).

Before beginning, it is important to mention the realm of the incomprehensible, which is sometimes depicted as three rays or arches above the top of the tree called Ain, Ain Soph, and Ain Soph Aur:

AIN: not/nothing

AIN SOPH: without limit/infinity

AIN SOPH AUR: infinite light without limit

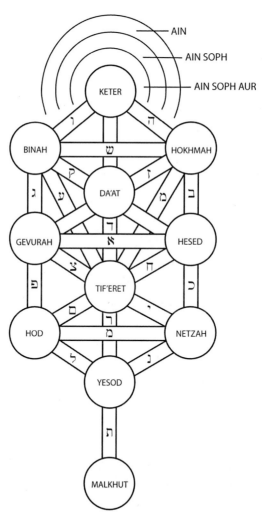

Figure 1: The Tree of Life

Keep in mind that if one were to completely dig up a tree in a manner that allowed the roots, the trunk, and the branches to be visible as a whole, the bottom and the top of the tree would look almost identical in size. What we can see in the pictorial representation of the Tree of Life is the filtering down of the great unknowable force of all existence into a comprehensible form. As above, so below!

Keter/Kether: (crown) represents the Great Divine, or Great Spirit, as best as we can understand. This is God as we have been taught and is neither male nor female.

Binah: (top left sphere) represents the Divine Feminine and the planet Saturn (understanding)

Hokmah/Chokmah: (top right sphere) represents the Divine Masculine and the stars of the zodiac from our perspective on earth (wisdom)

Gevurah/Geburah: represents the planet Mars (might, power, and the almighty)

Hesed/Chesed: represents Jupiter (mercy and grace)

Tiferet/Tiphereth: the sun (harmony and balance)

Hod: Mercury (mind, intellect, communication, and glory)

Netzah/Netzatch: Venus (love, victory, eternity)

Yesod: the moon (the foundation)

Malkut/Malkuth: The earth (the kingdom)

This is a very basic overview of the Tree of Life, so please do more research if you feel inclined, but what we have here is a visual representation of the Great Spirit filtering down (sometimes referred to as a lightning flash) the unknowable divine force into a Goddess and a God so that we can better relate and understand, while continuing to filter more specifically into planetary correspondences as well as human personalities and aspects (hence the beginning of the names of many gods and goddesses) to the sun, the moon, and finally to the earth and to each individual living creature.

Because a tree is virtually identical both above and below the ground, many mystics view the tree upside down. Both viewpoints are correct. Did God create us, or did we create God? As above, so below!

Section Four
MAGICK, ACTIVITIES, AND CRAFT

Believe, see, experience, and know
Secrets wait upon the breeze
Trust above and learn below
The ancient magick of the trees

Chapter 9

COMMUNICATION
AND SENSING

Understanding the symbolism of trees throughout countless cultures of human history is an enlightening study, but equally important is learning to form a personal connection with them in order to better comprehend the interaction of how the divine reveals itself to us through nature. This section is dedicated to aiding you in that endeavor. The meditations, rituals, and magickal exercises in this chapter are intended to help you develop a personal bond or relationship with trees. Some might think this sounds crazy, so let me begin by sharing a bit of recent scientific research that reveals the "sensing" abilities and intelligence of trees and plant life.

Plant neurobiology is the study of how plants communicate at all levels of biological organization. One of the founders and leaders in this field is the Italian botanist Professor Stefano Mancuso. In his lecture, which can be seen on YouTube in a video called "The Roots of Plant Intelligence," Mancuso reveals how plants can sense their surrounding environment and are able to communicate with other plants and animals. Mancuso shares how plants have often been underestimated throughout history due to a seeming lack of movement. But plants do have movement. Examples of this are the directional changes made by leaves as they lean and reach toward the sun, the opening, budding, and closing of flowers, and Mancuso reminds us of the movement of the carnivorous plant the Venus flytrap that captures and feeds off of ensnared insects. He also reveals how plants can communicate and sense their environment in a way that is more complex and sophisticated than many animals. Each plant has roots that reach deep into the soil, and each root apex (the location where the root grows) the plant continuously senses and monitors no less than fifteen chemical and physical parameters.

Concerning communication with animals and other non-plant life, Mancuso uses the example of how plants attract carriers such as bees to spread pollen from one flower to another, an essential process pertaining to the reproduction of the species. Ultimately, this field of study attempts to prove that plant life demonstrates intelligence and that plants have some type of cognitive function. In his work titled *The Power of Movement in Plants*, Charles Darwin attempted to explain that plants indeed have some form of brain or central intelligence system. Many ancient shamans, healers, wisefolk, oracles, midwives, Druids, medicine men and women, and other localized communal spiritual leaders of ancient days, now often referred to as witches, Pagans, country dwellers, heathens, heretics, mystics, and other names, were well in tune with nature and already knew this to be true. They spoke of how trees and plants communicate with humans and taught that we are equally able to communicate with them in return.

If plants can sense their surrounding environment and are able to communicate with other plants and animals, it only stands to reason that they may be able to communicate with us. Additionally, there exists much evidence supporting the notion that plants react to vocal tones and music, but that is too large a topic to get into here. The point is that you, too, can communicate and create a bond with the trees if you are open and willing to do so. Science is slowly beginning to catch up with what is called magick!

TREE TOUCH COMMUNICATION

Method 1

1. Choose and approach a tree that draws your attention.
2. Be willing and open-minded to listen.
3. Place your palms upon the trunk.
4. With reverence, ask the tree to communicate with you.
5. Do not ask a personal question about yourself but ask the tree to speak and tell you its story.

6. More than likely, you will not hear an audible message but will know intuitively what the tree has to say.

7. Leave a gift in return such as a wish of love and health, pour out a jar of water, offer some plant food, a song, or a vow to return and converse again. Whatever comes to mind will suffice, and often a hug is well accepted. There are other possibilities. Below are two examples from personal experience:

In my yard thrive two beautiful Colorado blue spruce trees, and often I go out and speak with them. They have shared that they've been present in our group ritual celebrations outdoors and that they protect the home from negative energies and unwanted beings. After I received this message, I looked up the magickal qualities of the spruce in an herbal handbook. Sure enough, the magickal properties listed were protection and warding off evil and negative energies. Trees will reveal to you their properties, and after all, this is one way that the magickal properties of trees were discovered to begin with. Coincidentally, the leaf tip projections of the spruce grow in the exact pattern of the Nordic rune Algiz, which is a symbol of protection.

Another example is when our group went on a camping trip to a nearby state park. Late that night several of us gathered one at a time around a very large oak and placed our palms upon the tree. When finished, each person shared what they felt the tree had revealed. Everyone reported that the tree felt sad and worried about something yet to come. Almost three months later, one group member who regularly visited the park went back to the campsite and reported to us that another tree, an even older oak about ten feet away from the one we had spoken to, had been cut down because it had a disease. We then understood why the tree had felt such sadness. It was losing a life-long companion.

Method 2

1. Choose a tree to communicate with.

2. Face the direction of east and step three to five feet away from the trunk.

3. With your pointer finger or with a nearby fallen twig, visualize a continuous flow of white or blue light down to the ground and walk around the tree clockwise until you arrive back at the starting point. If you prefer to skip this step, it is absolutely fine as the tree will still speak with you. It is merely a Wiccan method of keeping any other potential talkative beings from interfering.

4. Sit or stand with your back against the trunk of the tree.

5. Relax completely and begin breathing in through your nose to the count of four and out your mouth to the count of four. Repeat four times. This is to help you relax, focus, and open up.

6. Introduce yourself and ask that the tree speak to you.

7. Be patient and willing to listen.

8. You will intuitively know what the tree has to say.

9. When finished, give thanks, love, respect, or a token gift.

TREE AURA GAZING

Another wonderful and rewarding way to experience the magick of trees is to gaze upon its aura. An aura, simplified, is the energetic field or life force that emanates from a thing. The great Dion Fortune—psychologist, occultist, spiritualist, psychic, and author of many books such as *Psychic Self-Defense*, originally published in 1930—stated, "It is well known how often trees are objects of worship in all parts of the world. They have marked personalities and strong magnetic fields. In the spring, when the sap is rising, even non-psychics can often see the aura of a tree."

1. In daytime and favorable weather, venture outdoors and select a tree.

2. Position yourself forty feet or more away from the trunk.

3. Gaze into the sky just a bit past the highest boughs.

4. Choose and hold a focal point. Don't let your eyes wander.

5. You will begin to see the etheric/energetic pattern resembling the tree in the space above.

6. The aura will more than likely appear clear, blurry, and slightly distorted but will reveal a faint outline of the tree in the above and surrounding space like an astral or energetic blueprint.

7. You are now seeing the aura of a tree. You can also use this method to see the auras of people, animals, and even stones.

8. How does it make you feel? What impressions do you get?

9. If at first you feel that you are not successful, try again. Persistence will bring the breakthrough!

TREE ABSORPTION AND TREE THERAPY

Whenever you are feeling ill, stressed, depressed, or upset in any manner, a nearby tree just might be your best friend. A tree can relieve you of these burdens by absorbing the harmful energies and recycling them into positive ones. In fact, a study done at the Tokyo Medical University reveals that simply looking upon a tree, even through a window, can reduce anxiety and stress.

Professor Yoshifumi Miyazak of Chiba University, Japan's leading scholar in the field of forest medicine has helped develop a system of natural therapy called forest bathing or forest therapy, which is basically taking time to walk through the woods to enjoy and absorb the beauty of the surrounding natural environment. His studies suggest that this can lower blood pressure, lower the heart rate, and significantly reduce stress and anxiety. Tree or forest therapy mostly regards taking time to prevent illness and stress before it occurs and implies that we all need to take time out of our lives on a regular basis to enjoy nature, not only when we are ill or stressed. I would also like to add, from my own personal experience, that planting trees, flowers, or vegetables, caring for them, and watching them grow is a very therapeutic and rewarding endeavor.

TREE BREATHING

Consider the following activity to ease anxiety, depression, stress, pain, or to simply make a connection with nature. This is a soothing, simple, and powerful practice that can be done in your own back yard or in a nearby park.

• When the weather is favorable, locate a tall tree and sit with your back against its trunk. Begin to slowly breathe in through your nose and exhale out the mouth.

- Once you have done this at least five times, begin to imagine that each time you exhale, the tree inhales, and each time you inhale, the tree exhales. Let your mind be cleared and free of all concerns as you continue to do this for several minutes. It's as simple as that!

- When you are done, give the tree your love and blessings. Likely you will have made a new friend.

- By the time you walk away, you will notice a big difference in your breathing and will be at complete peace with your surroundings.

TREE ABSORBING

Tree absorbing is using a chosen tree to absorb a current stressor or harmful thought into its living form and removing it from you. Does this mean that if you let the tree absorb your worries or stresses that the tree will become ill? Absolutely not! The tree will absorb that which ails you and will release it back into the earth below, where these harmful energies can be recycled and transformed. Just think about the fact that trees absorb our waste CO_2 and transform it to oxygen. Our negative or unwanted waste does not hurt them. Give it a try, or a few tries if necessary.

1. Venture outdoors and find a tree that is healthy in appearance and large enough to sit beneath.

2. Approach the tree and introduce yourself. Tell the tree of your intention and ask for permission. You will instinctively know whether the tree agrees to aid you. In most cases, trees are glad to do so, but upon occasion they say no. If you are a smoker, please make sure not to have a lit cigarette near the tree because this often stresses them. Just think about forest fires and you will understand.

3. Sit with your back against the tree or lie on the ground near the trunk. If necessary, simply place your hands on the bark.

4. Take a moment to relax and focus upon what you want the tree to free you from.

5. Whether it is anxiety, stress, depression, or any type of emotional pain or worry, visualize this burden as forming into a sphere of light

within you as any color that seems appropriate. See this energy ball becoming stronger as your will to be rid of it increases.

6. See the sphere of light moving out of your body and into the tree until it is completely absorbed.

7. When you are finished, take a moment to give thanks to the tree and walk away.

8. Please note that in most cases, this activity needs to be repeated several times.

DISCOVER MAGICKAL CORRESPONDENCES BY INTUITION AND OBSERVATION

It is possible to discover some of the basic magickal properties of a tree by observation and intuition. For example, the leaves of some maple trees turn red in the fall, and due to the color correspondence, a maple leaf can be used for attracting love, romance, passion, and can be used for goals concerning change, willpower, and victory over struggles. The maple tree produces a sweet sap used to make syrup, and by this we can understand and trust the magickal correspondence of the maple concerning love based on sweetness and relate it to our sweethearts. Some trees, such as oak and locust, turn yellow in the fall, and yellow may be a correspondence of intellect, learning, optimism, and communication. Trees with thorns have protective properties but may also imply that a time of change and letting go is in store.

Many of our ancestors discovered the medicinal and magickal properties of trees and other plants by trial and error. They learned to base the correspondences on the shape and color of the leaves and the plant, such as a plant that appears to grow in the form of male or female genitalia sometimes have properties that can help to heal or stimulate the reproductive system. A plant with red leaves, stems, or berries may either help to cleanse the blood or poison it. It is very, and I mean *very* important, that you seek the advise of a physician or do intense research before employing such methods when it comes to using plants for medicine, for there are many poisonous look-alike species that can be deceiving. Much research is needed. I suggest that you focus on the magickal properties and the symbolic meaning of the trees.

- Examine the shape of the tree. Is it tall, short, wide, or thin? Do its branches reach up, down, or horizontally? What does that mean to you?
- What color are the leaves? Do the colors of the leaves change in the fall or does the tree remain green all year round? What color do the leaves change to?
- What does the shape of the leaf make you think of?
- What patterns can you find in the branches?
- What is the overall pattern of the tree?
- Even though each type of tree belongs to a family and genus, each individual tree has its own unique personality.
- Listen to what first comes to mind. This is often times correct so do not second-guess your initial intuitive impression.

TREE MEDITATION 1:
MEET AND GREET

You can do this meditation anywhere, whether outdoors, in a chair, or in your bathtub, but you may want to memorize the steps involved first or have someone guide you through the process.

1. Allow yourself to be completely relaxed.
2. Close your eyes or consider covering them with a blue or purple cloth to block out interfering light.
3. Free yourself from all distractions.
4. Allow any and all stress, concerns, worries, burdens, emotions, obligations, and responsibilities to disperse into the earth below.
5. Once relaxed and comfortable, inhale through your nose for the count of four or five, and then exhale out the mouth for an equal measure. Do this at least five times.
6. Visualize inhaling through the nose the white light of the divine, and as you exhale out the mouth, send love and gratitude back. Repeat five times.
7. See yourself sitting in a completely darkened room. The only light is coming from the thirteen small glowing stones that you are hold-

ing in your hand. Imagine how the stones feel. How do they sound when you shake them? Let one of the stones fall. Now you have twelve. Continue to drop one stone at a time, eleven, ten, nine, eight, seven, six, five, four, three, two, and one. Drop the last stone.

8. Suddenly, a doorway appears before you. On the other side you see a large tree.

9. Step through the doorway and stand close enough to the tree that you can touch it.

10. It is springtime and the leaves are beginning to bud. Perhaps you smell the scent of lilacs or **crabapple** blooms in the air. Wish the tree good morning.

11. The sun begins to rise higher and the temperature is getting warmer. It is summer, and the leaves are fully expanded and green. Bless the tree with gratitude and tell it good afternoon.

12. The sun is now beginning to set, and the leaves are changing color. Its fruits and berries are bright and ripe for the picking. Take one and eat it. How does it taste? Give thanks and bid the tree good evening.

13. The sun has now fully set, and the moon is shining above. The tree is barren of leaves and the first snow has fallen. Do not disturb the tree, but quietly offer your blessings of love and prosperity for the next year while thanking the tree for all it has provided.

14. Think for a moment about how you are like a tree. What do you have in common?

15. When you are ready, turn around and see the doorway behind you.

16. Step through the door. You are back in the dark room.

17. Open your hand and see the last stone that you dropped coming back to you. See it glowing ion your hand. Now the second stone returns, and then the third, the fourth, the fifth, the sixth, the seventh, the eighth, the ninth, the tenth, the eleventh, twelfth, and finally all thirteen stones are back in your hand and glowing.

18. Become aware of your body and surroundings.

19. Stomp your feet and open your eyes.

20. You have earned the love and friendship of the trees.

TREE MEDITATION 2:
SPIRAL JOURNEY TO THE THREE REALMS

1. Allow yourself to be completely relaxed.

2. Close your eyes or consider covering them with a blue or purple cloth to block out interfering light.

3. Free yourself from all distractions.

4. Allow any and all stress, concerns, worries, burdens, emotions, obligations, and responsibilities to disperse into the earth below.

5. Once relaxed and comfortable, inhale through your nose for the count of four or five, and then exhale out the mouth for an equal measure. Do this at least five times.

6. Visualize inhaling through the nose the white light of the divine, and as you exhale out the mouth, send love and gratitude back. Repeat five times.

7. See yourself sitting in a completely darkened room. The only light is coming from the thirteen small glowing stones that you are holding in your hand. Imagine how the stones feel. How do they sound when you shake them? Let one of the stones fall. Now you have twelve. Continue to drop one stone at a time, eleven, ten, nine, eight, seven, six, five, four, three, two, and one. Drop the last stone.

8. Suddenly, a doorway appears before you. On the other side of the door is a very large tree.

9. Step through the door and stand close enough to the tree that you can touch it.

10. As you stand before the tree in front of you, take a moment to know how it would feel to touch it. How does it sound or feel if you peeled its bark? Does any sap seep out? Are there any insects or birds living in the tree?

11. Suddenly, as you touch it, within the trunk appears an arching doorway. Step through the door and enter into the center of the tree.

12. You are faced with a choice of taking the stairs that lead up, down, or a forward path in the middle. Take the stairway down.

13. This is the realm of the subconscious, of dreams, ancestors, magick, and the shadow self.

14. Explore this place for a while and take note of how it makes you feel, how it appears to you, and what you encounter. Feel free to speak to those whom you may meet along the way and be at complete peace.

15. Call upon your shadow self to appear and join you for a time. For some, this can be a difficult experience, but know that you are safe and at liberty to leave at any time you choose. Your shadow is your subconscious self and/or the negative darker components of your personality including faults, vices, and things in your life that you don't like or acknowledge as well as the aspects of you that others see and don't care for. Take a moment to let your shadow reveal areas in your life that you can change or improve. Do not by any means dislike your shadow, but instead embrace it with love because it is a part of you. Harboring negative feelings toward your shadow may result in dire consequences that could manifest in your daily life or in your physical body.

16. If desired, ask for your spirit guide or guides to be present and show you what you need to know at this moment. Be ready to accept whatever is revealed.

17. Turn around and see the staircase leading you back to the center of the tree and ascend back to where you began. Walk the middle pathway until you come to a place or your own creation. It is a beautiful place where you feel at peace. It could appear as a library, a forest, a campground, near a mountain range or near the sea. There are infinite possibilities. This is your own happy place and looks exactly as you want it to. When you are there, take a moment to relax and make any alterations that you desire. Fill this place with love and happiness. There is nothing harmful or painful here.

18. This place is your inner sanctuary, a place of complete peace and harmony. You are like the trunk of a tree, grounded and centered in your current place in life.

19. Explore this realm for a while. What does it look like? The scenery can be changed at will.

20. Ask your spirit guide or guides to appear and speak with you. This is where you can receive instructions and advice concerning your health, goals, finances, and all things involved in your daily life.

21. When ready, turn around again and find the staircase leading upward to the right and climb the steps into the realm of light. This is the realm of the divine and your higher self or superconscious.

22. Examine this realm of light for a while and take note of how it appears. This is a happy place and where you may not only discover your fullest potential, but also speak with the Goddess, the God, spirit guides, and your ancestors. No harm may happen here. But take heed, nothing but a loving spirit with good intentions may enter!

23. When you feel like you have finished your journey, give thanks to those whom you may have encountered. Turn around and walk back down the staircase to the middle realm or center of the tree where you first entered, and then exit.

24. You are back in a place that resembles a darkened room.

25. Open your hand and see the last stone that you dropped coming back to you. See it glowing in your hand. Now the second stone returns, and then the third, the fourth, the fifth, the sixth, the seventh, the eight, the ninth, the tenth, the eleventh, the twelfth, and finally all thirteen stones are back in your hand and glowing brighter than before.

26. Become aware of your body and surroundings.

27. Shake your hands or stomp your feet. Bring your awareness back to the physical realm and open your eyes when you are ready.

TREE MEDIATION 3:
TREE JUMPING (REMOTE VIEWING)

This meditation is advanced and may take a great many attempts. Do not feel discouraged if you are not able to do it the first or second time around. Techniques as this require repetition, practice, and perseverance. Just keep in mind that persistence brings the breakthrough. Why not give it a try or three?

Before beginning, it is very important to be aware of a few things. This meditation is used to shift your "sight" to another location anywhere on earth where there is a nearby tree. First you must choose the place you want to see, and you must absolutely hold this location in your mind. You will need to be aware of the largest tree nearby where you are currently located. I also recommend that you choose to visit a place, in the meditation, where you can later go and see in person to confirm that your working was successful. If this is confusing, read over the steps involved and it will become clearer.

1. You will need to be free of noise, distractions, and people. Perhaps play some very light meditative music in the background at a low volume. Try to block out as much light as possible or just place a dark blue or purple cloth over your eyes. You may also consider burning some incense to help set the ambiance.

2. In your mind, see a white, purple, or blue circle around you.

3. Sit or lay down. Be as comfortable as possible.

4. Begin by breathing in through your nose for the count of four or five and exhale out of your mouth for the count of four or five. As you breathe let all concerns, worries, and stresses disappear into the background of irrelevance.

5. As you continue breathing in the nose and out the mouth, visualize breathing in the white light of the divine and exhaling all doubts.

6. Continue this breathing technique while visualizing violet or purple light as you inhale to open and awaken your third eye and to access your psychic abilities.

7. Visualize a white or silver cord extending up from your spine and reaching toward the stars. Now see the other end of this cord projecting down from your spine and deep into the earth below. This is for grounding and centering purposes.

8. See yourself sitting in a darkened room. In your mind, clap your hands three times.

9. Suddenly you are standing on a large hill or mound. Look around. You see a large tree at the base of the hill. You begin to walk down to it. Count backward from thirteen to one as you slowly step.

10. You are now standing at the base of the hill, near the tree. You realize it is the same tree that you saw in your own environment, before you closed your eyes. But now the tree has a portal of some sort. Open the door.

11. You may find a challenging spirit there. If so, you may be asked of your intentions. If your intention is to learn and love you will be able to pass, but if your will is to spy on another, you may be denied or questioned.

13. Once given access through this doorway, enter. You will encounter a set of stairs leading down. Follow the stairway to descend into the lower realm.

12. When you get to the bottom you exit the tree, you have arrived at the place you longed to visit, the location which you willed to view.

13. Take mental notes of what you are seeing and observing.

17. When you are ready to leave, go back and reenter the doorway in the tree from which you came. It will still be open.

18. Climb the stairs back up to the tree that lives near your location. Exit the tree and close the door.

19. Look around and find the nearby hill. Step back up the hill slowly counting from one to thirteen.

20. Clap your hands three times and find yourself suddenly sitting down back in the darkened room where you began. Shake your hands, stomp your feet, and come back to your waking state.

21. Just for fun, if you chose to see a place where you can physically go to, go and see if what you saw was accurate.

MEET THE GREEN MAN

If you are new to contemporary Pagan practice and spirituality, you may or may not be familiar with the Green Man. So, who or what is he? The Green Man has taken many forms over the ages and is of pre-Christian European origin. In a nutshell, the Green Man is the spirit of the divine as sensed in the collective life force of the trees, the plants, the forest, and is seen as the manifested voice or spirit form of the masculine consort to Mother Earth. He is the combined energies of the trees, plants, and wooded areas unified into an archetypal being or divine spirit that both is the breath of nature and breathes life into nature. The duality or union of the Green Man and Mother Earth is much like the "force" from Star Wars and is neutral in nature, being both destructive and constructive.

Images of the Green Man have been found in hundreds of European churches and cathedrals and are generally portrayed as a masculine face surrounded by green leaves. The Green Man represents not only the spirit or voice of the trees and wildlife but also represents life, death, rebirth, renewal, growth, and wisdom. A dear friend of mine, a fellow Pagan and Wiccan high priest, described the Green Man as the "spirit of the fields and the sound of the wind and the harvest." The Green Man has also been called Robin of the Wood, Jack in the Green, the Green Knight, the May King, the Oak King, and sometimes blurred and associated with Cernunnos, Herne, Daghdha, the horned god, the harvest lord, and others. The tale of Robin Hood is likely derived from the myth and symbology of the Green Man.

Developing a personal connection or rapport with the Green Man may awaken your higher self, your true purpose, magickal abilities, and collective memories of older times when we lived in harmony our environment. Connecting with the Green Man is a way of becoming one with nature and the divine. There are many ways to meet and connect with the Green Man. Here is a suggestion:

- Venture out to a nearby forest, park, or any location that is free of the sounds of traffic and daily human activity—any place where you feel connected to nature will suffice.
- When you are in the right place, relax, breathe deeply, and let all mundane concerns slip away into irrelevance.
- Sense the energy of nature around you and within you.
- Breathe in the air of nature and focus upon a time when humans once lived in harmony with the environment. Ponder upon the struggles and challenges that our ancestors endured.

- Imagine the Green Man as the teacher of survival skills and natural medicine.

- Call upon the Green Man to appear before you. He will most likely manifest in your mind rather than in the physical. You will sense his presence.

- Take a moment to greet the Green Man and allow him to speak to you.

- See yourself as a part of the Green Man, a part of Mother Earth, and allow the spark of nature to open and ignite within you.

- Take time to allow the energy of the trees and wildlife to merge with you internally. Perhaps visualize a green light or mist surrounding and entering you.

- When you feel ready, open your eyes and know that once you have made a bond with the Green Man, this internal connection to nature will never be severed or broken.

- Take note that you may begin to see images of the Green Man all around you from here on out.

Chapter 10

ACTIVITIES

TREE CROSS ATTUNEMENT

This is an exercise to attune yourself with the energies and spirits of the trees. It is best done outdoors but can be done anywhere.

1. Face the direction of north.
2. Visualize a brilliant orb of white light above your head. Below your feet shines a blue or green orb representing the planet Earth.
3. Raise your arms up above your head until your hands come together touching palm to palm with fingers pointing up. See your hands penetrating the white sphere above your head and allow a steady flow of divine light to move down into you.
4. Slowly lower your arms until your hands are pointing to the Earth below, allowing the light of the divine to fill and cleanse each part of your being as it flows through you along the way.
5. See the white light continuously flowing down from the sphere above and into the Earth below.
6. As the flow of light continues, raise both arms up and out so that they extend horizontally and line up with your shoulders as though you are forming the shape of a cross. If you were facing the north, your arms would be pointing east and west.
7. State, "I am like the tree. The light of the divine flows within me and through me. I have everything I need and enough to give to others. I am in balance with my life, with nature, and with the divine. So mote it be!"

8. Lower your arms again and give thanks.

9. Repeat regularly

EARTH GRATITUDE ACTIVITY

The purpose of this simple ritual is threefold: to let the earth know of your gratitude for what we have taken, to give something back, and to lift your voice to affect the collective conscious of humanity. Based on the magickal concept of "as above so below," the one or the few (the micro) can affect the whole (the macro) and vice versa. The spoken parts of this activity can be changed or expanded upon at will. I recommend giving offerings at each quarter when the time is appropriate, such as water, birdseed, bread, coins, fruit, flowers, crystals, or a personal vow. Let your heart guide you.

- Face the direction of north.
- Visualize a green light surrounding you and filling you with gratitude.
- Say, "I am one with the earth. From the earth I came and to the earth I shall return. I give thanks for what you have provided and in return I vow to care for you as best I can. So mote it be!"
- Face the direction of east.
- Visualize a yellow light surrounding you and filling you with clarity and new inspirations. Imagine a comforting gush of air brushing over you.
- Say, "I am who I am. I think for myself. I am a teacher and a student. I am always learning. I vow to be a voice of positive construction to all around me. So mote it be!"
- Face the south. Visualize a red light or flame engulfing you, filling you with willpower, passion, and confidence.
- Say, "I am the burning flame of passion and creation. I am a lover of life and all living creatures. I vow to be a source of love and compassion unto to all living beings as best as I am able. So mote it be!"
- Face the west. Visualize a blue light surrounding you. Imagine a steady flow of rain falling over you, cleansing you, and releasing all stress and worry.

- Say, "I am a being of water. I am the power of love and understanding. I am empathic and intuitive. The joy, the memories, and the tears of the earth flow through me and I greet them with mirth. I vow to do my best to be a vessel of understanding, compassion, and knowledge for all that thirst. So mote it be!"

- Move into the center of the space you have been working in or close your eyes and move into the center of yourself. Visualize a white light surrounding you.

- Say, "I am a being of spirit. I am part of the divine and the divine is a part of me. I am completely whole on all levels. I give you thanks for everything I have been given, for all I have now, and for all I will have. I give thanks for your blessings. I vow to give blessings back to you, to the earth, and to all living beings. Allow me to be a vessel of your light and I ask that you work through me. Please guide me and guard me along my path. Blessed Be!"

- Take a moment to think upon things that you can do to help others, yourself, and ways to give back.

TREE AND SONG MAGICK

Like the spoken word, music is powerful. Music can lift one's spirit or tear it down. We all relate to music in some form or other because music is a universal language. When combining the spoken word along with music and intent wonders can be worked. This is, after all, why we love to use chants in our celebrations and magickal workings. A long-time friend of mine and fellow high priest of Wicca once shared with me the magickal associations of each musical note, and I wrote them into my personal book of shadows. I do not know the original source of this information, but I can say that I have tested it (I learned how to read and write music from an early age due to playing violin since primary school), found it to be quite relevant, and have since found this information listed in other sources. The notes below are based on the natural tone and do not reflect flats or sharps:

A—Psychic development, vision, opening and balancing the third eye chakra

B—Resolution of conflicts and inner battles. This note pertains to the crown chakra.

C—Healing, blessings, and new beginnings. The note of C pertains to the root chakra.

D—Willpower and discord. The note of D pertains to the sacral (belly) chakra.

E—Energy, creation, and tapping into the inner magickal self. The note of E pertains to the solar plexus chakra.

F—Emotion, empathy, love, and growth. The note of F pertains to the heart chakra.

G—Unity, expression, accord, listening, absorbing, and learning. The note of G pertains to the throat chakra.

If you are not familiar with musical notes, I suggest that you download an app on your phone or other device such as a virtual violin or a virtual piano. With apps such as these you can see and hear the correct notes and utilize them in your workings. Perhaps consider trying to hum along with each note until you are able to match it correctly.

While keeping the above possibilities in mind, below is a song about the Druidic tree triad of oak, ash, and thorn (the hawthorn tree). Joseph Rudyard Kipling wrote the original version, but I have slightly changed the words and shortened it so that it is applicable for all people regardless of time, location, and political views. This is a great song or chant, primarily for Summer Solstice rituals, but may also be enjoyed at Beltane or Lughnasadh celebrations. Please remember that all trees are sacred and magickal, not only the oak, ash, and hawthorn.

Tree song 1 (based on the work of J. R. Kipling)
(Verse 1)
Of all the trees that grow so fair short or stout or tall
greater are none beneath the sun than oak and ash and thorn

(Chorus)
Oak and ash and thorn my friends
all on a midsummer's morning

surely we sing of no little thing
the oak and ash and thorn

(Verse 2)
All the trees in the forest grow, sacred below and above
all around may they always abound
the oak and ash and thorn

(Chorus)
Oak and ash and thorn my friends
all on a midsummer's morning
surely we sing of no little thing
the oak and ash and thorn

(Verse 3)
All the trees and leaves without
and all of the trees within
strong and tall they someday fall
but soon will rise again

(Chorus)
Oak and ash and thorn my friends
all on a midsummer's morning
surely we sing of no little thing, the oak and ash and thorn

(Verse 4)
Do not tell the church our plot
They may call it a sin
but we've been out in the woods all night
welcoming summer in
We bring you news to set the feast
good news for cattle and corn
now has the Sun come up in the east
and oak, and ash, and thorn...

(Chorus)
Oak and ash and thorn my friends
all on a midsummer's morning

surely we sing of no little thing
the oak and ash and thorn!

CREATE AN HERBAL GRIMOIRE

This exercise is not only fun and rewarding, but also helps you learn to identify the trees, create a bond with them, and provide an on-hand supply of leaves to use whenever the need may arise. To create an herbal tree grimoire, you will need a few items:

- A photo album or journal
- An old hardcover book that you can write in
- A pen or pencil
- A very large heavy stone or two
- Possibly a camera

When you have the time, go to a local park, an arboretum, or even your own back yard and collect specimens of different leaves. Take this book along with to help correctly identify each tree. It is best to find a fresh leaf that has already fallen, but if you must take a living leaf from a tree make sure to ask permission, do it with respect, and give the tree thanks and gratitude in return.

Insert the leaf specimen between two pages of a book and write the name of the tree it came from as well as the date and location it was gathered. Trust me, it is very easy to forget which leaf is which when you gather more than three and trying to recall each leaf from memory is more difficult than it may seem. Proper identification is crucial. I recommend, at least for beginners, to visit the nearest arboretum where the trees have been tagged and labeled.

Try to collect specimens from at least fifteen different types of trees, but keep in mind that here are many varieties of each. For example, there are well over one hundred types of maple, so count maple as one. If you can, try your best to find at least one specimen from the following list of trees: alder, apple, ash, aspen, birch, elm, fir, hawthorn, hazel, holly, maple, oak, pine, rowan (European mountain ash), spruce, and willow.

When you have done your best, each leaf needs to be pressed and dried for a minimum of seven days. Press and dry the leaves between paper sheets, such as in the book that you used to collect them, or place them between paper towels, but do not press them between wax paper! Wax paper will not absorb the moisture and the leaves will eventually rot. Next, you need to apply pressure to the leaves and a simple way of doing this is to pile a few books on top of the leaves and/or place a large rock on top. Be patient and let them dry and press for at least a full week. Finally, when the leaves are ready, carefully mount and store each leaf into an album and make sure to label each one correctly. Remember that you can always add more specimens later and there is no need to limit this to trees. My own herbal grimoire includes close to two hundred tree specimens alone.

RITUAL BURNING OF THIRTEEN SACRED WOODS

In the common twenty-six–lined version of the Wiccan Rede can be found the line; "Nine woods in the cauldron go, burn them fast and burn them slow." The nine woods referred to here are often thought to be birch, ash, oak, hawthorn, willow, hazel, grape, apple, and fir but there has been some debate. These nine woods have been taken from the Celtic tree calendar, however, all trees and plants are sacred and there is no reason to claim a mere nine. Below I have expanded upon this portion of the Rede and have written it as a chant unto itself to include thirteen types of woody plants rather than nine. I base my reasoning for choosing thirteen on the fact that it is impossible to include all woody plants, but nine is not enough and gives the impression that there are only nine. The number thirteen is also representative of witchcraft (thirteen full moons per year). The activity below is great for Beltane, Summer Solstice, Lughnasadh, Mabon, Samhain, and full moon celebrations.

Begin by collecting a small branch, twig, or even a leaf from each of the trees listed below. Once you have gathered a sample of each, read out loud the following as one by one each specimen is dropped into the flames:

Birch in the fire brings sight and intuition. New beginnings shall come to fruition.

Apple gives health, love, beauty, and youth, forgotten knowledge, and esoteric truth.

Hawthorn in the spring blooms sweet guarded flowers, burn to protect, release, and to empower.

Grape that grows upon the vine is delicious and divine, bringing laughter, knowledge, health, and wine.

Aspen quakes, shakes, and whispers of growth, confidence, guidance, and unconditional love.

Hazel finds the witch's heart. Magick, medicine, and blessings in them are.

Ash is mighty, magickal, and strong. In the fire, we hear an ancient song.

Alder serves to shield and protect. In the fire it grants an honest request.

Rowan is a tree of ancient knowledge and tale. Protection and magick make the fires prevail.

Oak is the king of wisdom and might, to fear, to laugh, and dance with delight.

Willow eases pain and sways in the wind, as we journey to other realms and back again.

Fir, spruce, and evergreens teach the greatest of mysteries.

Holly means jolly granting protection and love.

All trees are sacred below and above!

TAKE A SPIRIT WALK

A spirit walk is a magickal way of referring to a hike through the woods. By taking a spirit walk, one can attempt to identify as many trees as possible and perhaps even find a gift from nature such as a piece of wood to use for making a wand, a staff, a stone that beckons you, a feather, or a leaf or branch that resembles a rune. A walk through the woods is also a great time to perform one of the above mentioned meditations or other activities. To turn a hike through the woods into a spirit walk simply consider the following:

- Enter the woods with a reverent heart.
- Perhaps say a prayer and ask to see the beauty of nature in a way that you have never seen before.

- Try to identify as many trees, plants, flowers, birds, and other forms of life that you can.

- Take a few minutes to sit quietly near a tree and listen to the sounds of nature around you.

- Breathe the energy of nature in through the nose while allowing it to fill you with health, youth, and energy. Exhale out the mouth to release all the stresses, worries, and burdens of daily life while simultaneously sending blessings of gratitude back to the earth.

- On your journey, consider picking up any garbage or litter you may encounter to recycle or dispose of later.

- If you are blessed with a token gift from nature you will know it. For example, perhaps you will encounter a stone or a fallen branch that just seems to say, "pick me up and take me home." Even if you don't want it personally, maybe someone you know does so take it and pass it along.

- During your walk consider stopping near a tree and try to listen to what it has to say. You may be surprised.

- Most importantly enjoy the beauty of nature around you.

Chapter 11

WANDS, STAFFS,
AND AMULETS

MAKE A MAGICKAL WAND

At some point, each magickal practitioner may wish to make his or her own wand. A wand is not necessary by any means for magickal practice but can be extremely beneficial. Energy can be sent out through the fingers or projected mentally with proper visualization and intent, but a wand may help to focus and project that intent as well as add its own natural properties. A wand can be used for casting circles, directing energy such as invoking and banishing pentagrams, waving over the body to invite healing and blessings, placing near an area to ward off negativity or provide protection, placing near the bed to invoke dreams, to attract specific energies into an area, or even placed upon the altar to represent a direction or element based on intent and purpose.

For example:

North/Earth: A wand can represent earth because the wood comes from a tree that is rooted deep in the soil.

East/Air: A wooden wand can represent air because the leaves and branches of a tree move in the wind and the tree's aroma and pollens travel through the air.

South/Fire: A wand can represent fire because of its transformative properties as well as the fact that wood burns in a fire and transforms into glowing coals and later to ash.

West/Water: A wand can represent water because a tree absorbs and purifies the water in the soil nearby.

269

To begin the creation of a magickal wand, one must first choose a specimen. A good rule to go by is to find a piece that is about the length of your elbow to your fingertips. This is only for better control and focus but by no means necessary to conduct energy. It can be shorter or longer. Use what feels right to you. It is beneficial to go out into nature and find a specimen from a tree that has the specific magickal properties you are seeking, but if unable to do so, using a dowel rod purchased from a department store or a sawed-off wooden broom handle will suffice. If you find a branch that is much longer than the standard, and you like it as is, by all means use it. Besides, with a bit of work, it can easily be cut to your personal desired length or used as is. If you choose to shorten the wood, be careful to avoid harming yourself in the process. Personally, I have found it much easier to work with a branch that is fairly straight, but this is not necessary. Some practitioners, in fact, prefer a crooked or curved specimen. A straight piece of wood, at least for me, makes it easier to visualize the energy flow. Whatever you choose, just make sure the specimen is thick or hard enough that it will not break or snap under light pressure.

If possible, it is good to find a specimen that has recently fallen to the ground or one that has already died but still attached to the tree. In this case, check to make sure it is not rotten or infested with termites. I have made many wands from specimens that have fallen, but sometimes it is necessary to cut off a living branch just to ensure that it is not rotten or feeble. If you choose to do this, the tree needs to be asked permission first while stating your intention, and then the branch must be allowed to completely dry before working with it, and the drying process could take up to six months.

Regarding what type of wood to use, please note that some practitioners have made very powerful wands from pieces of wood that simply called to them without knowing what type of wood it is. This is certainly fine to do for general practice because all trees are sacred, and all wood will help to focus energy, but to create an even more powerful wand, I suggest choosing which type of wood you would like your wand to made from first, because most trees correspond to various magickal properties. If you decide to choose a specific tree, the next obvious step is to go out and find the tree. Below are just a few examples of some of the most common woods used to make a wand or even a staff. Please refer to the last chapter of this book for the correspondences of many additional trees.

Alder: shielding, protection, overcoming obstacles, and courage

Apple: awakening otherworld senses, fertility, knowledge, youth, beauty, health, love, spiritual work, and manifesting goals

Ash: strength, energy, facing difficulties, wisdom, endurance and survival

Birch: new beginnings, youth, spiritual evolution, and devotion

Hazel: magick, witchcraft, healing, change, letting go, honesty, and purity

Oak: leadership, laughter and joy, mysteries, magick, wisdom, strength, might, power, victory, and mastering your own life

Pine/Fir/Spruce: longevity, protection, clearing unwanted energies, banishing harmful energies or malevolent spirits, connecting to all worlds and understanding the mysteries as revealed through nature and observation

Rowan (European mountain ash): magick, power, and protection from evil, psychic attack, and all harmful energies

Sycamore: invoking the divine, new beginnings, intuition, love, and healing

Willow: journey to other worlds, spirit communication, astral projection, healing, intuition, psychic abilities, easing pain, vision, confidence, love, magick in general, and balancing emotion

Below are some helpful tips to follow once you have chosen the right type of wood for you, and by the way, nobody says you can have only one wand. Why not have many? I do.

1. Safely cut the wood to the length that you desire.

2. Carefully shave off the outer bark of the branch, and then consider using sand paper to create a smooth surface.

3. If you would like any additional decorations, carefully carve, paint, or wood burn any art or magickal symbols onto the wood.

4. Many practitioners choose to attach a pointed crystal of some sort to the top of the wand to further amplify the energy being sent out and also to incorporate the magickal properties of the stone, but this is not necessary. Honestly, although I do have several wands and staves

that I work with, I have had great success with a small twig I just picked up in the yard without knowing what tree it came from and without modifying it in the slightest way.

5. I recommend using polyurethane to coat the wood once finished solely for hardening the wood and protecting it from external damage while leaving an inch at the bottom and at the top in its natural state. This will also add a brilliant luster. I suggest adding three coats, one at a time, and allowing 24 hours between each coat to dry. This of course is by no means necessary and some prefer to keep the wood in its natural state.

6. Now you may attach any feathers, amulets, charms, or other symbolic adornments to your wand if desired.

7. Once you feel your wand is complete, it is time to bless and empower it.

BLESSING, CONSECRATING, AND EMPOWERING A WAND

There are numerous ways to bless and empower your wand. If you are new to the practice of magick or simply do not consider yourself as a Wiccan or a witch, consider using one of the following simple ways to cleanse and charge your wand:

1. Bury your wand in a shallow patch of soil for twenty-four hours. This will allow the earth to absorb any possible prior energies or influences. The wood will still retain its natural inherent magickal properties.

2. Set your wand in a pile of salt for twenty-four hours.

3. Allow the wand to bask beneath the sunlight in the day and under the moonlight at night.

4. Hold the wand in your hand and visualize a white light descending over the wand and see all impurities flow out and into the earth.

5. Simply call upon whatever name you give to the higher power and ask for cleansing and blessings.

6. Once you have done one of the above techniques, hold the wand in your hand and concentrate on the purpose of the wand. Keep your focus and hold your intent until you feel that the wand is ready.

The above options are simple, and anyone can use them. However, I prefer a different technique that is based in Wiccan practice. Even still, there are many other possibilities, but the following is my personal favorite. This can also be used for any object such as a stone, a piece of jewelry, a staff, athame etc.

1. Set up a magickal altar or workspace

2. Upon the altar should be a representation of earth such as a pentacle or a bowl of salt or dirt, a representation of air such as burning incense or a feather, a representation of fire such as a lit candle, a goblet or chalice filled with water, and a representation of the God and Goddess.

3. Start in the east and cast a circle clockwise with one or two fingers pointing to the ground while visualizing a white light projecting to the surface. The direction of east represents creation and the natural flow of new energy upon the earth because it symbolizes the rising sun in the morning and new beginnings. This is opposite in the southern hemisphere.

4. Pass your wand through the smoke of the incense or touch it to whatever you have chosen to represent air and say something similar to this; "By the power of air, I consecrate and empower this wand (or name of tool) and ask for your blessings."

5. Quickly pass the wand through the candle flame and say, "By the power of fire, I consecrate and empower this wand and ask for your blessings."

6. With your fingertips splash a bit of water upon your wand and say, "By the power of water, I consecrate and empower this wand and ask for your blessings."

7. Touch the wand to the representation of earth and say, "By the powers of earth, I consecrate and empower this wand and ask for your blessings."

8. Raise your wand into the air above your head or place it close to your heart and say, "In the name of the Goddess, the God, and the Great Spirit, I ask that you bless and empower this wand to be used in your service and in my magickal workings."

9. Visualize a white, blue, purple, or golden light descending onto your new magickal tool.

10. With authority state, "So mote it be!"

11. Open the circle by starting once again in the east and moving counter-clockwise and draw the energy used to cast the circle back into you or disperse it back into nature.

12. It is done.

Enjoy using your wand and show it off to your friends and fellow practitioners if you wish, but take care to keep it guarded and limit how many people can hold it because you don't want it to absorb any possible harmful energy.

REGARDING THE MAGICKAL STAFF

The meaning and purpose of a staff is threefold. To begin, the staff may be used in magickal workings and practice much like a wand or athame (a double-edged blade) and can be a tool with which to direct energy.

In addition, the staff has historically been a symbol of elderhood and leadership in the magickal arts and is generally not carried by a beginner. One reason for this is that the staff is a bit more difficult to use than a wand. Another is that it takes much more time, thought, and dedication to create one. In general, the length of a staff is relevant to the height of the individual, and if one is young and still growing, he or she will outgrow it. The staff itself is tall and this alone represents adulthood and even more; it represents magickal maturity and one who walks between the worlds. The staff is also a symbol of the World Tree that penetrates the realms of above and below and we can find numerous examples in mythology and sacred texts where it was an elder that carried a staff such as Moses and Aaron, Merlin, and the Egyptian Pharaohs. Many deities of ancient mythology also carried a staff or something similar that may possibly represent this very same principle such as Thor's hammer, Poseidon's trident, Hermes's caduceus, Zeus's lightning bolt, and can also be a symbol of elderly wisdom such as the papal cross carried by the Pope or the walking stick or cane of our seniors.

An interesting example can be found in the Old Testament of the Bible, Exodus 7:8–13. Moses and his brother Aaron faced the Egyptian Pharaoh who demanded they display a miracle. Aaron threw down his staff and it transformed into a serpent. The Pharaoh's magicians and wise ones (wizards) in turn threw down their staffs and these also transformed into serpents. Aaron's staff swallowed up the others. Moses was eighty years old and Aaron was eighty-three. In ancient times the serpent was a symbol of wisdom, knowledge, and age. If you feel the need to create a magickal staff, simply follow the same instructions used for making a wand.

I hope that most will keep the symbolism of the staff sacred and choose not to create one until the time is right, but if you really feel compelled to do so, by all means proceed.

MAKE A MAGICKAL HERBAL TREE TRIAD

It has been said, although likely invented or made up after their time, that the Druids used a combination of three plant types to create a magickal herbal amulet, sachet, or incense. Regardless of whether or not the Druids actually used this method is of little importance because it can certainly be quite effective if made with proper knowledge and intent. The formula is very simple; use equal parts of either the dried leaves, blossoms, or wood from a tree, from a flower, and from a non-tree herb. This combination of plant specimens (tree/flower/herb) can be carried in a sachet or placed under a pillow or over a doorway to attract or repel specific energies, burned as an offering, burned to create a sacred fire, used to create sacred space, or used as a correspondence to boost magickal workings.

Below are three examples; however, I suggest that you do additional research to create your own as there are infinite possibilities and combinations:

To Attract Love and Beauty
- One part apple blossoms, leaves, or wood
- One part rose leaf or petal
- One part lavender

To Protect and Ward off Evil

- One part spruce or pine needles, or oak, hawthorn, locust, or rowan
- One part sage
- One part fern, geranium, or marigold

To Draw Luck and Money

- One part aspen or maple
- One part cinnamon or ginger
- One part chamomile flower

The examples above represent three of the most commonly desired workings and include non-tree herbs and flowers. However, it is just as effective to use three different types of trees only. Please refer to the next chapter to choose three or more equal parts or combinations of the dried wood, leaves, flowers, or even sawdust to create a magickal tree herbal combination, and for the specifics of each tree, please browse through the detailed properties and descriptions provided in the field guide in section two.

Chapter 12

QUICK GUIDE TO MAGICKAL AND MEDICINAL PROPERTIES OF TREES

MAGICKAL PROPERTIES

Below is a quick reference list to help utilize the magickal properties of trees. However, it is of dire importance you understand that the trees will not aid, assist, or guide you if your intentions are harmful. In addition, please remember that nobody should take a part of a tree without asking permission first and revealing to the tree what you plan to use it for, but if your heart is in the right place, most trees will grant you permission. If, however, you get the feeling that a tree does not approve, then I suggest you leave the tree alone and move on to another. Do not take from a tree just because you can. There may be repercussions. If it is the wood you seek, look for fallen twigs, branches, or those that may still be attached to the tree but no longer live. If you want the leaves or needles, I suggest looking on the ground first and gathering those that have fallen. Only when this is not an option, and you have the tree's blessing, should you cut a living leaf or twig. Make sure to give love and gratitude in some form or other back to the tree. It is foolish to think one can take without giving in return. The truth is that we are not above nature but are a part of it.

For any of the below possibilities, you can simply use either the leaves or wood of one tree or combine two or more. There is no limit. This type of magick operates in accord with the law of proximity; in other words, the magickal properties cause and create effects in the nearby location. If you wish to keep your home safe from harmful energies, choose one of the following and place the wood, leaves, or needles over a door, window, or anywhere close to the area you wish to protect. If you want to ward negativity and harmful energies from your car, place the wood, leaves, or needles within the vehicle. If you wish to attract or repel specific energies wherever you go, carry the wood, needles, or leaves with you in a sachet. It is the same concept when using crystals or stones. For an extra boost of empowerment, I suggest you hold the leaves, needles, or wood in your hand, free your mind of stress, worries, anger, resentment, jealousy etc., and then ask the spirit of the tree to work with you while focusing on your intention and mentally projecting this intent into the specimen. This is a simple method of charging and aligning your intentions with the natural vibrations of the plant. Be warned, if your intention is to harm, all that you do will fall back upon you when you least expect it and the only harm you will cause is to yourself. Magick has a universal built-in system of checks and balances and cannot be manipulated for long even if it does not seem apparent for some time.

All-Purpose Magick: apple, cedar, ginkgo, holly, lilac, maple, oak, pine, rowan, sandalwood, sycamore, willow

Acceptance/Self-Esteem: alder, arborvitae, aspen, birch, cherry, cypress, fir, ginkgo, grape (vine), grapefruit, horsechestnut, ironwood, katsura, larch, lemon, lilac, lime, linden, maackia, maple, oak, olive, palm, poplar, quince, willow, yellowwood, ylang-ylang

Ancestors and Burial: apple, arborvitae, birch, cypress, elder, elm, ginkgo, Kentucky coffee tree, pagoda, redwood, sycamore, willow, yew

Astral Projection: catalpa, ginkgo, lilac, poplar, willow

Awakening/Enlightenment: apple, birch, bodhi, boxelder, cherry, holly, ironwood, lemon, lilac, lime, mango, maple, myrrh, ylang-ylang

Banishing: arborvitae, aspen, fir, hawthorn, larch, lilac, linden, locust, oak, pine, rowan, spruce, sweet gum, sycamore, hazel, yew

Beginnings: birch, cherry, elm, ironwood, olive, Kentucky coffee tree, larch, lilac, magnolia, sycamore, willow

Binding/Defense: arborvitae, aspen, buckthorn, cedar, devil's walking stick, dogwood, elder (do not burn), euonymus, ginkgo, hawthorn, holly, larch, lilac, linden, maackia, monkey-puzzle, oak, olive, peach, pine, rowan, spruce, sweet gum, sycamore, witch hazel

Courage: alder, aspen, black gum, euonymus, Joshua tree, oak, walnut, yellowwood

Creativity: beech, birch, cherry, ginkgo, grapefruit, holly, mahogany, maple, willow

Curse Breaking: arborvitae, bamboo, bodhi, buckthorn, cedar, elder (do not burn), euonymus, fir, hackberry, hawthorn, holly, larch, mimosa, oak, pine, rowan, sumac, spruce, yew (don't touch without gloves)

Depression (to reverse): apple, apricot, cedar, cherry, fir, oak, orange, pear, pine, plane tree, spruce, tulip tree, yellowwood, most fruit trees

Divination: apple, arborvitae, baobab, beech, buckeye, cherry, cottonwood, elm, fig, ginkgo, hawthorn, holly, hornbeam, horsechestnut, laurel, lemon, lilac, lime, magnolia, mimosa, orange, plane tree, pomegranate, rowan, totara, willow, witch hazel

Dreams: apple, ash, aspen, baobab, elm, holly, hop tree, lilac, linden, magnolia, mimosa, myrrh, poplar, willow

Exorcism: acacia, arborvitae, aspen, bamboo, buckthorn, cedar, cinnamon, dragon's blood, elder (do not burn), fir, ginkgo, hackberry, juniper, larch, lemon, lime, myrrh, pine, oak, palm, rowan, spruce, sumac

Faith: acacia, almond, apple, banyan, cherry, cinnamon, cottonwood, holly, olive, palm, pine, sycamore, most trees in general

Health/Healing: apple, apricot, ash, avocado, bamboo, banana, baobab, black gum, boxelder, catalpa, cedar, cherry, chestnut, cinnamon, cork tree, cypress, elder (never burn), eucalyptus, fringe tree, ginkgo, grapefruit, hop tree, hornbeam, katsura, larch, laurel, lemon, lilac, lime, linden, locust, magnolia, mahogany, mango, maple, mimosa, monkey puzzle, myrrh, nutmeg, oak, olive, orange, pear, pepper tree, persimmon, pine, plum, pomegranate, poplar, redbud, redwood, rowan, sassafras, sumac (be cautious as there is a poisonous variety), sycamore, terebinth, totara, tulip tree, walnut, witch hazel, ylang-ylang

Legal Matters: alder, bamboo, hickory, linden, oak, palm

Longevity: apple, apricot, cherry, cypress, fir, ginkgo, holly, maple, peach, pear, pine, redwood, spruce, yew, most evergreen trees

Love/Fertility: apple, apricot, ash, aspen, avocado, banana, birch, black gum, boxelder, catalpa, cedar, cherry, chestnut, cinnamon, cork tree, dogwood, dragon's blood, elm, fig, ginkgo, grapevine, holly, honeysuckle, katsura, lilac, linden, locust, maackia, magnolia, mango, maple, mimosa, monkey puzzle, myrrh, myrtle, nutmeg, orange, pawpaw, peach, pear, plum, pomegranate, quince, redbud, serviceberry, sycamore, tulip tree, willow

Luck/Fortune/Wishes/Success: banyan, beech, boxelder, buckeye, buckthorn, cashew, chestnut, cork tree, dogwood, euonymus, fig, ginkgo, hickory, holly, honeysuckle, horsechestnut, larch, linden, maple, nutmeg, oak, orange, palm, pear, persimmon, pomegranate, poplar, rowan, walnut

Money: almond, banana, boxelder, buckeye, cashew, catalpa, cedar, chestnut, cinnamon, ginkgo, grapevine, honeysuckle, horsechestnut, maple, myrtle, nutmeg, oak, orange, pecan, pine, pomegranate, poplar, sassafras

New Beginnings: birch, boxelder, cedar, cinnamon, coffee tree, elm, fir, ginkgo, ironwood, larch, lilac, magnolia, maple, pomegranate, sycamore, willow

Peace and Comfort: alder, apple, arborvitae, aspen, avocado, beech, birch, ginkgo, hornbeam, horsechestnut, ironwood, katsura, lemon, lilac, lime, linden, maackia, maple, myrrh, myrtle, oak, palm, willow

Protection: acacia, alder, apple, arborvitae, ash, aspen, bamboo, birch, bodhi, cedar, chestnut, cinnamon, devil's walking stick, dogwood, dragon's blood, ebony, elder (do not burn), elm, eucalyptus, fig, fir, ginkgo, hackberry, hawthorn, hemlock, holly, honeysuckle, hornbeam, ironwood, kauri, larch, lemon, lilac, lime, linden, locust, mahogany, maple, mimosa, mulberry, myrrh, Norfolk pine, oak, olive, Osage orange, palm, pawpaw, pepper tree, pine, plum, pomegranate, quince, redwood, rowan, spruce, sweet gum, willow, witch hazel

Psychic Abilities: apple, elder, elm, lilac, magnolia, mimosa, redbud, rowan, willow

Purification/Cleansing: apple, arborvitae, birch, buckthorn, cedar, cherry, cinnamon, cypress, ebony, elder (do not burn), fir, ginkgo, hackberry, hawthorn, holly, larch, lemon, lilac, lime, mango, mimosa, myrrh, oak, palm, pepper tree, pine, plum, spruce, rowan, willow

Reincarnation/Past Life Recall: acacia, aspen, birch, cedar, fir, ginkgo, holly, ironwood, larch, lilac

Sleep: elder, hop tree, linden, willow

Spirit Communication: almond, apple, aspen, banyan, baobab, beech, birch, catalpa, cedar, coffee tree, devil's walking stick, elm, fir, ginkgo, hawthorn, holly, hop tree, hornbeam, ironwood, Joshua tree, larch, lemon, lilac, lime, linden, monkey puzzle, pomegranate, spruce, sweet gum, sycamore, willow

Success: apple, chestnut, euonymus, hornbeam, larch, oak, orange, poplar, rowan, walnut

Youth/Beauty/Longevity: apple, apricot, avocado, baobab, Canadian hemlock, cedar, cherry, fir, ginkgo, grapefruit, holly, Joshua tree, katsura, lemon, lilac, lime, maackia, mango, maple, monkey puzzle, myrtle, Norfolk pine, orange, peach, pine, redwood, spruce, sycamore, tulip tree, willow

QUICK REFERENCE TO MEDICAL AILMENTS

Below is a quick reference list of thirteen physical ailments and the trees that can be used to combat those said ailments. This is a generalized list and there are many more that can be found in the field guide (chapter four). It is necessary to keep in mind that this is a magickal guide to incorporating trees into your spiritual and magickal practices and that this book is not by any means meant to avoid visiting your doctor. I am not a physician and I do not suggest that you utilize the medicinal properties of trees without consulting a professional practitioner of medicine. What I do suggest is that you use these trees as a magickal correspondence to aid in spell work and magickal goals that may pertain to healing. Also, it is important to note that as science and medicine continues to advance, more and more healing properties and benefits of trees are continuously being discovered, and so therefore, there may be additional health and healing properties of trees that have not been included. Once again, please be careful, do additional research, and speak with a professional first if you decide to employ the medicinal properties of trees. Sometimes only the leaves contain the beneficial properties that you seek, and sometimes those properties are only found in the bark, or only in the fruit, or only in the roots or flowers etc. It is not enough to assume that any part of a given tree will be helpful. In fact, many times certain parts of trees can be harmful and toxic while other parts beneficial. Lastly, this list and all the information throughout this book pertains to the tall woody plants called trees and does not include other non-tree plants. If you want to know more or are curious about where I gathered the information for this book, please refer to the bibliography or consider doing your own research.

Blood Pressure: apple, cherry, cork tree, hawthorn, linden

Burns: apple, aspen, Canadian hemlock, linden, poplar

Cough/Chest Colds: catalpa, cherry, elm, eucalyptus, fir, ginkgo, larch, magnolia, maple, mulberry, pear, pine, red cedar, sassafras, walnut

Diarrhea: alder, cork tree, dogwood, elm, hackberry, linden, London plane tree, poplar, sweet gum

Fever Reduction: alder, ash, aspen, cherry, cork tree, cottonwood, dogwood, elm, fringe tree, ironwood, lilac, tulip tree, willow

Headaches/Pain: apple, aspen, cork tree, cottonwood, elder, fringe tree, shagbark hickory, poplar, viburnum, willow

Heart Problems: apple, cherry, Cornelian cherry dogwood, hawthorn, plum

Inflammations: alder, aspen, linden, poplar, willow, witch hazel

Laxatives: ash, buckthorn, catalpa, crabapple, fringe tree, hickory, Kentucky coffee tree, peach, plum

Minor Cuts/Wounds: alder, beech, catalpa, Canadian hemlock, cork tree, cotton wood, elm, fringe tree, hackberry, hop tree, hornbeam, pagoda tree, poplar, Rowan (European mountain ash), sweet gum, sycamore

Mouth (Gums, Teeth, Throat): alder, apple, birch, persimmon, sassafras

Rheumatism: alder, birch, buckthorn, cork tree, hickory, sweet gum

Urinary/Bladder: ash, cork tree, hornbeam, larch, peach, pear, tulip tree

OTHER NOTABLE TREES

Acacia

Family: Fabaceae

Number of Species: Over 800

Properties: The acacia tree, which closely resembles the locust tree, is also called the gum Arabic tree, thorn tree, Egyptian thorn, or whistling thorn. It was considered sacred to the Egyptian god Osiris. The ancient Egyptians used the wood for crafting boats as a symbol of the journey of the soul after death. It is said that the ancient tribes of Israel used the wood of the acacia tree to construct the Ark of the Covenant, the tabernacle, and the altar within the ancient temple (see Exodus 25:23). Place a branch or twig of acacia wood over or near the bed to ward off harmful spirits or energies. Burn acacia wood along with sandalwood to arouse psychic abilities.

Almond

Family: Rosaceae

Number of Species: About 40

Properties: Almond nuts, leaves, and wood can be used in money spells, fertility rights, patience development, and connection with the divine. Carry almonds to attract money or other treasures. Sweet almonds may cure or reduce fever, however bitter almonds are toxic to humans if not boiled and can cause serious health problems or even death. Almond wood is excellent for crafting a wand or a staff, and some traditions claim this wood as superior for such tools. In ancient Biblical times, the nearby Pagan cultures considered the almond tree, as well as the pomegranate, to be sacred to the Great Mother Goddess. Its scientific name *Amygdalus* comes from the Sumerian words *amaga*, meaning Great Mother. Ironically, the Biblical staff of Aaron, and possibly that of Moses, was made of almond wood and referred to as the staff of God (see Numbers 17:8 and Exodus 19:9). The almond tree may also be seen as a symbol of the light of the divine as one of its ancient names (Aramaic) is *luz*, meaning light.

Apricot

Family: Rosaceae

Number of Species: Over 400 species of prunus

Properties: Also called wild apricot and golden apple, the leaves, flowers, and pit can be carried or used to attract love or draw in healing energies. The fruit is very edible, minus the seeds, which contain cyanide; they are round like a small peach, yellow-orange with a tint of red. Seeds may fight cancer, but they also contain cyanide, therefore one must consult a physician prior to consuming in order to learn the proper dosage. The fruit contains vitamin A, calcium, phosphorous, iron, and traces of sulphur, sodium, manganese, bromine, and cobalt.

Avocado

Family: Lauraceae

Properties: Also called *Ahuacotl* (Aztec), alligator pear, and persea. Use for love, lust, beauty, fertility, and all types of magick. Wands made from avocado are very powerful, and this wood is all-purpose, magickally speaking. If you grow an avocado plant from the pit and care for it in your home, you will invite the energies of love and peace into your dwelling. Avocado fruits are high in potassium, fiber, vitamin B6, vitamin C, E, and much more.

Bamboo

Family: Poaceae

Number of Species: About 1,450

Properties: The common bamboo, or golden bamboo, is not a tree, but a grass that grows up to 100 feet in height. The wood and leaves can be used for protection, healing emotional wounds, breaking curses, or to bring good fortune. Place bamboo wood over your door to bring good luck and protection from harmful energies. To break a curse, crush the wood into a powder and burn it while knowing that as the wood burns, so does the curse. Carry a piece of bamboo wood with you to repel harmful unwanted energies.

Banana

Family: Musaceae

Number of Species: At least 70

Properties: Use for health, fertility, prosperity, and increasing potency. The leaves, fruit, and flowers can be carried to attract monetary gain and prosperity. Sometimes financial gains come in disguise. Banana wood can be used to make a wand or staff. Bananas actually grow on very large plants and are not technically trees.

Banyan

Family: Moraceae

Number of Species: About 850

Properties: The banyan tree is the national tree of India and is also called Indian fig, arched fig, and the Vada tree. In many ancient cultures, the banyan tree has been seen as a representation of the World Tree, the Tree of Knowledge, and the Tree of Life. The wood is an excellent specimen for making a staff. Sitting beneath or touching a banyan tree with reverence will bring good luck.

Baobab

Family: Malvaceae

Number of Species: 8

Properties: Connecting to the spirit world, associated with the moon and the element of water, healing, and intuition, sometimes used for burial rites as this tree is considered a gate to the spirit world. In South Africa there is a baobab tree over 2,000 years old and is known by the locals as the "Tree of Life." This particular tree is so large that it takes 30 or more people holding hands to surround it. The leaves of the baobab tree are rich in vitamin C and calcium. The bark and seeds have been used to treat colds and fever.

Bodhi

Family: Moraceae

Number of Species: About 850 species

Properties: Protection, wisdom, fertility, meditation, and enlightenment. The bodhi tree, also called pipal tree, bo tree, and sacred fig, is sacred to Vishnu and Buddha and it is said that both were born beneath this tree. Walk counter-clockwise at least three times to break a curse or to remove harmful energies. Burn the dried leaves during meditation to receive wisdom and enlightenment. This tree is very sacred to Hindus and Buddhists.

Cashew

Family: Anacardiaceae

Properties: Carry cashews to attract prosperity and money or use as a correspondence in this type of magick.

Cinnamon Tree

Family: Lauraceae

Properties: Spirituality, love, passion, desire, success, healing, blessing, protection, cleansing, purification, money, and increasing psychic abilities. The inner bark of the cinnamon tree is used to obtain the cinnamon spice. There are several related species that can be used to obtain cinnamon, but only one true cinnamon tree. Cinnamon spice has been mentioned several times in the Bible as an ingredient for making anointing oil. Burn or carry cinnamon leaves, incense, or spice to invite positive spiritual vibrations, to promote healing, to attract money, and to stimulate psychic abilities. Place cinnamon in an area to protect from harmful energies.

Devil's Walking Stick

Other Names: Hercules club, angelica tree, prickly ash (though not an ash), prickly elder, toothache tree, pigeon tree, shot bush

Number of Species: More than 800

Family: Araliaceae

Magickal Properties and Lore: Protection, endurance, strength, unconditional love, can represent both the God and the Goddess, but beware, this tree is very sacred to the divine and also the nature spirits; in general, it should not be used. If you come across this tree, give it love and blessings and win the favor of the tree spirits. Be careful of the thorns.

Medicinal Properties: Roots and fruit have been used to treat toothaches, boils, snakebites, and eye and skin problems, but this requires very special procedures as the berries and bark are toxic to humans and even touching this tree can irritate the skin. Flowers provide nectar and pollen for honeybees, and the berries are a source of food for birds and other wildlife but are not safe for humans.

Dragon's Blood Tree

Family: Asparagaceae

Number of Species: At least 40

Properties: Protection, exorcisms, potency, and love. Burn the resin or an incense to attract love or to drive away harmful energies. To induce quiet and peace in a household, mix powdered dragon's blood with sugar and salt and then seal up the mixture in a bottle or jar and keep it hidden.

Ebony

Family: Ebenaceae

Number of Species: 500–700

Properties: Protection, purification, and magickal power. Ebony wood can be used to make an incredibly powerful wand. It has been said that one should not stand beneath an ebony tree during a storm. The name ebony is derived from the Egyptian name for the tree *hbny* and/or the Greek name *ebenos*. The name of the genus, *Diospyros*, comes from the Greek words *dios* and *pyros*, meaning the fruit of god or divine fruit.

Eucalyptus

Family: Myrtaceae

Number of Species: 400 to 700 species of evergreen trees and shrubs

Properties: Also known as gum tree. Used for natural and magickal healing, protection, balance, and vitality. Hang a branch or twig over your bed to help promote the healing of fevers, colds, and other illnesses. Leaves can be carried for protection. The wood of the eucalyptus is used to make the magickal musical instrument called the didgeridoo that considered sacred to many shamans.

Fig

Family: Moraceae

Number of Species: Over 800

Properties: Use for fertility, conception, impotency, divination, protection, and love. Folk legend has it that by writing a question on a fig leaf, one can derive a yes or no answer. If the leaf dries slowly, the answer to the question is yes and a good sign; but if the leaf dries rapidly, the answer is no. Fig branches, twigs, and leaves will bring protection to the home as well as good luck. Place a fig branch or twig near your door if you travel in order to encourage a safe return. Share a fig with a loved one to strengthen your relationship and to promote love. The fig tree is mentioned numerous times in the Bible and is said to have clothed Adam and Eve after partaking the fruit of the Tree of Knowledge (see Genesis 3:7).

Grape

Family: Vitaceae

Number of Species: About 60

Properties: Although not a tree, this wood is too wonderful not to include. It is associated with joy, delight, fertility, love, health and healing, metal powers, and money. Grapes are sacred to the Moon Goddess, Dionysus, and Bacchus. Eat grapes to enhance fertility or share red grapes with those you love, or place grapes upon the altar for magickal workings to give an extra boost of power. Carry dried twigs for the same purposes.

Grapefruit

Family: Rutaceae

Properties: Health, healing, longevity, optimism, energy, weight loss, and inspiration. The grapefruit has also been called the "forbidden fruit" or *chakotra*.

Honeysuckle

Family: Caprifoliacea

Number of Species: 180

Properties: Honeysuckle is not a tree, but due to its easy access and powerful properties, it is worthy of mention. The honeysuckle has many magickal properties. Use for protection, good fortune, money, psychic abilities, balance of the divine masculine and feminine, and safety. Carry honeysuckle flowers to attract money and love. Gently crush the flowers, with permission of course, and rub the resulting extract on the forehead between the eyes to awaken or increase psychic abilities. Plant a honeysuckle near the home to draw good luck, positive energies, and nature spirits and to ward off harmful energies. Place a twig or small branch over the door to ward harmful energies and possibly to deter fevers and colds.

Joshua Tree

Family: Agavaceae

Properties: Survival, perseverance, connecting with the divine, longevity, and beauty. The Joshua tree grows in the Mojave Desert and is also called the yucca palm tree and *izote de desierto*. Mormon settlers named the tree after the Biblical story of Joshua, who reached his hands up to the heavens in a gesture of prayer due to the apparent shape of the tree.

Kauri

Family: Aruacariaceae

Number of Species: About 20 species of tall growing coniferous evergreen trees

Properties: Relationships, connecting with the divine, symbolic of "as above so below," protection, shielding, love, and emotional healing; can be used for general magick.

Laurel

Family: Lauraceae

Number of Species: 2–3 species of laurel tree

Properties: Healing, easing both physical and emotional pain, divination, and comfort. Also called sweet bay, and bay leaves are often used for cooking such as in soups. The leaves and other parts of this tree were used in ancient Greek and Roman ceremonies and considered sacred to Gaia, Daphne, and Apollo. Burn bay leaves while employing any form of divination to encourage a trance-like state to induce prophetic and psychic abilities.

Lemon

Family: Rutaceae

Properties: All-purpose magick. Use for discovering the truth, discovering spirit guides, starting over, longevity, healing, enlightenment, exorcism, discovering the truth of a matter, protection, purification, cleansing, love, joy, and divination. Mix lemon juice with water and contain the mixture in a spray bottle to purify an area from harmful energies. Add lemon juice to a ritual bath to purify the body. The dried leaves and fruit peels can be carried in a sachet to promote inspiration and clarity and to attract love. Share some freshly squeezed lemon or lime juice with water as a drink or a tasty treat with a loved one to strengthen the bonds of family, friendship, and unconditional love.

Lilac

Family: Oleaceae

Number of Species: 20–25 species and over 1,000 varieties of this small tree or shrub

Properties: Love, rebirth, protection, exorcisms, fertility, healing, psychic abilities, and past-life recollection. The essence of the flowers can cleanse and balance all the chakras, particularly the heart, help focus the mind, and aid in opening spirit communication. The message of the lilac is to learn to maintain a balance of the mind, emotion, the mundane, and the spiritual. Consider adding the flowers to bath water. Plant a lilac near the home or carry the wood or leaves to ward off evil and negativity. The wood makes a very powerful wand. This strong wood has been used for making musical instruments and engravings. Lilacs are often planted for ornamental purposes and their wonderfully fragrant flowers. These flowers are sometimes used in salads or for seasoning food. Used to reduce fevers and to treat malaria.

Lime (see Lemon)

Magnolia

Family: Magnoliaceae

Number of Species: About 200–210

Magickal Properties and Lore: Love, healing, fertility, renewal, faithfulness and fidelity, discovering what has been lost, and sexuality. Keep leaves, flowers, or bark near your bed to help maintain a faithful relationship (on your part). The flower essence opens psychic abilities and deepens intuition. Use this essence to open your abilities to retrieve lost items, memories, and ideas. There are both deciduous and evergreen varieties of magnolia trees. The seeds provide food for birds and mammals, and deer love the to eat the leaves and twigs. Magnolias are often used as ornamental trees for their beautiful flowers, leaves, and shade. The wood is very strong and quite valuable. Magnolia flowers can be used to help respiratory infections, congestion, and sinus headaches.

Mahogany

Family: Meliaceae

Number of Species: 3

Properties: Use for protection, healing, and inspiration. Mahogany wood is very valuable for making furniture, boats, musical instruments, and can be used to craft a wonderful magickal wand.

Mango

Family: Anacardiaceae

Number of Species: About 69

Properties: Love, longevity, health, and beauty. In Hinduism, mango blooms are considered sacred to the goddess Saraswati, and the fruits are sacred to the god Ganesh and seen as a symbol of enlightenment and purification. Mangoes are one of the most well-known tropical fruits around the world and have been cultivated in India for at least 4,000 years. They were brought to Brazil and Mexico and thrive in Central America.

Monkey Puzzle

Family: Araucariaceae

Number of Species: 15

Properties: Caring for others, devotion, love, longevity, healing, otherworld communication, resolution of conflicts, and banishing. This tree is close to extinction and has been seen as a symbolic representation of the bridge between the physical and spirit worlds. The monkey puzzle tree, also called the Chile pine, native to South America, is a conifer covered with so many spiny scales that it is impossible to climb even for a monkey. This tree is actually home to many parrots that feed on the nuts. It grows in a pyramidal shape.

Myrrh

Family: Bureraceae

Properties: Intuition, dreams, meditation, empathy, emotion, love, healing, protection, exorcism, healing, purification, cleansing, and general spiritual concerns. Myrrh is an all-purpose magickal tree. Burn myrrh incense to purify and cleanse a place or the body of unwanted energies and to bring peace and comfort. Myrrh has been valued as sacred throughout much of antiquity. Myrrh is sacred to Yahweh, Adonis, Aphrodite, Isis, Ishtar, Astarte, and the Great Mother Goddess in general. Myrrh is one of the ingredients mentioned in the Bible to create anointing oil (Exodus 30:22).

Myrtle

Family: Myrtaceae

Number of Species: At least 3,000 species of trees and shrubs.

Properties: Love, youth, weddings and handfastings, fertility, healing, money, peace, and joy. Carry the dried leaves or flowers in a sachet to attract love or money. Place the leaves, flowers, or wood on the altar as an additional magickal correspondence. Carry myrtle wood or place the wood near the bed to extend youth and beauty. Plant a myrtle tree or plant near the home to invite peace and love. A myrtle branch makes for a very great wand. The myrtle tree has long been considered sacred in many ancient cultures. In the ancient Sumerian text called the *Epic of Gilgamesh*, myrtle was named as one of the sacred trees that grow in the grove of the gods. Myrtle is considered sacred to Artemis, Aphrodite, Venus, and Zeus.

Norfolk Island Pine

Family: Araucariaceae

Number of Species: 40

Properties: Protection, exorcisms, longevity. Keep and care for a Norfolk pine to ward off harmful energies and spirits. The Norfolk pine is commonly sold as a houseplant during the Yule/Christmas season, but is actually a tree that can grow up to 200 feet in height. The tree is native to the Norfolk Island in the South Pacific, east of Australia. This is a very ancient tree that once thrived in the days of the dinosaurs. It is a tropical evergreen and cannot survive cold temperatures. It needs a lot of sunlight and constant moisture. If you want to keep and grow one, make sure the soil stays moist, but don't over water it, and make sure it has ample sunlight. If you want it to grow taller, it must be replanted into a larger pot each year or the pot will stunt its growth.

Nutmeg

Family: Myristicaceae

Properties: Money, luck, relationships, health and healing. Carry a nutmeg to attract good luck and to ward off colds and sickness. Use in magickal workings that deal with money and finance, for instance, grind a nutmeg and blend with base oil such as canola oil or olive oil, and rub the mixture on a green candle to charge it and give an extra boost to the work.

Olive

Family: Oleaceae

Properties: Healing, peace, fertility, protection from evil, to bring luck. Olive is a very sacred tree within many religions.

Orange

Family: Rutaceae

Number of Species: At least 15

Properties: Love, divination, luck, money, healing, beauty, youth, and vitality. Add dried orange peels to a bath regularly to appear more attractive and to preserve youth and beauty. It has been said that if you eat an orange while concentrating on a yes or no question, you can then count the seeds to determine the answer. If there are an odd number of seeds, the answer is yes, and an even number of seeds means no. The problem with this type of simple divination is that when people get an answer they don't want to hear, it is common to dismiss it as nothing but superstition and untrue. Don't ask a question if you are not willing to accept an answer that you don't like. Share an orange with a loved one or friend to strengthen the bond or simply to promote health, as oranges are rich in vitamin C. A Christian legend from Spain tells a story when Mary, Joseph, and young Jesus were traveling and they encountered an orange tree that was guarded by an eagle. Mary asked the tree to give them a fruit and the eagle fell asleep. Mary was then granted three oranges, one to represent the father, one to represent the mother, and one to represent the son.

Pagoda Tree

Family: Leguminoseae or Fabaceae

Number of Species: Almost 20,00

Magickal Properties and Lore: Also called Japanese pagoda, Chinese scholar tree, and scholar tree, a Chinese myth states that using this wood attracts evil spirits, demons, and death. Best that you do not take the wood from this tree carelessly. Leaves, flowers, and fruit have antibacterial, diuretic, and antispasmodic properties.

Palm

Family: Arecaceae or Palmaceae

Number of Species: More than 2,500

Properties: Also called tree of peace, palm is associated with protection, peace, victory, strength, learning, and fertility, and it calms the soul. Leaves prevent negative energies and evil spirits from entering the area where the leaves or wood are placed. Palm wood makes a very powerful wand or staff and is sacred to both Christians and ancient pagan cultures such as the Romans. It has been said to represent the "Tree of Life." Palms are valuable for oils, coconuts, dates, syrup, and wood. Palm sap is sometimes used to make wine. The coconut palm produces very edible and delicious fruit.

Pepper Tree

Family: Anacardiaceae

Properties: Purification, protection, and healing. Also called California pepper tree, false pepper, American pepper, Peruvian mastic, Peruvian peppertree, pirul, *escobilla*, *molle de Peru*, and peppercorn tree. This tree has been used for centuries by Latin-American natural healers (curanderos) in healing rituals. Gently brush the branches over the body of the person in need of healing to absorb the ailment into the wood and then burn to release the ailment. Burn the dried leaves to purify and cleanse an area of unwanted or harmful energies. This wood can be made for a great healing wand.

Pipal (see Bodhi)

Pomegranate

Family: Lythraceae

Number of Species: 2

Properties: Luck, wishes, wealth, fertility, divination, protection, healing of blood-related issues, love, new beginnings, otherworld journeys, the afterlife, and connecting with our ancient past. The pomegranate has also been called Carthage apple, grenadier, malicorio, pound garnet, and the "fruit of life." Pomegranate is sacred to Persephone, Ceres, Dionysus, Aphrodite, Venus, Hera, and Astarte. Eat the seeds to promote fertility and to promote healthy blood. Make sure to make a wish before eating. Carry a branch, twig, or a piece of wood to attract money. Hang a branch or twig of pomegranate over or near a door to ward off harmful energies and spirits. The pomegranate was used by the ancient Israelites in the creation of the robes for the priests (Exodus 28:33). This tree has also been written about in many other ancient sacred texts.

Quinc

Family: Rosaceae

Properties: Love, joy, protection, marriage, happiness, and fertility. The ancient Greeks called the fruits of this tree "golden apples." This tree is Sacred to Venus, Aphrodite, Freya, Zeus, Hera, and Marian. Carry the seeds, leaves, or wood to protect against energetic, spiritual, and bodily harm. Use the leaves, flowers, wood, or fruit in love workings or handfastings. This tree has a rich ancient mythical history.

Sandalwood

Family: Santalaceae

Properties: Sandalwood is also called sandal and santal; it is an all-purpose magickal tree.

Terebinth

Family: Anacardiaceae

Number of Species: 10

Properties: Healing, burial rites, and the sacred feminine mysteries. The terebinth is also called turpentine tree and is the tree that produces the pistachio nut. The terebinth is considered sacred to Jehovah and Allah. The ancient Hebraic name for this tree is *Elah* (which conveys a feminine meaning) has been confused or mistranslated as *Elon* (oak) to give it a masculine association. In Genesis 18:1 and Genesis 35:4, the oak tree is mentioned but was likely a mistranslation for terebinth. A possible reason for the mistranslation was to remove the sacred feminine from divinity.

Totara

Family: Podocarpaceae

Number of Species: 75

Properties: Healing, divination aid, longevity, ancestors, wisdom, and respect for elder hood. This tree is very ancient and said to have remained unchanged for at least 70 million years. It is considered sacred to Maori, Tane Mahuta, the sun god, the Green Man, and the lord of the forest.

Ylang-Ylang

Family: Annonaceae

Number of Species: About 2,500

Properties: Fertility, truth, perseverance, hope, and intuition. Ylang-Ylang is sacred to the Goddess, and as a sign of this, its scent is strongest at night. Many perfumes are made from this tree. Meditate near this tree or use the scent of the oil or incense during meditation in your home to assist with cleansing and repairing the aura and chakras, to discover the truth or clarify a situation, or to increase or develop empathy, intuition, psychic, and magickal abilities.

BASIC IDENTIFICATION
AND GLOSSARY

aggregate fruit: A fruit that is composed of many tiny berries such as a mulberry.

alternate: Leaves on a twig that alternate and do not grow directly across from each other.

analgesic: An analgesic is a drug used to relieve pain such as aspirin, but in this case, it is a natural pain reliever that can be found in the bark of the willow, aspen, and poplar trees.

antiseptic: An antiseptic prevents a wound or sore from becoming infected by inhibiting or destroying the growth of bacteria.

apex: The tip or terminal point of a leaf

aromatherapy: The use of plant oils or other parts of a plant, generally by heating or burning, to release the essence through the air so that the properties of the plant are absorbed into the body by means of inhalation.

astringent: A chemical that shrinks bodily tissues and therefore helps to reduce the outward flow of blood or other secretions. Astringents are good for slowing the blood from a minor cut or wound.

bark: The dead external protective covering of the trunk and branches of a tree or shrub.

berry: A fruit with two or more seeds and a soft flesh-like exterior.

blade: The flat part of a leaf; also called the lamina.

bough: The branch of a tree.

branch: The thin woody part of a tree that generally bears the leaves and flowers.

broadleaf tree: A tree with flat and thin leaves that usually shed annually.

capsule: A thin, dry, walled fruit containing more than one seed.

catkin: Sometimes called aments. Clusters of incomplete unisexual flowers. They are dense, caterpillar-like, and sometimes fuzzy. Birch and willow trees are good examples of catkin-producing trees.

clustered needles: Clustered needles are a group of needles growing from a central point, such as pine needles.

compound leaf: A leaf with more than one blade and all blades are attached to a single leaf stem, such as those of the ash tree.

conifer: A tree that bears cones such as the firs, the spruce, and the pines.

crown: The upper part of a tree containing the branches, leaves, and stems that form the visible shape and size of a tree.

deciduous: Trees that drop their leaves annually.

decoction: The resulting liquid after mashing and boiling a part of a plant to extract oils, compounds, and chemical substances.

diaphoretic: A substance that induces or encourages perspiration.

disk: A flat fruit resembling a disk that contains a seed such as the fruits of the elms.

diuretic: A substance that promotes urination such as coffee.

drupe: A fleshy fruit that generally contains a single seed embedded within a protective outer shell (also called a pit). Examples are peaches, cherries, and walnuts.

elliptic: An elongated oval shape, generally twice the length of the width.

entire: The margin of a leaf with smooth, untoothed edges.

evergreen: A tree whose leaves or needles remain living on the tree all year long

family: A group of related *genera* (see genus). In terms of proper taxonomy, the family is always capitalized and always ends in *-aceae*.

foliage: The leaves of a plant or tree

fruit: A reproductive growth structure that contains one or more seeds.

furrowed bark: Bark on a tree with deep channels and grooves.

genus: A closely related group of plants within the same family that share comparable characteristics such as similar flowers and fruits (plural is genera). In terms of proper scientific taxonomy, the genus is always capitalized and italicized. For example, the genus of any type of maple tree is classified as *Acer.*

infusion: The result of steeping an herb into water, oil, or alcohol, such as an herbal tea.

invasive: A plant that reproduces and spreads over a large area rapidly. This is generally an undesired activity.

leaf base: The point where a leaf attaches to the petiole.

leaflet: A leaf like subdivision of a compound leaf.

leaf scar: A mark that remains on a twig where a leaf was previously attached.

lobe: The projection that shapes a leaf.

margin: The edge of a leaf.

midrib: The central vein of a leaf.

needle: A long and narrow leaf generally pertaining to coniferous trees.

nut: A fruit with a hard exterior containing one seed.

opposite: Leaves that grow directly across each other on the same twig.

oval: The shape of a leaf or leaflet that grows in the form of an oval. It is twice as long as it is wide and both ends are rounded.

ovate: The shape of a leaf or leaflet similar to an oval but is broader near the base like an egg.

palmate: Blades, lobes, veins, or leaflets of a compound leaf that stem from the base of a leaf and resemble the shape of a hand with all fingers pointing out.

petal: The part of a flower that resembles a leaf and is usually brightly colored.

petiole: The stalk of a leaf that connects the leaf to the twig.

pinnate: Leaves, leaflets, or veins of a leaf that grow in a way that resemble a ladder or a feather such as the honey locust.

pith: The inner portion of a twig.

pod: The dry fruit of a tree that holds many seeds like a pea-pod, such as the fruit of the honey locust and Kentucky coffee trees.

poultice: The extraction of herbal chemicals, usually through heat, and absorbed into a cloth to be applied to a wound, sore, or inflamed skin.

sachet: A small cloth bag containing herbs or stones.

samara: A winged fruit containing a seed such as those of the maples and ash. These are often called "helicopters."

sessile: A leaf that is attached directly to the base and lacks a stalk.

shoot: A young and still growing stem or twig.

simple leaf: A single leaf that is not compound.

sinus: The indentation or space between two lobes of a leaf.

species: A specific plant within a genus. In terms of scientific taxonomy, the species of a plant is italicized in lower case following its genus. For example, all maples belong to the genus *Acer*, but a red maple is classified as *Acer rubrum*.

spur: A short stubby twig, sometimes sharp and resembling a thorn, and can bear clusters of leaves.

stalk: The thin stem or main axis of a plant that supports a flower, leaf, or fruit.

teeth: The notches on the margin (edge) of a leaf, generally pointy and divided into tooth-like projections and can be categorized by various sizes as blunt, course, fine, and sharp.

trunk: The central supporting stem of a tree.

twice-compound: A compound leaf structure where the leaflets have smaller stems and leaflets of their own.

BASIC VISUAL EXAMPLES

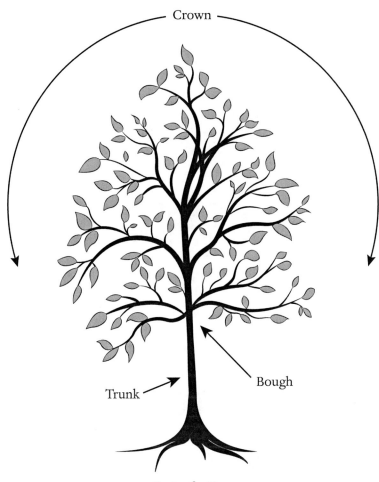

Parts of a Tree

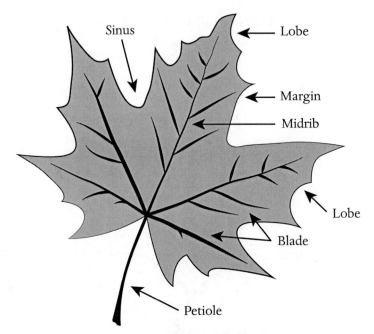

Sinus

Lobe

Margin

Midrib

Lobe

Blade

Petiole

Parts of a Leaf

Simple Leaf

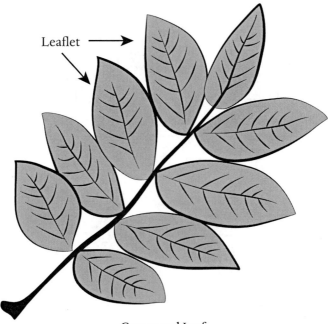

Leaflet ——→

Compound Leaf

Palmate Compound Leaf

Twice Compound Leaf

Opposite Leaf

Alternate Leaf

BIBLIOGRAPHY

Andrews, Ted. *Nature-Speak: Signs, Omens, and Messages in Nature*. Jackson, TN: Dragonhawk Publishing, 2004.

Arbor Day Foundation. *What Tree Is That? A guide to the more common trees found in Eastern and Central U.S.* Nebraska City, NE: Arbor Day Foundation, 2008.

Beyerl, Paul. *The Master Book of Herbalism*. Custer, WA: Phoenix Publishing Inc., 1984.

Blamires, Steve. *Celtic Tree Mysteries: Secrets of the Ogham*. St. Paul, MN: Llewellyn Publications, 1997.

Bopp, Judie, Michael Bopp, Lee Brown, and Phil Lane Jr. *The Sacred Tree: Reflections on Native American Spirituality*. Twin Lakes, WI: Lotus Light Publications, 1989.

Bowes, Susan. *Life Magic: The Power of Positive Witchcraft*. New York, NY: Simon & Schuster Editions, 1999.

Caldecott, Moyra. *Myths of the Sacred Tree*. Rochester, VT: Destiny Books, 1993.

Carter, Mark. *Stalking the Goddess*. Alresford, Hants, UK: Moon Books, 2012.

Coombes, Allen J. *Trees: The Visual Guide to More than 500 Species of Trees from Around the World*. New York, NY: DK Publishing, 1992.

Crockett, James Underwood. *Evergreens*. NY: Time Life Books, 1971.

Cunningham, Scott. *Cunningham's Encyclopedia of Magical Herbs*. St. Paul, MN: Llewellyn Publications, 1985.

Cunningham, Scott. *Earth Power: Techniques of Natural Magic*. St. Paul, MN: Llewellyn Publications, 1983.

———. *The Complete Book of Incense, Oils, & Brews*. St. Paul, MN: Llewellyn Publications, 1989.

Dirr, Michael A. *Manual of Woody Landscape Plants: Their Identification, Ornamental Characteristics, Culture, Propagation and Uses*. Champaign, IL: Stipes Publishing L.L.C., 2009

Drew, A.J. *A Wiccan Bible: Exploring the Mysteries of the Craft from Birth to Summerland*. Franklin Lakes, NJ: New Page Books, 2003.

Erdoes, Richard, and Alfonso Ortiz. *American Indian Myths and Legends*. NY: Pantheon Books, 1984.

Farrar, Janet and Stewart. *The Witches' God*. Custer, WA: Phoenix Publishing, 1989.

Ferm, Vergilius, ed. *Living Schools of Religion*. Paterson, NJ: Littlefield, Adams & Co., 1965.

Fortune, Dion. *Psychic Self-Defense*. York Beach, ME: Samuel Weiser, Inc., 1992.

Frye, Northrop. *The Great Code: The Bible and Literature*. New York, NY: Harcourt Brace Jovanovich Publishers, 1981.

Graves, Robert. *The White Goddess*. NY: The Noonday Press, 1988.

Grimassi, Raven. *The Wiccan Mysteries: Ancient Origins & Teachings*. St. Paul, MN: Llewellyn Publications, 1997.

Guinness, Alma E., ed. *Joy of Nature: How to Observe and Appreciate the Great Outdoors*. Pleasantville, NY: Reader's Digest, 1977.

Hageneder, Fred. *The Meaning of Trees: Botany, History, Healing, and Lore*. San Francisco, CA: Chronicle Books LLC, 2005.

The Holy Bible: New International Version. Grand Rapids, MI: Zondervan Publishing House, 1984. Copyright 1973, 1978, 1984 by International Bible Society.

Kilmer, Joyce. "Trees." In *Trees and Other Poems*. New York: George H. Doran Company, 1914.

Kloss, Jethro. *Back to Eden*. Loma Linda, CA: Back to Eden Books, 1982.

Linford, Jenny. *The Tree: Wonder of The Natural World*. NY: Barnes & Noble, Inc., by arrangement with Parragon Books Ltd., 2006.

Little, Elbert, L. *National Audubon Society Field Guide to North American Trees: Eastern Region*. NY: Alfred A. Knopf, Inc, 1980.

Lowery, Linda, and Richard Keep. *The Chocolate Tree: A Mayan Folktale*. Minneapolis,: Lerner Publishing Group, Inc, 2009.

Matthews, John, and Will Worthington. *The Green Man Tree Oracle: Ancient Wisdom from the Spirit of Nature*. New York, NY: Metro Books, 2008.

Monroe, Douglas. *The 21 Lessons of Merlyn: A Study in Druid Magic & Lore*. St. Paul, MN: Llewellyn Publications, 1992.

Moura, Ann. *Green Witchcraft: Folk Magic, Fairy Lore & Herb Craft*. St. Paul, MN: Llewellyn Publications, 1996.

O'Connell, Mark, and Raje Airey. *The Complete Encyclopedia of Signs & Symbols: Identification and Analysis of the Visual Vocabulary that Formulates Our Thoughts and Dictates Our Reactions to the World Around Us*. London, UK: ' Hermes House, 2005, 2006.

Penczak, Christopher. *The Living Temple of Witchcraft, Volume Two: The Journey of the God*. Woodbury, MN: Llewellyn Publications, 2009.

———. *The Temple of High Witchcraft: Ceremonies, Spheres and the Witches' Qabalah*. Woodbury, MN: Llewellyn Publications, 2007.

Pepper, Elizabeth. *Celtic Tree Magic*. Middletown, RI: The Witches' Almanac, LTD., 1996.

Phillips, Roger. *Trees of North America and Europe: A Photographic Guide to More Than 500 Trees*. NY: Random House, Inc., 1978.

Scheffel, Richard L., ed. *ABC's of Nature*. Pleasantville, NY: The Reader's Digest Association, Inc., 1984.

Silverstein, Shel. *The Giving Tree*. NY: Harper & Row, 1964.

Smith, Joseph. *The Book of Mormon: Another Testament of Jesus Christ*. Salt Lake City, UT: Intellectual Reserve, Inc., 1981.

Stewart, Amy. *Wicked Plants: The Weed that Killed Lincoln's Mother & other Atrocities*. Chapel Hill, NC: Algonquin Books of Chapel Hill, 2009.

Tekiela, Stan. *Trees of Illinois: Field Guide*. Cambridge, MN: Adventure Publications, Inc., 2006.

Tyson, Donald, ed. *Three Books of Occult Philosophy*. St. Paul, MN: Llewellyn Publications, 2003.

Valiente, Doreen. *Natural Magic*. Custer, WA: Phoenix Publishing Inc., 1975.

Webster, Richard. *Flower and Tree Magic: Discover the Natural Enchantment aroundYou*. Woodbury, MN: Llewellyn Publications, 2008.

Weiner, Michael A. *Earth Medicine-Earth Foods: Plant Remedies, Drugs, and Natural Foods of the North American Indians*. New York, NY: The Macmillan Company, 1972.

Zell, Oberon. *Grimoire for the Apprentice Wizard*. Franklin Lakes, NJ: New Page Books, 2004.

Online Sources

"Ancient Egypt: The Mythology." Accessed September 22, 2010. http://www.egyptianmyths.net/tree.htm.

Atsma, Aaron. "Flora 2: Plants of Greek Myth." The Theoi Project: Greek MythologyAuckland, New Zealand, 2000–2011. Accessed November 18, 2010. http://www.theoi.com/Flora2.html.

"Benefits of Buckthorn Herb." Liveandfeel.com, 2006–2013. Accessed May 27, 2012. http://www.liveandfeel.com/medicinalplants/buckthorn.html.

Bond, Annie B. "Your Celtic Tree Horoscope." CARE2.COM, INC. January 15, 2007. Accessed January 13, 2011. http://www.care2.com/greenliving/your-celtic-tree-horoscope.html.

Brand, Mark H. "Plant UConn: Database of Trees, Shrubs, and Vines." Accessed July 12, 2012. http://www.hort.uconn.edu/plants/index.html.

"Celtic Tree Calendar and Ogham." July 04, 2010. http://www.angelfire.com/wizard2/celticoghamtrees/

Christenson, Allen, J. "The Sacred Tree of the Ancient Maya." Provo, UT: 1997. Accessed July 07, 2010. http://maxwellinstitute.byu.edu/publications/jbms/?vol=6&num=1&id=133.

Dale, C. James. "In Japan, healthy minds rejuvenate in healthy forests." October 08, 2010. Accessed January 21, 2013. http://www.theglobeandmail.com/life/travel/destinations/in-japan-rejuvenate-in-healthy-forests/article4266258/.

DragonOak.com. "Magical Properties of Trees and Wood Magick." Accessed November 15, 2010. http://www.dragonoak.com/Magical-Wood-Properties.html.

Fields, Rick. "Who is the Buddha? The Life Story of the Historical Buddha, Siddhartha Gautama." Accessed Aug. 12, 2018. https://tricycle.org/magazine/who-was-buddha-2/.

Mancuso, Stefano. "The Roots of Plant Intelligence." TEDGlobal: 2010. October 15, 2010. http://www.ted.com/talks/stefano_mancuso_the_roots_of_plant_intelligence.html.

Musselman, L.J. "Trees in the Koran and the Bible." Accessed 08, 2010. Norfolk, VA. http://www.fao.org/docrep/005/y9882E/y9882e11.htm.

Parsons, John J. "Hebrew for Christians: The Letter Yod." Accessed September 22, 2010. http://www.hebrew4christians.com/Grammar/Unit_One/Aleph-Bet/Yod/yod.html.

Prontes, Isabel. "Elder Tree Facts." Accessed August 12, 2010. http://www.gardenguides.com/117135-elder-tree.htm.

Robbins, Stuart. "Exposing PseudoAstronomy: Sizes of Solar System Objects." December 18, 2008. Accessed November 26, 2011. http://pseudoastro.wordpress.com/tag/sun-400-times-larger-than-the-moon/.

Root, Jeff. "Earth and Moon to Scale." February 18, 2003. Accessed November 26, 2011. http://www.freemars.org/jeff/planets/Luna/Luna.htm.

"Sacred Trees." Accessed November 11, 2010. http://www.goddessnames.net/sacredtrees.html.

Smith, Richard Gordon. "Ancient Tales and Folk-lore of Japan." Accessed Dec. 27, 2018. http://www.sacred-texts.com/shi/atfj/atfj04.htm.

Swanson, Jan. "Hermetic Qabalah: The Qabalistic Tree." April 2007. Accessed Dec. 29, 2018.

"The Story of the Sacred Tree." September 11, 2010. http://nwindian.evergreen.edu/curriculum/SacredTree.pdf.

"The Trees of Illinois Wesleyan Arboretum." Accessed May 03, 2010. http://www.iwu.edu/treemap/.

"Trees of North America." Accessed May 31, 2010. http://treesof-northamerica.net/.

Witcombe, Christopher L.C.E. "Sacred Places: Trees and the Sacred." Sweet Briar College, VA: 1998. Accessed July 08, 2010. http://witcombe.sbc.edu/sacredplaces/trees.html.

TO WRITE TO THE AUTHOR

If you wish to contact the author or would like more information about this book, please write to the author in care of Llewellyn Worldwide Ltd. and we will forward your request. Both the author and publisher appreciate hearing from you and learning of your enjoyment of this book and how it has helped you. Llewellyn Worldwide Ltd. cannot guarantee that every letter written to the author can be answered, but all will be forwarded. Please write to:

Gregory Michael Brewer
⅍ Llewellyn Worldwide
2143 Wooddale Drive
Woodbury, MN 55125-2989

Please enclose a self-addressed stamped envelope for reply,
or $1.00 to cover costs. If outside the U.S.A., enclose
an international postal reply coupon.

Many of Llewellyn's authors have websites with additional information and resources. For more information, please visit our website at http://www.llewellyn.com